D0900551

ADDITIONAL PRAISE FOR

Remembering Medgar Evers: Writing the Long Civil Rights Movement

"*Remembering Medgar Evers* is both an all-important testimony to the necessity of the memory of the man, the moment, and the movement and a compelling explanation of Medgar's relevance and persistence in black cultural production. Culling not only factual accounts from contemporary media sources but also creative responses from writers and musicians, Gwin memorializes the long civil rights struggle in Mississippi and the role Medgar's life and death played in it. She skillfully merges the theoretical work of American literary and cultural studies with a moving analysis of the power of righteous social action and political justice in the United States."

—THADIOUS M. DAVIS, author of *Southscapes: Geographies of Race, Region, and Literature*

"In *Remembering Medgar Evers*, Minrose Gwin has woven an intricately textured appreciation of that stunningly brave man, his tortured time, and the deeper meaning of his arduous life and brutal murder. Toiling in relative obscurity to overcome white supremacy in Mississippi, brought down by a racist assassin who publicly exulted for decades thereafter, Evers was both unique and representative of black Americans' unfinished march toward full equality. Gwin makes sure that we cannot forget either reality."

—HODDING CARTER, University Professor of Leadership and Public Policy, University of North Carolina–Chapel Hill

"A worthy tribute to one of the civil rights era's most important and overlooked figures, an essential interrogation of Medgar Evers–themed works of some of the most important American artists of the last half century and an intelligent examination of art meets activism."

—FRANK X WALKER, author of *Turn Me Loose: The Unghosting of Medgar Evers*

Remembering Medgar Evers

Mercer University Lamar Memorial Lectures No. 53

MINROSE GWIN

Remembering Medgar Evers

WRITING THE LONG CIVIL RIGHTS MOVEMENT

THE UNIVERSITY OF GEORGIA PRESS

Athens & London

A SARAH MILLS HODGE FUND PUBLICATION
This publication is made possible in part through a grant from the Hodge Foundation
in memory of its founder, Sarah Mills Hodge, who devoted her life to the relief and
education of African Americans in Savannah, Georgia.

All of the author's royalties from the sale of this book will go to
the Medgar Evers Institute.

Copyrights and acknowledgments appear on pages 175–76,
which constitute a continuation of this copyright page.

Published by The University of Georgia Press
Athens, Georgia 30602
www.ugapress.org
© 2013 by Minrose Gwin
All rights reserved
Designed by Walton Harris
Set in 11/14 Filosofia
Printed and bound by Thomson-Shore
The paper in this book meets the guidelines for permanence and
durability of the Committee on Production Guidelines for Book Longevity
of the Council on Library Resources.

Printed in the United States of America

17 16 15 14 13 P 5 4 3 2 1

Library of Congress Cataloging-in-Publication Data

Gwin, Minrose.
Remembering Medgar Evers : writing the long civil rights movement / Minrose Gwin.
    p.   cm. — (Mercer University Lamar Memorial lectures ; no. 53)
Includes bibliographical references and index.
ISBN-13: 978-0-8203-3563-6 (hardcover : alk. paper)
ISBN-10: 0-8203-3563-0 (hardcover : alk. paper)
ISBN-13: 978-0-8203-3564-3 (pbk. : alk. paper)
ISBN-10: 0-8203-3564-9 (pbk. : alk. paper)
1. Evers, Medgar Wiley, 1925–1963. 2. Evers, Medgar Wiley, 1925–1963—Influence.
3. Evers, Medgar Wiley, 1925–1963—Songs and music. 4. Civil rights movements—
Mississippi—Jackson—History—20th century. 5. African Americans—Civil rights—
Mississippi—Jackson—History—20th century. 6. African American civil rights
workers—Mississippi—Jackson—Biography. 7. Civil rights workers—Mississippi—
Jackson—Biography. I. Title.
F349.J13G85 2012
323.092—dc23 [B] 2012022118

British Library Cataloging-in-Publication Data available

For Myrlie Evers-Williams,
whose courage and vision
call us to remember the past
and look to the future

The struggle of man against power
is the struggle of memory against forgetting.

— MILAN KUNDERA, *The Book of Laughter and Forgetting*

A KEEN FOR MEDGAR

We sing no blues for you
   No man!
We sing no blues for you
   No man!
Blues is dead—but not you
   No man!
   Not you.

You'll always live—forever
    Always live—forever
    Wherever freedom lives
    There's where you are,
    Right where you are.

Blues may die—but not you
   No man! Not you!
You'll always live forever!
   and
We sing no blues for you
   No blues
For you.

— JIM WILLIAMS

CONTENTS

Remembering Medgar Evers

CHAPTER ONE

"He leaned across tomorrow"

MEDGAR EVERS AND THE FUTURE

Medgar Wiley Evers's lifelong struggle for social justice and his cold-blooded political assassination on June 12, 1963, raise large questions around history, memory, and mourning. Yet these questions are situated in a foreshortened time and place: the racially divided city of Jackson, Mississippi, during the spring and early summer of 1963. More broadly, the Evers story is situated in a remarkable historical moment of alternative political imagination: the U.S. civil rights movement of the 1950s and 1960s. Like the movement itself, this book is both broadly construed and locally inflected. Evers's life and death call us to consider the historical legacy of political revolution. He was a larger-than-life hero and a martyr whose death ricocheted throughout the sixties in the assassinations of other strong human rights and civil rights leaders. At the same time, his is the story of a specific man in a specific place, a young man with a wife and children and a dog named Heidi, a man who liked to fish for bass and grow prize plums on a tree in the backyard, a "servant leader" who was a good listener and spent much of his time exposing and documenting heinous crimes against his people, urging them to have courage, patience, and optimism—to hold their heads high and look to the future.[1] As we enter the fiftieth anniversary year of Evers's death, we may consider how such a man is remembered or forgotten, how mourning summons some to the act of imaginative writing, and how such art born out of trauma and martyrdom may call forth not only remembrance of the American and southern past but also social action in the global present. In this sense, the closing lines of Gwendolyn Brooks's poem "Medgar Evers" capture the ongoing momentum of Evers's life and death:

> Roaring no rapt arise-ye to the dead, he
> leaned across tomorrow. People said that
> he was holding clear globes in his hands.[2]

While this book is not a biography of Evers, it is an attempt to unveil the power and vitality of an imaginative trajectory that, like Brooks's poem, has remembered his life of service and mourned his untimely and violent death.[3] It foregrounds, within the context of what Jacqueline Dowd Hall and other historians have called "a long and ongoing civil rights movement,"[4] the aesthetic challenges and ethical complexities of a body of writing—fiction, poetry, memoir, and drama—that emerged in response to the civil rights leader's life and death and that surge forward in history, right up to the present moment. I also examine aesthetic production in the journalistic writings about Evers, flawed and obscure though they be, and in songs ranging from early 1960s gospel and protest music to contemporary hip-hop rhythms and folk melodies, with performers ranging from global entertainers to local southern bands. Certain of the texts I discuss, such as James Baldwin's and Eudora Welty's writings, have gained historical resonance as they have moved through the decades and multiple generations of readers. Other writings of the sixties, many of the heartfelt condolence letters and memorials in the Medgar Evers and Myrlie Evers Archives in the Mississippi Department of Archives and History, remain, in their obscurity, locked inside the vault of history, having been read by only a few people, and most of those very long ago.[5] Whether in the form of poetry, fiction, memoir, drama, journalism, film, song, letter, or memorial, these writings present tangled aesthetic challenges and ethical complexities, reminding us of the reverberating impact of the nation's and the South's hard and broken past.

Wherever they are found, stories about Medgar Evers are at heart local—and rightly so. The local: is it not the starting point for the collective work of memory and mourning, the *where*, *what*, and *who* of any story about the past? If we are to understand, even in small measure, how either social visions of justice or repressive systems of power are reproduced and revised over time, it seems crucial to attend to the local as the source of material and cultural specificity—the stuff of everyday life—out of which real people's embodied knowledges emerge and come to be represented and performed imaginatively. As Ralph Ellison's Invisible Man ends up saying, "Who knows but that, on the lower frequencies, I speak for you?"[6] In this sense, to be deeply located in the everyday life of a place, as Evers was, is to be broadly human. Location is, after all, as Eudora Welty so famously remarked, not only "the crossroads of circumstance" but "the heart's field."[7] As I hope will become apparent, I'm thinking about the local not only as a space of comings and goings, of routes as well as roots, but also as itself a route that is both temporal and spatial, just as memory is. In my discussion of Jackson, Evers's home and the site of his death, the local isn't just a place; it is also a confluence through which memory and history flow.

In his own times Medgar Evers's "heart's field," as well as his "crossroads of circumstance," was his home state of Mississippi, and with the exception of his service in World War II, he lived there his whole life, in his last year refusing the NAACP's offer to relocate him and his family to California: "This," he said, "is home. . . . The things that I don't like I will try to change."[8] For Evers and other activists involved in the state's arduous civil rights struggle in the spring and summer of 1963, the seething state capital of Jackson had become a mire of tension, violence, and horror: a "crossroads of circumstance" both daunting and threatening. Demonstrating adults and children were being shoved into reeking garbage trucks and hauled to livestock pens at the fairground—"Mississippi's concentration camp," as Medgar Evers's widow, now Myrlie Evers-Williams, called it[9]—becoming the butt of racist jokes by bigoted newspaper columnists. Mayor Allen Thompson had just asked city voters to approve a bond issue of five hundred thousand to one million dollars to build more detention facilities to hold racial demonstrators.[10] Participants in the Woolworth's lunch-counter sit-ins, including Tougaloo Southern Christian College student Anne Moody, one of the writers I discuss in this volume, were frozen in place on the covers of the nation's newspapers, their condiment-splattered bodies hunched in self-protection before an angry white mob. A boycott of white-owned businesses had ratcheted up the rhetoric of racism from city officials. Jackson, in the words of local poet Margaret Walker, was a

City of tense and stricken faces
City of closed doors and ketchup-splattered floors,
City of barbed wire stockades,
And ranting voices of demagogues,
City of squealers and profane voices;
Hauling my people in garbage trucks.[11]

If social practice, past and present, defines and shapes place, then Jackson of the early 1960s can be seen as the spatial embodiment of apartheid.[12] And it bears emphasizing that, during the height of the civil rights encounters in the U.S. South, located spatial practices were obviously the precise points of struggle — where African Americans could live, sleep, ride, eat, sit, drink, study, work, worship, vote — in short, where black citizens could *place* themselves in their daily lives. Along with voter registration, economic parity, and matters of courtesy, these were Evers's primary concerns as the first NAACP field secretary in Mississippi, a post many had called a suicide mission.

Danger was nothing new for Evers, who had put his life on the line for years. As early as 1958, Adam Nossiter points out, a Mississippi Sovereignty Commission memo titled "Medgar Evers, Race Agitator" included a suggestion from Governor J. P. Coleman that "spot checks be made of the activities of Medgar Evers, both day and night, to determine whether he [was] violating any laws."[13] In 1954, after serving in a segregated army unit on the European front in World War II and while he was employed by the Magnolia Life Insurance Company in Mound Bayou, Mississippi, Evers, under direction from the NAACP (by then he was an active member of the organization), made an unsuccessful attempt to enter the University of Mississippi law school.[14] He later helped James Meredith accomplish that goal. In Meridian he was beaten for refusing to move to the back of a bus. As field secretary he supported and/or organized economic boycotts and lunch-counter and library sit-ins in Jackson and voter registration drives throughout the state. Wearing the clothes of a fieldworker, he made dangerous trips on backcountry roads to rural Mississippi communities to investigate incidents of racial murder and mayhem for the NAACP.

By the spring of 1963, especially as the white merchant boycott began to grip Jackson, threats against Evers's life and those of other civil rights activists in the state had proliferated. Racial tension in Jackson, the South, and the country in general was at fever pitch. The front-page headline in Jackson's *Clarion-Ledger* on June 11, the day before Evers's murder, was "[George] Wallace, U.S. Gird for Historic Clash." Earlier on the night Evers was shot, President Kennedy had addressed the nation on the federal/state confrontation over the integration of the University of Alabama. On the personal front, the material and cultural spaces that Medgar and Myrlie Evers inhabited with their three young children in 1963 ranged from urgently dangerous (even the police were trying to run Medgar over as he went about his business) to socially uncomfortable. On their own Guynes Street, few families were happy about the Everses' presence in the neighborhood. Many of their neighbors—doctors, lawyers, business professionals, and teachers living in the first black suburb of Jackson, with its modest new tract homes in a two- to three-block area flanked on the north and south by white lower-middle-class subdivisions—hadn't wanted the Evers family to locate there six years earlier; rumors of a petition to keep the Everses out had reached them before they moved in. In 1963 there was growing fear that the area would become a drive-by target for racist thugs instead of the pleasant middle-class neighborhood its residents had envisioned for their children to grow up in.[15]

In the city of Jackson, white violence and anarchy were supported, even encouraged, by state and local government officials whose major outlets were the two white-owned Jackson newspapers, the morning *Clarion-Ledger* and the afternoon *Daily News*. These papers were much more virulently segregationist in their news coverage of civil rights issues than most other Mississippi newspapers (with few exceptions, something of a feat in the 1960s), to the degree that the *Columbia Journalism Review* concluded in 1967 that their biased coverage of the civil rights struggle qualified them for the title of "quite possibly the worst metropolitan newspapers in the United States."[16] The White Citizens' Council of Mississippi, the white-collar twin of the KKK founded in 1953 to maintain white supremacy, was supported by the Hederman family network, which controlled both newspapers and owned one of the Jackson television stations.[17] The governor of Mississippi and the mayor of Jackson were members, and Evers's killer, Byron De La Beckwith of Greenwood, was a charter member.

A "Bigger and Better Bigots Bureau," the Council had become a virtual arm of the state and received state funds through the Mississippi Sovereignty Commission, a state spy agency, formed in 1956 with the avowed purpose of upholding the racial status quo.[18] In a 1962 editorial Hazel Brannon Smith, the Pulitzer Prize–winning editor of the *Lexington Advertiser*, called for abolishing both the Sovereignty Commission, with its "statewide network of paid spies," and the "vicious and dictatorial Citizens' Council (which tries to destroy anyone who does not conform totally and absolutely to its line)" and was "no less dreaded and feared than the Gestapo of Hitler's Germany and the paid informers of the Communist conspiracy."[19] As Nossiter notes, the goals of both the Commission and the Council were accomplished through a "paranoid, dirty war against suspicious outsiders, civil rights workers, blacks seeking their rights, and men and women suspected of carrying on interracial liaisons" that made Mississippi into a virtual police state.[20] In all, as James Silver, a history professor at the University of Mississippi, wrote in 1963, "Within its own borders the closed society of Mississippi comes as near to approximating a police state as anything we have seen in America."[21] (Silver was fired from the university for his progressive book *Mississippi: The Closed Society*.)

Like much of the South, Jackson and Mississippi were clearly in the clutches of a white supremacist fascism, and in this regard it is important to note that the civil rights movement had begun to emerge at the very moment in history that people throughout the world were confronting the devastating aftereffects of Nazism in Western Europe and their parallel in the Jim Crow laws of the American South. Certainly the comparison between Nazi Germany and the U.S. South had become painfully apparent to Evers the World War II veteran, as it had to many African Americans. Hall points out that

> African Americans and their allies were among the first to grasp the enormity of the Nazi persecution of the Jews and to drive home the parallels between racism and anti-Semitism. In so doing, they used revulsion against the Holocaust to undermine racism at home and

to "turn world opinion against Jim Crow." A "rising wind" of popular anticolonialism, inspired by the national liberation struggles in Africa and Asia that erupted after the war, also legitimized black aspirations and linked the denial of civil rights at home to the exploitation of the colonized people around the globe as well as to racially exclusive immigration naturalization laws.[22]

Evers, who himself had witnessed the results of Nazi atrocities in Europe, had noted a specific connection to Nazism in the actions of the Citizens' Council. In a sizzling news release from NAACP headquarters in Jackson on March 16, 1955, he wrote that his investigations of the punishments meted out to blacks who attempted to register to vote showed conditions akin to those that existed "during Hitler's reign and the Nazi hey-day when the Jews were terrorized and executed," adding,

> as paradoxical as life would have it, some of these same persons who were beaten and terrorized by the Nazis are assisting the die-hards of the Citizen's Councils in bringing about economic pressure on Negroes who pay their poll taxes and register in Humphry County.
>
> The National Association for the Advancement of Colored People is very strongly opposed to such Hitler-like tactics and we shall employ every legal means possible to combat them.[23]

At the height of the demonstrations in Jackson, when Evers watched six hundred demonstrators, mostly children, herded into garbage trucks by police in riot gear and locked up at the state fairgrounds, he exploded: "Just like Nazi Germany. . . . Look at those storm troopers."[24]

NAACP director Roy Wilkins echoed Evers's sentiments when he spoke in Jackson at a mass meeting the next day, saying, "In Birmingham, the authorities turned the dogs and fire hoses loose on peaceable demonstrators. Jackson has added another touch to this expression of the Nazi spirit with the setting up of hog-wired concentration camps. This is pure Nazism and Hitlerism. The only thing missing is an oven."[25]

Evers, in fact, seems to have thought of himself as an underground resistance fighter through his own investigative narratives of injustice. Like the Old Testament prophet Micah decrying a corrupt and violently exploitative social order in Jerusalem—whom Margaret Walker would create as his biblical double in her poem "Micah"—Evers testified to the racial violence and inequities within the state by filing reports to the national office of the NAACP, which were then sent out in news releases across the country.[26] At the same time he forged his own contacts with reporters outside Jackson, who themselves were dubbed "outside agitators," and passed information on to them.[27] When black individuals, usually men or boys, were murdered in rural counties, he risked his life to investigate the murders on his own. "He placed himself between the wounded, the beaten, the frightened, the threatened, the assaulted, and the white racist society that invariably had everything its own way," Myrlie Evers would later write. "He investigated, filed complaints, issued angry denunciations, literally dragged reporters to the scenes of crimes, fought back with press releases."[28]

A story related by Tom Dent, New Orleans writer, editor, and activist, reveals Evers's persistence in these tasks. When Clyde Kennard, who had been jailed for trumped-up charges of theft after attempting to enter the University of Southern Mississippi, was finally released from prison after being denied treatment for the cancer that would kill him several months later, it was Evers who picked him up at Jackson's University Hospital—the hospital where Evers would spend his own last moments. First Evers had to wait at the "colored desk" to get Kennard's release papers, and then stood an additional two hours at the "colored only" prescription desk waiting for Kennard's medicine. Dent writes, "[Medgar] had to wait until every white patient's prescription had been filled before they would serve him. . . . When we left the hospital that afternoon, Medgar was angry. Yet, he was still Medgar, that is, he was not so bitter that he couldn't offer a ride to the Negro section, to two women who had been waiting at the prescription desk with him," trying unsuccessfully to persuade them to offer statements about their own abuse at the same "colored only" window.[29]

Evers's reports and news releases indicate that he himself was a storyteller whose outrage boiled up off the page as he recounted the struggles and persecutions of his people. Hearing and retelling testimonial stories of violence, he set the gold standard for the accuracy and fullness of memory in the face of willful forgetting or misremembering. He took photographs of mutilated bodies, including that of fourteen-year-old Emmett Till, and he called news reporters in the middle of the night to alert them to crime scenes. As Evers-Williams describes, he felt keenly his responsibility as a witness to racially motivated killings of and atrocities against the "unsung heroes and heroines in Mississippi."[30]

In December 1955 he began his report titled "Killing of Clinton Melton, Negro, by Elmer Kimbel, White," as follows: "Saturday night, December 3, 1955 was another night of terror in the county of Tallahatchie and the town of Glendora. An 'innocent' Negro man, World War II veteran, father of four small children (ages range from 5 months to 5 years), and husband of an attractive wife, was shot to death by a white man." After recounting the story of the white man who pulled a shotgun and blasted Clinton Melton in the face for, purportedly, filling his car with too much gas, Evers continues: "The four children, Deloris Melton, 5 years; Clinton Melton, Jr., 3 years; Vivian Melton, 2 years; and Kenneth L. Melton, 5 months, were left fatherless by this fiendish killing." He relates a statement from Melton's widow, who would herself be dead in March 1956 after the car she was driving ran into a ditch (a death Evers also investigated). She said she did "not want the NAACP to come into the case" because of the fear of reprisals against her and her family, as there had been in the Emmett Till case. Before her death she had planned to abandon the family home and leave the county. Evers ends the Melton report with a poignant statement; for him, he writes, "The experience shall be of long memory."[31] Similarly, Evers's report on the 1956 murder of Edward Duckworth in Smith County begins thusly: "The continuing violence of Negro citizens in Mississippi is as much alive today as it was in August when Emmit [*sic*] L. Till was 'lynched.'"[32]

If government-sanctioned violence and anarchy weren't enough to contend with, an iron-handed control of the dissemination (or lack thereof) of national news in Mississippi, and certainly in the Jackson area, was almost as constraining. State and local governments in Mississippi, all white controlled, had commandeered, with a few exceptions, most media outlets in the state. Television viewers throughout Mississippi lived in a vacuum when it came to national news of race relations. As Myrlie Evers describes in her memoir *For Us, the Living*: "The blackout of television news on civil rights had gone so far that network news programs originating in New York were systematically interrupted with signs indicating technical difficulties whenever the news turned to race. We had been denied all of the network documentaries on civil rights. We were cut off from news developments within our own state. The only news we received on race relations was the distorted news the local stations decided we should have."[33] The blackouts had begun in September 1955, soon after the 1954 *Brown v. Board of Education* decision, when Jackson's NBC affiliate WLBT had flashed a "Cable Difficulty" logo on the screen while civil rights attorney Thurgood Marshall talked about school integration on NBC's *Today* show. Soon after, other stations followed suit with the "Sorry, Cable Trouble" sign appearing regularly during newscasts and documentaries about race relations, integration, and violence against African Americans.[34]

With the flow of information from the outside world severely limited, the Sovereignty Commission spying on progressives throughout the state, the KKK and Citizens' Council terrorizing blacks throughout the South, and the murders of Till, Melton, Duckworth, and others going unpunished, southern African Americans generally and civil rights activists in particular "were frightened to death," as Evers-Williams would say almost half a century later, in a 2007 NPR interview. "It's hard to imagine for us today how dangerous it was to question the southern system. . . . [I]t was unheard of to take that kind of risk."[35]

Within this frame of apartheid politics, vigilante violence, and fascist control, Evers's murder at the hand of white supremacist Byron De La Beckwith gestured both forward and backward in history. It was the first death by assassination of a public figure in what would prove a long, grim trajectory of political killings of major American leaders of the sixties. Although Evers was known in his time as a man of exceptional determination and courage—his death, funeral services, and NAACP-managed burial at Arlington Cemetery were widely covered in the national media—his murder actually acquired weight and resonance as it moved through history, becoming what many have seen as the harbinger of a decade of political bloodshed on a wider stage.[36] Beckwith's two mistrials by juries of white men in the winter and spring of 1964 (both unpleasant surprises to his high-powered defense team,[37] which had expected acquittal, despite the crystal-clear body of evidence linking Beckwith to the crime), followed by his reindictment in December 1990 and conviction in 1994, moved the Evers murder from the southern past to the present, as have other highly publicized belated convictions of racially motivated murders and bombings of the 1960s. The Evers story was further popularized by the book *Ghosts of Mississippi*, Maryanne Vollers's 1995 account of the murder and trials, and the 1996 film by the same name. In the summer of 1963, though, Evers was the highest-ranking public figure in the civil rights movement to be murdered.[38] Myrlie Evers describes her husband's murder as "an official act, for Medgar's energies were all directed against the official state of things in Mississippi. . . . It is almost as though the assassin had been appointed by the state to carry out the execution of an enemy of the state, an execution that the state could not, in all good public relations, openly carry out itself."[39]

At the same time, Evers's murder was a reenactment of southern history, a haunting replica of three centuries' killings of southern black men and youth who had been snatched from their homes and families and unspeakably brutalized. Beckwith shot Evers in his own driveway, as he was about to enter his own home—a spatial invasion that runs directly counter to Americans' purported belief in the sanctity of home and family. As Bobby DeLaughter, the assistant district attorney in Beckwith's third and conclusive trial in 1994, would say years later in what seems a deeply ironic understatement, "I feel indignant when I think about anybody being shot in the back after ambush in the driveway of their home with their wife and small children inside. I feel indignant reading about these children coming out, crawling through a pool of blood in the carport and saying daddy, please get up. I get indignant about that."[40]

The story of Evers's assassination has been widely told. When, soon after midnight on June 12, he drove into the carport of his modest house at 2332 Guynes Street and got out a stack of T-shirts imprinted with "Jim Crow Must Go," Beckwith lay in wait for him in a thicket of honeysuckle in an overgrown vacant lot across the street, which Evers and other neighbors had complained to the city about for some time.[41] As Vollers imagines the scene, Evers in his white shirt must have been a perfect target as he retrieved some T-shirts and paperwork from his blue Oldsmobile, breaking his own rules that everyone in his family get out on the passenger side in the carport, keeping the car between the person and the over-grown vacant lot across the street, and go directly into the front door of the house, which had been placed on the side with safety in mind. Beckwith shot him in the back, just below the right shoulder blade. "The slug tore through him, then through a window and a kitchen wall, before it glanced off the refrigerator and landed on a counter."[42] The mortally wounded Evers, who was thirty-seven, fell on his driveway and dragged himself to-ward the door as his wife, then pregnant with the couple's fourth child, and the couple's young children ran outside to find him lying in a pool of blood.[43] His last words were "Turn me loose." He died shortly thereafter in University Hospital, the University of Mississippi teaching hospital in Jackson, where his own doctor, Albert Britton, was not allowed to treat him because he too was black.[44] In some tellings of the story, Evers was at first turned away because hospital officials said they had no "colored" blood.[45]

This is a version of Evers's assassination told repeatedly, with varying degrees of accuracy. The most widely read of these narratives, Vollers's account, reenacts this scenario while also focusing, problematically, on Beckwith's exceptional racism and the hands-wiped-clean catharsis of his 1994 conviction for the state of Mississippi. Civil rights historian Renee Romano believes that the newly reopened civil rights trials of the 1990s, such as Beckwith's third trial for the murder of Evers, tell their own stories, molding in our times what she and Leigh Raiford term "a consensus memory" of the white South that emphasizes "old, unrepen-tant racists" while "ignor[ing] the social context of white support for segregation."[46] Another point of entry into the story of Evers's murder is found in Reed Massengill's *Portrait of a Racist: The Man Who Killed Medgar Evers* (published with a question mark after the title before Beckwith's conviction and without it afterwards), a biography of Beckwith by the killer's nephew-in-law, based on letters, interviews, and family history. Nossiter's historical study *Of Long Memory: Mississippi and the Murder of Medgar Evers* probes the Evers assassination for what it has to tell us about southern culture and politics and considers the huge schism be-tween black and white: "the two Mississippis [that] continue to view his-tory—and the present—through different prisms."[47] Nossiter's thought-ful and provocative book notwithstanding, though, the story of Medgar

Evers himself has until recently received less attention than the events surrounding his death and the subsequent attempts to bring Beckwith to justice undertaken by white men such as William Waller in the sixties and later the indignant DeLaughter, whose courage and determination made him the hero of *Ghosts of Mississippi*, the 1996 film.

Unlike books about Evers's death that probe the psychology of either white Mississippi or Byron De La Beckwith, Michael Vinson Williams's much-needed and carefully researched biography, *Medgar Evers: Mississippi Martyr*, which was published after this book was in production, focuses on Evers's life. Williams shows how Evers "was defined by his childhood, the examples his parents provided, the racism he encountered, and the freedoms he experienced overseas. Each of these life experiences helped focus his attention on combating racism and making the country live up to its democratic creed." Besides the racism and the introduction to racist violence Evers experienced as a child, Williams shows how his work in insurance sales in Mound Bayou, Mississippi, coming on the heels of his service in World War II, gave Evers "a close and personal look at the depth of black oppression" and therefore a deep awareness of how much needed to be done to achieve racial justice in his home state.[48] Williams sketches the fine line Evers walked in dealing with the NAACP national leadership's reluctance to work with other civil rights organizations in Mississippi throughout the late 1950s and early 1960s and his genuine admiration for Dr. Martin Luther King Jr. and other activists, both national and local. In late 1962, Williams reports, Evers found himself, as local efforts to boycott white businesses took hold of Jackson, "caught in the middle of the growing divide between the NAACP leadership in New York and the youth of Jackson, and the growing tensions between the two groups nearly pulled him in two."[49] In all, Williams paints a nuanced picture of Evers's leadership, which was itself coming to rich fruition by the time of his assassination. Williams depicts Evers's strategic effectiveness, dogged dedication, and sheer love for his home state as pivotal in changing "Mississippi's oppressive climate to one conducive to political and social progress." Even so, Williams observes, "the legacy of Medgar Evers has yet to receive full analysis because his impact and participation in the civil rights struggle has yet to be completely explored."[50]

Williams's book is an important corrective to this gap in our knowl-

edge about Evers's impact on civil rights history. But, as Williams himself points out, there is still much work to be done. Despite the fact that
Evers's murder ushered in a decade of political assassinations and set
fire to a powder keg of racial unrest throughout the nation, his brief but
eventful life of quiet service and remarkable courage has been consigned
to the periphery of both mainstream U.S. history and civil rights history. When a biracial jury was being selected from residents of Panola
County, Mississippi (north of Jackson), for Beckwith's 1994 trial, Vollers
observed that "most potential jurors could argue convincingly that they
knew nothing or next to nothing about either Beckwith or Evers."[51] As
the contemporary hip-hop group Dälek asserts in the 1990 song "Who
Medgar Evers Was," "Tell the truth, you never knew who Medgar Evers
was."[52] In his introduction to the 2005 volume of letters and speeches
titled *The Autobiography of Medgar Evers*, Manning Marable likens Evers
to "the nearly invisible and underappreciated women servant-leaders"
of the movement, who practiced transformational leadership by leading through example and dedication, thereby inspiring others to become
involved in political activity. He eschewed the limelight, "modestly pre-
ferring that others bask in public recognition while he labored on the
sidelines." Marable points to the fact that "in most standard textbooks of
African American history, Evers is either barely mentioned or completely
ignored. . . . Even in memoirs and commentaries by veterans of civil-
rights struggles, Evers barely merits any attention." Only a "modest body
of literature and films" has kept Evers's legacy alive, most of them fairly
recent.[53]

This is an effacement, if not erasure, noted time and again by his
widow. In the NPR interview cited earlier, Myrlie Evers-Williams said,
"Medgar was the forebear to Dr. King and others who have gotten so much
publicity. He was so brave."[54] In another interview with *Democracy Now!*
on the forty-fifth anniversary of her husband's death, she expressed her
feelings more bluntly: "It's been very difficult to hear people talk about
the civil rights movement and the leadership as though it started in 1964,
when it really did not." Later in the interview she added: "I just want so
badly for historians and particularly for our younger generation to know
more about Medgar and the role he played, because it is almost devastating to see and hear mentioned things of the civil rights movement that

give the appearance that nothing happened until 1964."[55] Her preface to *The Autobiography of Medgar Evers* clearly states that she wanted to bring together Evers's writings because of a lack of knowledge about him and other civil rights leaders of the fifties. She tells this poignant story:

> While touring a southern college campus before a lecture, I stopped along the way to dialogue with some students. I asked, "Do you know who Medgar Evers was?" A puzzled look crossed the faces of the students. They all agreed that they had never heard of him. One young man guessed, "Was he one of those old baseball players in the Negro League?" Another asked, "Did he play basketball?" I responded, "No, he was a civil rights leader in Mississippi until his assassination in 1963." They looked at me with a nano-second of discomfort, shrugged their shoulders, and walked away saying, "Never heard of him."
>
> Although this incident happened two years ago, it is firmly embedded in my memory as is my almost frantic search for Medgar's inclusion in corporate booklets and calendars distributed during Black History Month (February); the search for more than a sentence about him in books on civil rights leaders.[56]

Evers-Williams said in a 2010 interview, in fact, that she has made a life's work out of keeping Evers's memory alive, because she knew that if she didn't, "he would have been forgotten within one year of his death—one year."[57] Her continuing frustration was prefigured and shared. In 1988, decades after writing the story called "Where Is the Voice Coming From?" which became the most famous work of 1960s literature about the Evers murder, Eudora Welty, another Jacksonian, would worry that Evers and the movement were being forgotten, even at the local level. In an interview in 1988, well before the resurgence of interest in the Evers murder case that came from Beckwith's retrial and conviction, the author said she feared that the past had been obliterated for young Mississippians: "When this museum mounted the first ever exhibition on the civil rights movement in Jackson, it had marvelous posters, photographs, everything. School children—black and white—were invited to come. None of them had ever heard of civil rights. They didn't know there had ever been a time when there weren't any. They never heard of

Medgar Evers. It was amazing. They passed through this as if it were a glass wall."[58]

Despite Evers's own determined commitment to testimonial and memory, as well as the broad scope of his activism, it has been said, with varying degrees of irony, that Medgar Evers the man was worth much more to the movement dead than alive. The symbolic effect of his death—his grieving young widow and children at the graveside and in the Oval Office with President Kennedy, his funeral services in Jackson and Washington, his veteran's burial at Arlington—swept the nation in much the same way that Emmett Till's murder, which Evers had had a crucial role in publicizing, and the youth's brutalized face in his coffin appearing on the cover of *Jet* magazine in 1955 had horrified the country. Nossiter, in fact, believes that, for the most part, in the remembrances of the people who knew Evers in his last days, "the transformation from activist to martyr-symbol had begun even before his death . . . making his murder a logical culmination for his life."[59]

Evers's assassination galvanized support for civil rights and brought enraged African Americans into the streets across the country. In more than one sense, as James Baldwin would discern, Evers's murder as another reiteration of the lynchings of black men and youth was specifically resonant in terms of the Till murder. There are strong links between the two killings. In his relatively new role as NAACP field secretary—he'd taken the post on November 24, 1954—Evers in fact "worked exhaustively" on the Till murder, which occurred in Money, Mississippi, on August 28, 1955.[60] Moreover, in his hometown of Decatur, Mississippi, Evers's own boyhood experience of witnessing the aftermath of a lynching of a family friend, James Tingle, who was dragged from his home, hung, and shot, left an indelible mark. Tingle's blood-stained clothes were placed on a fence near the road down which Medgar and his brother Charles walked twelve miles to school, and according to Charles Evers, this sight had a profound effect on both brothers. Moreover, emboldened by the gory display, white children in the bus spit, shouted, and threw rocks at the two of them, "who dove into the ditches to avoid being hit."[61]

The exhibition of the brutalized black body is mired in a complex history of white voyeurism. Russ Castronovo has pointed to "the aestheticized violence of lynching" of the late nineteenth and early twentieth centuries and has shown how the media in the United States "had no qualms about doing something aesthetic with politics by presenting African American dehumanization as a source of white pleasure."[62] In a similar vein, Toni Morrison notes that the story in much white American literature of the bound and suffering black person has resulted not in ethical commitment by whites but rather a contemplation of the (white) modernist predicament and a unifying nationalist impulse in American literature; "that narrative is used for the construction of a history and a context for whites by positing history-lessness and context-lessness for blacks."[63] An example of both Castronovo's and Morrison's observations might be the film *Ghosts of Mississippi*, which, despite the avowedly good intentions of its director, Rob Reiner, not only slights Evers's life and marginalizes African Americans, including Myrlie Evers-Williams, as civil rights heroes but focuses on the white figure, Bobby DeLaughter, as the true hero/savior of the Evers story. Marable, in fact, argues that the film ironically fails to explain Evers's political ideas or the motives behind white racism and makes Evers "a ghost in his own film, because the audience cannot hear him in his own words."[64] The story of white men's valor in bringing an old racist killer to justice, certainly no mean feat in Mississippi history, erases the long haul of the civil rights struggle and Evers's laborious, dangerous work—the more complicated story of a movement that stretches far into the future and deep into the past: the kind of activism that puts one foot in front of the other and keeps on walking.

Citing this more complicated story of activism, Jacqueline Dowd Hall has called for a "more robust, more progressive, and *truer* story" of the civil rights movement. This more expansive movement would extend in time beyond the U.S. South and beyond "a single halcyon decade" and into our present and our future. She calls for new forms of storytelling of "an undefeated but unfinished revolution," one that is "harder to cast as a satisfying morality tale" and "harder to simplify, appropriate, and contain."[65] In line with Hall's call for a "harder" civil rights movement and Marable's observation that imaginative writing has been the most obvious site of memory in the Evers story, Christopher Metress argues that literary texts open the door to "a more expansive sense of the materials of civil rights history" by enriching "our understanding of the black freedom struggle of the mid-twentieth century" and, in their complex renderings of the past, offer "greater possibilities for the movement to speak more effectively to the challenges of our time."[66] I want to suggest that the forms of storytelling we find hovering around the Evers story exemplify what might be called an aesthetics of memory, an aesthetics that operates both inside and outside of the forward motion of time and thereby links civil rights history to a more expansive, open-ended conception of human rights struggles in the past, present, and future—struggles that are precisely located in the past and in place but that also travel through both time and space.

It is this cultural work of the imagination and its testimony to the lives of those who lived in the past that prevent us from buffering ourselves against the violence of the southern past and call us to remember the civil rights movement in some of its nuance and complexity. By way of this process, history is thus formed by and feeds into collective memory, and as Raiford and Romano suggest more generally, "history and memory necessarily challenge and blur each other's boundaries."[67] Writing from a literary perspective, Jefferson Humphries sees this blurring as a literary endeavor at heart, observing that "history is nothing but memory elevated to the status of myth, a kind of literature in reverse."[68]

The recursive relationship between history and memory is complicated by the civil rights movement's central place in contemporary culture, which has made it "ripe for appropriation" by advertisers, institutions, and political groups.[69] Clearly the movement and its expression of African American cultural trauma and triumph have become overarching metaphors that transfer to many causes—conservative and progressive—that have little to do with the kind or severity of race- and class-based oppression that triggered the movement and in some cases run directly counter to the aims of the movement itself. Hall, for example, stresses how "the movement's meaning has been distorted and reified by a New Right bent on reversing its gains."[70] As Romano and Raiford argue, "the effort to determine what is known and remembered about the past . . . is an effort to claim and exert power" in the present and for the future; cultural remembrance of the civil rights movement as a shining example of American democracy has been used to foment hegemonic forms of nation building.[71] In mainstream American culture, what Raiford and Romano call "consensus memory" also creates dominant narratives of the movement: Dr. Martin Luther King Jr. is the "good" leader (after having been posthumously groomed for the role) and Malcolm X the "bad." The exceptional African American individual, such as Rosa Parks, heroically fights oppression by refusing to move to the back of a bus, but the activism and sacrifice by many in the black community, for example, Claudette Colvin, who refused to give up her seat nine months before Parks did, goes unrecognized.[72]

By its very nature, memory is capricious, fluid, creative, and unpredictable. As such, it is readily available to the aesthetic impulse, the performative urge. Writings about the heroism and martyrdom of Medgar Evers illustrate how memories of a historical event are often disseminated through the workings of the imagination, which are in turn folded back into the ever-fluctuating flow of collective memory, shaping how history is received and perceived over time and how, in its migratory turn back to the present, memory shapes stories yet to be told and received. But what memories emerge and survive when a black child growing up in Mississippi in the early 1960s sees a racist cartoon in the local white newspaper? Or a young person, white or African American, reads story after story about the purported criminal behavior of black men? How do such memories get transmitted generationally? It would be tempting in this story of Evers's legacy to focus only on the positive: the fiction, poetry, memoirs, drama, memorial writings, and songs that call us to remembrance of a hero who died a hero's death, that engage us in the act of mourning Evers's tragic death and celebrating his extraordinary life. But the story of Evers's everyday life and struggle, grounded in the crossroads of circumstance of his beloved state and its capital city, was also writ large in the journalism of those places. *Jackson Daily News* editor Jimmy Ward's wounding racist humor and the Jackson papers' cartoons, layout, and design were also performances of race that were cultural conduits of memory for African American as well as white readers — conduits of negative images and language that have thrown long shadows into their readers' futures and the futures of their children and grandchildren.

In 1960s Jackson, Mississippi, such media-driven narratives, though of fleeting circulation, performed "'acts of transfer,' transmitting so-cial knowledge, memory, and a sense of identity."[73] Tucked tidily away for years in archival microfilm or on dusty periodical shelves in re-search libraries, they nonetheless live in the memories of many whites and African Americans who read them, memories that have been passed along to future generations and re-performed in complicated ways. It is part of the work of this book to excavate such disparate texts and their manipulations of individual and collective memory. These narratives about Evers and the events leading up to and following his death move across the historical sweep of a good half of the past century in American and southern history, yet they also fold back into the African American history of diaspora and slavery and, in contemporary times, economic exploitation and racial violence.

For the most part, though, this book is about writings that mourn and memorialize a great man. I also ask whether or to what degree mourning and testimony require the embodiment found in aesthetic forms—how the work of the imagination, no matter how rough edged and unsophis-ticated, may lead readers toward larger questions of justice through the re-membering of a regional and national history of racial trauma and cul-tural mourning. Many of these larger concerns around human-inflicted trauma, cultural mourning, and aesthetic production have been turned over in the fields of trauma studies and memory studies. Yet, despite the quantity of writing about the southern past, a need remains for specific frames of reference, or what Iwona Irwin-Zarecka has called "frames of remembrance."[74] These frames, which allow us to examine the work-ings of memory more precisely, are needed to set analytical parameters around questions of collective memory of racial trauma experienced by southern African Americans.

Such parameters are especially important for southern studies be-cause the racial divide between what is considered important to remem-ber and what is not, especially in regard to the civil rights movement of the 1960s, has been vehemently drawn along race lines, a fact noted by sociologists but too little marked in southern and American liter-ary studies.[75] The cultural space of the U.S. South has long existed as an American repository of disapprobation and mourning, one that can be grounded in removals and diasporas, forced unpaid labor, human interventions in family structures, and violent deeds and institutions. This southern archive of history has been both manipulated and disavowed. Moreover, well into the twenty-first century, racial violence still marks the cultural narrative of the South. Events such as the dragging murder of James Byrd in Jasper, Texas, a noose hanging from a tree on the grounds of a high school in Jena, Louisiana, the killing of Trayvon Martin in Sanford, Florida—all reverberate back through southern history.[76] Such events gather a psychological momentum that brings with it a coalescence of collective memory, which casts deep shadows over the future, even in a so-called postracial age. Frank X Walker's brilliant collection of poems, *Turn Me Loose: The Unghosting of Medgar Evers* (forthcoming), takes measure of these long shadows of southern history and the bifurcated forms of memory they elicit in lingering contemporary arguments about the meaning of the Confederate flag, antebellum plantation life, and Jim Crow.

In these pages I focus these wide-ranging questions around collective memory by looking at how a variety of writers of literature and song over the past half century have engaged the aesthetic challenge and ethical predicament posed by a historical moment of grave crisis and mourning: Medgar Evers's violent and tragic death. I want to consider, too, how such a moment as the Evers assassination becomes a continually shifting frame of remembrance that reveals just how incompletely and imprecisely the border is spliced historically between past and present—and spatially between the U.S. South and the rest of the world—when it comes to cultural memory of human-inflicted trauma in a long and ongoing civil rights movement. These aesthetic responses to civil rights history can produce ethical directives for the future. Frank X Walker's stunning book of poems, the most recent and extensive work of literature about Medgar Evers discussed here, is a striking example of such a response as it points toward a future in which reconciliation must always be balanced by the hard work of remembrance. In the final poem of the collection, "Heavy Wait," Mississippi is depicted as an elephant in need of "a memory as sharp as her ivory tusks / with as many wrinkles as her thick thick past."[77]

At the same time, Evers's life as a servant leader reflects Hall's observation that "remembrance is always a form of forgetting." She notes that "the dominant narrative of the civil rights movement—distilled from history and memory, twisted by ideology and political contestation, and embedded in heritage tours, museums, public rituals, textbooks, and various artifacts of mass culture—distorts and suppresses as much as it reveals."[78] Such forgetting is necessary to narratives that unify,[79] and Evers's life's work, often slighted in civil rights histories, seems often to fold imperceptibly into the narrative of a foreshortened movement with a few outstanding leaders, rather than a long and ongoing effort on many fronts by large and diverse segments of activists. The amnesia of the third batch of potential Beckwith trial jurors (African American and white) makes this point. As Nossiter reports: "When the district attorney asked a panel of fifteen potential jurors, plain-looking country people in bargain-store clothes, whether anyone knew anything of Evers, no one raised a hand."[80]

On the same local scene today, though, Evers seems anything but forgotten. Jackson's airport and one of its main streets are named after Medgar Evers, and in the airport an alcove displays an exhibit dedicated to his memory; the Evers house is itself a museum on the self-guided civil rights tour; the post office across the street from where Beckwith was taken after his conviction in 1994 is named after Evers; Medgar Evers Library offers Medgar Evers T-shirts for sale and has a larger-than-life Medgar Evers statue out front. More broadly, around the country, memorial sites range from Medgar Evers University in New York to a Medgar Evers Swimming Pool in the state of Washington, and most recently, to the U.S.N.S. *Medgar Evers*, a navy supply ship dedicated in October 2009 by Secretary of the Navy Ray Mabus, who was a fourteen-year-old white boy in northern Mississippi when Evers was killed and who later became governor of the state.

But there is also the question of how forgetting is calculated. Spatially, Jackson proper seems just as split as it ever was. According to the 2010 census, only about 18 percent of its population is white, and the past decade has seen the loss of thousands of city residents.[81] The once-thriving African American center of commerce and exchange, the Farish Street neighborhood, is for the most part a boarded-up ghost town and haven for drug merchants.[82] As I discuss in chapter 2, the 3.6 miles between Eudora Welty's large, gracious Tudor home in the Belhaven section of Jackson and the Everses' modest ranch-style home on Margaret Walker

Alexander Street (changed from Guynes) is still a long, long way in terms of economic advantage, cultural opportunity, and living conditions. Major streets in the black part of town are cluttered with abandoned businesses and empty strip malls. In some areas, it is difficult to find a place to eat or do the laundry. Only a handful of white children attend the Jackson public schools; historically progressive Millsaps College, on its pretty hillock in Welty's neighborhood, has a twelve-foot-high fence encircling it. And Jackson isn't alone; the demographics and tax bases of urban centers across the country have been drastically altered by crumbling tax bases caused by white, middle-class flight. All of this requires a vigilant forgetfulness, the kind of forgetfulness that makes whole populations invisible except in moments of crisis, such the aftermath of Hurricane Katrina in New Orleans, when our cities' overwhelming poverty and despair rise, unbidden, to the surface of the American consciousness.

Evers's legacy turns us to resonant questions about the future. If cultural memory is "a practice, an act of imagination and interconnection,"[83] which is shared by social groupings that share historical commonalities and embodied experience, one question that follows is how historically and imaginatively imbued memories of the civil rights movement that emerge from African American history and memory might also shape a broader sense of relation and responsibility to global issues, past and present. Many of our civil rights leaders, including Evers, who was influenced in early manhood by the African freedom struggles, had a more expansive sense of the power and scope of the movement. In our own times the movement casts light on other human rights struggles and failures and helps us see them, in their particularity, as part of a larger whole. In this sense, the concept of an ongoing civil rights struggle illustrates Kelly Oliver's belief that "we need to find the conditions of the possibility for justice—for the impossible to become possible in the future—in the past." Oliver suggests, in a reversal of causality, that our vision of the future shapes how we perceive the sense of possibility felt and acted upon by others in the past: "we revisit the past for the sake of a different future." In returning to the past in our quest for a more just future, we read "the conditions of the possibility of that future into the past" and thereby "open up alternatives to the present." Part of this recursive process, too, is how a certain vigilance in studying history evolves out of our imagining of our own present moment as already past and thinking of present-day work for social change as "an imaginary encounter with a possible future."[84]

Remembered, Evers's life's legacy pivots to the future, linking us to other human rights struggles, both local and global, and helping us see them as part of a larger, longer, more complex history. This is why his legacy matters. Deeply located in place, a Mississippi and a South he insisted on laying claim to as his and his people's, Evers was a man of plural singularity, a rock-solid worker whose behind-the-scenes tactics inched the Mississippi movement forward incrementally but sometimes almost imperceptibly. He was a leader without bodyguards or police escorts; he wasn't one for grand speeches, though he could speak eloquently; he was more often than not alone in dangerous situations. He blended in, standing alongside his people even as he led. At home, he answered his phone and patiently argued with racist crackpots on the other end of the line, much to his wife's consternation.[85]

On a broader scale, the Evers story—and the role of hero/victim at the center of it—engages questions around human-inflicted trauma, particularly the question of the ethical responsibility of cultural memory to grave historical moments of wounding and loss. In recent years the contemporary field of thought that has come to be called trauma studies has moved in two different and often contentious directions around questions of contagion and proliferation, especially as they involve human-inflicted trauma. Can trauma move from one site or person to another? Can cultures actually be connected through trauma, albeit differently located and experienced? Those who would be inclined to answer yes to these questions have argued on various fronts that trauma can be an experience of wounding that is not strictly delimited by either personal or symbolic victimhood, that actually can be transmitted and disseminated among cultures and subjects in extraordinarily complex and immutable ways that may not always be purely biographical or historical.[86] Other scholars feel, quite strongly, that trauma is so precisely particularized historically and culturally that theories emanating from such events can never be applied to other sites of wounding.[87]

Aesthetic production—and its ebullient though vexed affiliations with memory, history, and mourning—seems very much at the heart of these questions about human-inflicted trauma: its legacy in memory and its cogency for arguments about justice. If a powerful and beautifully written piece of writing about historical trauma—Margaret Walker's poem "Micah" about Evers, for instance—is another way of knowing that event, how does such a text make complicated ethical claims on the reader *through* its aesthetic energies? What might those claims entail? How might aesthetic responses to a specific event of wounding, Medgar Evers's assassination by Byron De La Beckwith on June 12, 1963, translate the specificity of that event into something larger than itself, just as Evers's life and death may be translated into a larger story of ongoing social responsibility?

An attention to the significant but tangled role of aesthetic production in the work of remembering traumatic events summons us back, as I said earlier, to an attentiveness to the local and its crossroads of circumstance. By the spring of 1963 Medgar and Myrlie Evers were barricading themselves inside their modest ranch-style house. They had taught their three small children to fall to the floor and crawl to the bathroom at the sound of gunshots or other disturbances. With an attention to the nuances of positionality and place, I consider in the second chapter of this book the specific relationships of writers James Baldwin, Margaret Walker, and Eudora Welty to that local scene of threat and fear: Baldwin's harrowing 1963 visit with Evers in backwoods Mississippi that resulted in the author's linkage of the murders of Emmett Till and Medgar Evers in Baldwin's 1964 play *Blues for Mister Charlie*; Walker's 1970 poetic representation of Evers as the vociferous Old Testament prophet Micah who decries the violence and corruption of Jerusalem (Jackson); and Welty's portrait in "Where Is the Voice Coming From?" of a white racist who crosses over into Jackson's first black suburb (whose paved streets he envies) to murder Evers, whose fictional name is Roland Summers. I don't argue that simple proximity to the local led to a closer alignment to the Everses' experience, but I do suggest that the local—both as what Welty called "the crossroads of circumstance" and "the heart's field"—is an

integral part of the equation of these authors' very complicated affiliations with the scene of terror on Guynes Street. I ask how writing is affected by its authors' entanglements around proximity and position and
how such entanglements affect the way we remember Evers.

In the third chapter I examine the aesthetic components—layout, design, photography—of Jackson's white- and black-owned newspapers,
which, in Evers's final months and directly after his death, created op-
positional narratives of race fueled by vast differentials in institutional
and economic sources of power, and in doing so vied with one another to
produce competing narratives of social justice. Today we might discount
the place of these newspapers in a study of collective memory. After all,
most are difficult to locate and read in microfilm or, more recently, online; they are of their own times, one might argue, not ours. In this study,
though, these newspapers are viewed as *"lieux de mémoire,"*[88] archival
sites of cultural memory, to be sure, and certainly sites that themselves
remain for us today hidden from view. But I also argue that their traces—a
phrase here, an allusion there, perhaps a striking picture or story, but
mostly deeply felt beliefs about race and the civil rights movement—remain strongly present in the collective memory of their readers and what
Marianne Hirsch would call the "postmemory" of their readers' descen-
dants and, moreover, have spilled out far beyond Jackson, Mississippi, or
even the South.[89]

In stark contrast to the white Jackson newspapers, which manipulated
visual representation to convey their racist messages, many of the other
texts I work with in chapters 4 and 5—memoirs by civil rights activists
such as Anne Moody and Myrlie Evers-Williams herself and songs from
the sixties and our own times—are forms of what Brett Ashley Kaplan calls
"aesthetic mourning." As Kaplan notes, aesthetic mourning may "en-
courage us to think critically" about difficult histories.[90] There is indeed
an urgency about aesthetic mourning that manifests Morrison's insis-
tency that art should be "unquestionably political and irrevocably beautiful at the same time."[91] Grounded in topical folk music and black freedom
songs, which supported and instigated the civil rights movement, music
by today's rappers and folk singers joins in keeping the Evers story alive
in a forgetful world.

Moody's 1968 memoir of her own involvement as a college student in the civil rights movement, *Coming of Age in Mississippi*, and Myrlie Evers's 1967 coauthored memoir, *For Us, the Living*, bear witness to the grueling day-to-day hardships and terrors of civil rights work, work that resulted in Moody's physical and emotional breakdown and Myrlie Evers's devastating loss of her husband and home. Kai Erickson has observed that trauma can both "create community" and damage it, sometimes irreparably.[92] Moody's and Myrlie Evers's memoirs, published only a few years after Evers's death, reveal the initial damage to the movement in Mississippi from his assassination but also served as rallying calls to that damaged and traumatized community to tap into the growing strength of a national movement for racial justice.[93] In this regard they fulfilled a function similar to many of the slave narratives of the mid-nineteenth-century abolitionist period, Moody and Evers-Williams both testifying to the personal cost of living under white institutions of oppression and violence, as well as rallying their readership to overturn these systems of violent subjection.

Yet the deeply complicated relations of racial trauma and aesthetics in these and other memoirs and songs of the sixties do not, in the psychological sense, work through trauma neatly or completely. The nature of trauma is its resistance to a departure into history; often trauma persists stubbornly in the present, as if it were just happening, again and again. In such cases trauma hovers like an echo, uncannily reproducing itself, like the profoundly ironic echoes of the song "We Shall Overcome" in the last lines of both Moody's and Myrlie Evers's books or, more recently, the jarring beat of Dälek's "Who Medgar Evers Was." These writers and performers—past and present—resist a departure from the past, repetitively acting out rather than working through the trauma of civil rights history, eschewing any conveniently therapeutic trajectory.[94]

With the notable exception of the newspapers, all of these texts form a constellation of aesthetic production around Evers's life and death that continues to witness not only to the harsh realities of working in the movement but also to the very process of witnessing itself.[95] Even more recent memoirs serve a testimonial function, among them Willie Morris's flamboyantly titled *The Ghosts of Medgar Evers: A Tale of Race,*

Murder, Mississippi, and Hollywood, as well as other creative nonfiction texts in which white writers from the South wrestle with the meaning of the Medgar Evers story or, as in the case of Massengill's *Portrait of a Racist*, with the engorged racism of the murderous Beckwith that both horrifies and fascinates the author (his nephew-in-law).[96] Morris's story of his tangled emotions as a southern white man—and arguably Welty's chilling story of a cold-blooded killer—offer up another kind of witness, not to the vicissitudes of being black in the 1960s South but to the guilt and anxiety of being cloaked in a southern whiteness that won't wash off, a whiteness that is both frightening and monstrous, that is itself a stain.

That stain soaks through to recent fiction discussed in the final chapter of this book. Two novels, both by white women from Mississippi, reiterate the story of white racism in 1960s Mississippi as presented in Evers's struggles and death: *The Help* by Kathryn Stockett (2009) and my own novel *The Queen of Palmyra* (2010). Both books question a culture of blindness and forgetting. A less optimistic book, *The Queen of Palmyra* asserts that the weight of Mississippi history still lies heavy and poses the loaded question of how to address and be responsible to an irreparable past. Likewise, Frank X Walker's *Turn Me Loose* is intent on "unghosting" history; writing in the voices of Myrlie Evers, Byron De La Beckwith and his two wives, and even the bullet that killed Evers, Walker circles and recircles the mystery of racism, marking its strange wanderings through human psyches and social institutions, its "legal lynchings."[97] As discussed in the final chapter, the forty-nine poems in *Turn Me Loose*, which I learned about just as I was finishing this book, mark a milestone in literary work about Evers and, by urging twenty-first-century readers to remember Medgar Evers and the racist violence that took his life, splice a jagged border between past and present.[98] As Michelle Hite notes in her epilogue to Walker's book, "If we are to finally lay him to rest, to satisfy his request to *turn him loose*, we must remember."[99]

Many of us in the humanities believe that art does cultural work—that art can and does feed the empathy and what Oliver calls the "response-ability" required for social justice in the real world of our present.[100] Increasingly, questions about how art can matter in a world engorged by transnational capitalism have become more pressing. As Morrison indicates in her many statements about the relationship of art and ethics, it is art's responsive and responsible rendering of history and memory that is a key to the affective, cognitive, and political processes that form systems of ethics and justice. The way history comes to *matter*, in all the nuances of the term, in aesthetic production and the impulse to memorialize, can create, for better or worse, a present and a future that matter in a world that is deeply stained by violence but also awash in possibility.

The field of Holocaust studies struggles with the question of how an incomprehensible number of murders should be represented and remembered: how the multitudes can and should be mourned one by one. The final larger question the Evers story calls us to is that of individual sacrifice. How does the one individual, a man whom many in this country remember and perhaps many more have forgotten or have never heard of, become more than one? As Myrlie Evers notes, "Medgar was carefully chosen. No other victim would have served at that moment in time. Medgar was killed specifically because of what he represented, of what he had become, of the hope that his presence gave to Mississippi Negroes and the fear it aroused in Mississippi whites."[101]

From all accounts, Medgar Evers knew he was going to die for his work in the Mississippi civil rights movement. What does it mean that one man or one woman dies, knowingly, in the cause of representing the many in the face of injustice? Cultural mourning and memory kept alive through writings and stories are as much spatial as temporal; they exist in both the past and the present, yet they move us toward a future that will inevitably become the past. What kind of future will that be, and what kind of history will it produce?

Art is deeply connected to the world and, as such, provides a migratory path toward global thinking. Evers's life, "the everydayness of race, memory, and injustice" that it signifies, resides in these texts.[102] The fact that much of this writing focuses on Evers's death does not diminish the importance of that life; to the contrary, it reveals what kind of man he was, both in life and in death, within the context of a double vision of two civil rights movements: the one he gave his life for and the one he could only begin to imagine. It was often said, emphatically, that Evers was a *man*.[103] Certainly this is a clear reference to his courage, but it is important to understand that his was both a singular and a plural heroism. Evers was both a leader and a member of the community he served. He walked the streets of his community with police and criminals alike hounding him, drove the dark and dangerous backcountry roads of Mississippi to hear the stories, stood in the "colored line" to get medicine for his desperately ill comrade, talked to anyone who knew his phone number, kept his cool. He modeled for southern African Americans a new form of cultural identity that both drew from the past and broke with it. The future always in his mind's eye, "he leaned across tomorrow."

In recent years the U.S. South and its deeply flawed history have become integral parts of global thinking about human-inflicted carnage and trauma and questions of justice, responsibility, and intervention. These are the aspects of Evers's story—its presentness and its prescience—that still draw us in. How, indeed, should we mourn and celebrate Medgar Wiley Evers and his plural singularity? How do we remember him, both as the one and the many? And where should remembrance lead?

CHAPTER TWO

Where Are the Voices "Coming From"?

JAMES BALDWIN, MARGARET WALKER, EUDORA WELTY, AND THE QUESTION OF LOCATION

January 4, 1963: On a tour of the troubled South, New Yorker and world traveler James Baldwin meets Medgar Evers, NAACP field secretary for Mississippi, for the first time. They are young men about the same age: Baldwin is thirty-eight, Evers thirty-seven. In the coming days Baldwin will nervously accompany Evers into DeKalb County, Mississippi, to investigate a murder. Baldwin is a cosmopolitan man; he has lived in some of the major cities of the world, but he is terrified as the two of them weave their way along the backcountry roads. Evers is looking into the case of a black man who was killed by a white storekeeper because "the white storekeeper liked his wife."[1] Evers's report on the case will go to the NAACP headquarters in New York and from there to news media across the country. Baldwin comes away from the experience with a deep admiration for Evers, calling him "'a *great* man . . . a beautiful man' and sens[ing] in him a resignation that sprang from an inner knowledge that he was 'going to die.'"[2] The DeKalb County murder, along with Baldwin's visit to a country church with Evers on the same trip, will form part of the plot and setting of Baldwin's 1964 play *Blues for Mister Charlie*.[3] At the time of Baldwin's death more than two decades later, he will be working on a book about Medgar Evers, Malcolm X, and Martin Luther King called *Remember This House*.[4]

June 12, 1963: In her Jackson, Mississippi, home at 741 North Congress Street on the white side of town, renowned fiction writer Eudora Welty, a gentle and progressive individual with a keen interest in local politics, hears the news reports that Medgar Evers has been murdered. Shocked, horrified, and furious, she sits down at her typewriter and produces the voice of Evers's hate-filled killer in an attempt to explain to the world the twisted logic behind such a horrific crime. The result is the famously riveting short story "Where Is the Voice Coming From?" published about three weeks later in the *New Yorker*. When Beckwith is arrested on the second of July, as the July 6 issue of the magazine is in press, Welty and her editor have to make hasty revisions over the phone. Her portrayal of the details of the murder is too close to the truth, although as time will show, she gets the class identity of the killer wrong, making him "a Snopes" instead of "a Compson"—a mistake that would trouble and unsettle her for the rest of her life.[5]

June 13, 1963: Another Jackson writer, Margaret Walker, a prize-winning poet and author of the often-cited poem "For My People," is in Iowa City working on a doctorate at the University of Iowa, although her family lives only a few doors down Guynes Street from the Everses. Like Welty, she is deeply angered and grieved to hear of Evers's murder. Writing in her journal, Walker calls it the "worst tragedy of the whole Movement for equality . . . tragic and overwhelming in its horror." A few nights later, Walker writes, she is horrified when watching "Eyewitness to History" on television and the first face she sees is that of her fourteen-year-old son, Sigis, in the Everses' yard. When she talks to Sigis on the phone, he reports, "Mother, the blood is all over the place."[6] In 1970 her chapbook of poetry about the civil rights movement, *Prophets for a New Day*, will contain a poem about Evers titled "Micah," which likens Evers to the vociferous Old Testament prophet who also decried the social injustice he saw around him.

All three of these writers' narratives of the Evers murder are informed by the authors' relationships to the local scene in Mississippi, the place and cultural space where Evers lived and worked. Walker and Welty each wrote passionately and directly about Evers's murder. Baldwin's play took a longer, indirect trajectory, starting out as a drama about the 1955 murder of fourteen-year-old Emmett Till. Yet the author, fresh from his harrowing time with Evers in Mississippi, was clearly writing both from and about Evers's murder as well as Till's, creating a work in which their deaths merge into the histories of many such murders of southern African American men and boys. To paraphrase the title of Welty's famous story about Evers's murder, these three writers' voices were "coming from" their own complicated senses of proximity to and distance from the local. Indeed, the *local*—Mississippi, Jackson, the Everses' Guynes Street—folds into the *locations*, that is, the personal proximities and affiliations of these writers vis-à-vis the Evers story, and profoundly shapes their telling of it.

There's been a wealth of theoretical discussion about location, but I'd like to return to Welty's statement in which she calls location "the crossroads of circumstance, the proving ground of 'What happened? Who's here? Who's coming?'" that is "the heart's field."[7] In the discussion that follows, I consider geographic, cultural, and emotional proximities of these three writers to "the crossroads of circumstance" and "the heart's field" of Evers's specifically located life experiences. I also ponder how the local may be conceptualized as both an aesthetic and a geographic component in the cultural work of remembrance that leads to a "longer, harder" vision of a civil rights movement that extends temporally into our own times—our here and now and our future—and spatially to other human rights struggles. How do the various forms of proximity and distance occupied by these three writers in relation to Evers's "heart's field" shape the acts of remembrance, mourning, and social action to which their writings summon us as readers?

In an introduction to a reading of *Beloved*, Toni Morrison once said that she wrote her novel about slavery to find out "what it must have been like."[8] Similarly, we may ask what it must have been like to walk in the shoes of Medgar Evers and other civil rights activists who were so firmly planted in the local. I raise this question in relation to Renee Romano and Leigh Raiford's observations that civil rights history more often than not has been rendered in terms of exceptional individual action in the moment rather than long-term community activism, that the long and exhausting hard work of local organizing and everyday jeopardy and sacrifice—the kind of work that Medgar Evers was known for—hasn't been fully narrated as part of the civil rights story. Evers was a leader who worked without fanfare or bodyguards. He was careful and thorough, negotiating as best he could the interests of local activists with the national offices of the more conservative NAACP (no mean feat) and eschewing the limelight himself while persistently removing the veil from the racial crimes he uncovered and publicized. As I have suggested, Evers was a leader of plural singularity in that he was very much a man of the people, one man who worked hard alongside others to push the movement forward slowly and painfully. What was it like for him to live and work collaboratively on the local scene of Jim Crow Mississippi in both transparent and non-transparent ways? In her writings and in interview after interview up to the present, Myrlie Evers-Williams has emphasized the terrible fear that gripped her husband, their family, and their community. Mapping the terror of a landscape of violently enforced racial apartheid, she writes in her memoir: "A map of Mississippi was a reminder not of geography, but of atrocities, of rivers that hid broken bodies, of towns and cities ruled by the enemy. No spot was safe, no road without its traps, and Medgar was a constantly moving target." On this map a history of mayhem is inscribed. The years, she writes, "were stamped with the names of the murdered, the months were inked with those of the beaten and maimed. Affidavits testifying to the routine cruelty of white Mississippians toward Negroes piled up in Medgar's files. Each represented an hour, a day, a week of Medgar's life in a surrealist version of Hell."[9]

In the summer of 1963 the Everses were living under a state of siege. They had selected the lot for their house because it was between two houses and not at the end of Guynes Street, which in turn was linked to a busy road with an easy escape route.[10] They had added to their modest house two special features for safety—a side entry door from the carport and bedroom windows high off the ground. They didn't plant bushes or trees near the house; they got their German shepherd named Heidi and fenced in the small bare backyard, where the children could only play if Heidi was present. As the tension heightened, they became victims of threatening phone calls, gunshots into the house, rocks, and a fire bomb.

Their street had burned-out streetlights that the city had neglected to replace. If the family members were out after dark, they were not to leave the porch light burning because it would provide more of a target from the overgrown lot across the street; after barricading themselves inside the house, they often would sit on the floor to watch television, rather than on the sofa. The children were instructed that if they heard gunshots they were to drop to the floor and crawl to the bathroom.[11]

Evers-Williams would say twenty-five years later, in a commemorative issue of *The Crisis*, "We both knew within our hearts that at some point in time the chances were very good that he would be taken from us. . . . It was something that we lived with on a day-to-day basis."[12] In an interview with British writer Nicholas Hordern a decade after her husband's assassination, she said that the level of psychological tension that she and her husband were under in the days leading up to his death was so excruciating that when he came home at night, they would just sit together and hold each other and cry.[13] The week before Evers's murder had been clotted with local tension. Riot police had lined the street in front of the Masonic Temple as Lena Horne and Dick Gregory spoke to overflow crowds, who didn't yet know that the national headquarters of the NAACP had withdrawn its support for demonstrations and stopped authorizing bail. That Monday Evers had learned that he was on a KKK hit list. On Tuesday a Jackson police car almost hit him as he crossed the street.[14] On the national scene, Governor George Wallace had folded under pressure from Washington and allowed black students to enter the University of Alabama under the protection of the National Guard, and that night President Kennedy had given a speech about the immorality of segregation, calling for white Americans to search their consciences on the subject of race.

On the last full day of her husband's life, June 11, Myrlie Evers, then a few weeks pregnant with their fourth child, got up at 5:00 a.m., ironed ten or twelve shirts, and answered the constantly ringing phone with pleas of people whose children had been jailed. "I had an obsession of keeping my house clean," she said, "keeping clothes and keeping everything ironed, keeping everything right up to par because I had this premonition that something was going to happen, and I wanted everything to be in order when it did. You know it was a subconscious kind. . . . Rather like writing a will . . . but I felt awful, and I was ill and as it turned out I didn't have things spotless, and I was exhausted."[15]

While Myrlie Evers dragged herself through her household labors that morning, James Baldwin was relaxing in Puerto Rico after an intense round of lectures and civil rights rallies on the national and international stages since his January visit to Mississippi and other parts of the South. On May 12 he and a group of activists in the arts had had an unpleasant and unproductive meeting with Attorney General Robert Kennedy; the May 23 issue of *Life* had featured his Congress for Racial Equality (CORE) tour of the South with a group of memorable photographs, including one of him in Durham, North Carolina, with an abandoned child; he'd given electrifying talks and interviews, traveling from the east coast to Los Angeles, making incendiary comments and speeches along the way about the terrible state of things in the South and the failure of the president and attorney general to intervene. The *Life* article headlined his battle cry: "There's a bill due that has to be paid."[16] Such comments had resulted in a national web of intense federal surveillance and an ever-thickening FBI file.

Baldwin's position as what biographer David Leeming calls a "prophetic witness who cried out across the gulf between the races"[17] depended on his ability during the early sixties to move in and out of the dangerous South; he was a translator of the local to the global and vice versa. Both an emissary, at his own peril, from the larger, more progressive national and international scenes to the interior of the southern—often rural southern—civil rights struggle and a reporter of that struggle to the world at large, he seemed to see himself as a traveling witness, a black man who visited sites of danger such as DeKalb County with Evers, offered inspirational support from a racially marked and therefore dangerous visitor's position, and then went out into the larger world to report what was happening in the dark of night on Mississippi country roads or Birmingham city streets. This zeal for social justice manifests itself in *Blues for Mister Charlie*.[18] As he writes in the prefatory note: "We are walking in terrible darkness here, and this is one man's attempt to bear witness to the reality and the power of light."[19]

More generally, Baldwin's modus was to enter and then withdraw from the civil rights struggle, just as he traveled back and forth between the United States and abroad. In a 1970 interview Baldwin says that he returned to the United States from Paris because of the civil rights movement, adding, "I got tired and I began to be ashamed, sitting in cafes in Paris and explaining Little Rock and Tennessee. I thought it was easier to go home." In the same interview he says he left the United States again "when Malcolm X was killed, when Martin Luther King was killed, when Medgar Evers and John and Bobby and Fred Hampton were killed. I loved Medgar. I loved Martin and Malcolm. We all worked together and kept the faith. Now they are all dead. When you think about it, it is incredible. I'm the last witness—everybody else is dead. I couldn't stay in America. I had to leave."[20] Moreover, in his public role as spokesman for civil rights, Baldwin felt so personally threatened by the string of assassinations that he thought he might well be next. Over time, he went as far away as he could go—to Israel, Istanbul, France.

In his own personal life, Baldwin seemed to have conflicting impulses about his own sense of locality, his place on the map. Like Morrison in her essay "Home," Baldwin seemed to associate home with conflicts around race. He saw the local as a gateway to the larger political arena. In "The Harlem Ghetto" in *Notes of a Native Son*, he writes not about the place where he grew up but rather about the black press and the vexed relations between African Americans and Jews. There is indeed more about Harlem—his birthplace and home—in the next essay in the volume, "Journey to Atlanta." In a 1961 letter to his literary agent, Baldwin writes from Israel about an upcoming trip to Africa and the sense of his own rootlessness it evokes:

the fact that Israel *is* a homeland for so many Jews . . . causes me to feel my own homelessness more keenly than ever. (People say: "Where are you from?" And it causes me a tiny and resentful effort to say: "New York"—what did *I* ever do to deserve so ghastly a birthplace?—and their faces fall.)

But just because my homelessness is so inescapably brought home to me, it begins, in some odd way, not only to be bearable but to be a positive opportunity. It must be, must be made to be. My bones know, somehow, something of what waits for me in Africa.[21]

This uneasiness with home and its association with race and racially based oppression coalesce in Baldwin's deep fear of the U.S. South and may have been partly responsible for slowing Baldwin's pace in writing *Blues for Mister Charlie*. The play was based, as Baldwin explains, "*very distantly indeed*, on the case of Emmett Till—the Negro youth who was murdered in Mississippi in 1955" (my emphasis). Director Elia Kazan had suggested in 1959 that Baldwin undertake a play about Till, and Baldwin had agreed to write it, but over the years his efforts had stalled again and again. In his prefatory notes Baldwin writes that, although the germ of the play had been "bugging" him for years, he was afraid to write it. At first he thought this reluctance came from a fear of failure in committing to a new form, but then he began to understand that his real fear was much deeper—he felt compelled, as Welty had been in the writing of "Where Is the Voice Coming From?" to enter the psychology of white racism, and he feared he "would never be able to draw a valid portrait of the murderer" and "a spiritual darkness which no one can describe." Yet, as he says, he came to understand that "we have the duty to try to understand this wretched man; and while we probably cannot hope to liberate him, begin working toward the liberation of his children. For we, the American people, have created him."[22]

Baldwin was always quick to acknowledge that racism and racist violence were not strictly southern or even national phenomena. Arguably, though, his January 1963 foray into Medgar Evers's local scene—the visit to Jackson, the trip to the backwoods, the murder investigation, the whispered meetings with frightened African Americans, the complete lack of any hope of bringing the murderer to justice in a time when southern juries were made up of white men only—may well have caused him to perceive Mississippi as the place where all his fears as a black man living in his times coalesced, the place where so many black men and boys had been pulled from sleep, as Emmett Till had been, to face a lynch mob that did its work with impunity. Trudier Harris notes, in fact, the "tremendous fear that accosted him every time he ventured South" and connects

Baldwin's fear of the South with his fear of emasculation and castration.[23] Those fears and the sense of helplessness they evoked seem to have frozen Baldwin's efforts over the years to write the play.

If so, anger and grim determination trumped fear when, on June 12, 1963, Medgar Evers was gunned down in his own driveway by yet another hate-filled white man. Evers's assassination deeply angered Baldwin and spurred him, at long last, to sit down and write his play. As he says in the prefatory note: "When he [Evers] died, something entered into me which I cannot describe, but it was then that I resolved that nothing under heaven would prevent me from getting this play done." The play is inscribed "to the memory of MEDGAR EVERS, and his widow and children, and to the memory of the dead children of Birmingham," a reference to the Sixteenth Street Baptist Church bombing the September following Evers's murder that resulted in the deaths of four choir girls.[24]

Baldwin wrote most of the play in Puerto Rico and finished it in New York. After being plagued by problems during rehearsals, mainly by the author's insistence that he maintain control over the production, *Blues for Mister Charlie* opened on Broadway to mixed reviews less than a year after Evers's death. Baldwin had insisted on low prices for admission, a move that filled the theater but resulted in insufficient income to cover production costs, and the Actors Studio production company tried to close the play a month after its opening. Baldwin managed to get private financial backing for the play to keep it open until the end of August. A short time later the Aldwych Theatre presented a disastrous performance in London.[25] Reviews were more negative than positive, perhaps because, as Calvin Hernton noted in 1970, of the mirror *Blues* held up to white behavior: "In regard to the Negro, when the white man is portrayed as a barbarous, unmitigated bigot, we not only label the art form as 'controversial,' we also cry out that it is not 'art'; we call it 'propaganda.'"[26]

Mississippi casts a long historical shadow in *Blues for Mister Charlie*, with traces of Medgar Evers in its shape. As Baldwin's prefatory note to *Blues* also illustrates, Evers's murder was a ghostly replica of three centuries' killings of southern black men and youth, the kind of violence Baldwin himself had so feared when he'd made his trip south in January 1963. (On New Year's Eve 1962, he'd called his friend the actor Rip Torn because he was so frightened about going south the following day. The next morning Torn put him on the plane with a bottle of scotch to calm his nerves.)[27] This fearsome local scene in *Blues*, called "Plaguetown, U.S.A.," with its "power to destroy every human relationship," is inescapable and powerfully tied to Medgar Evers. For Evers, his family, and other activists, "Plaguetown" was home, present in every threatening phone call, every move they made. In the prefatory note Baldwin writes: "I once took a short trip with Medgar Evers to the back-woods of Mississippi. . . . Many people talked to Medgar that night, in dark cabins, with their lights out, in whispers; and we had been followed for many miles out of Jackson, Mississippi, not by a lunatic with a gun, but by state troopers. I will never forget that night, as I will never forget Medgar."[28] In an interview about a year later, Baldwin said of the trip with Evers: "We rode around those back roads for hours talking to people who had known the dead man, trying to find out what had happened. And the Negroes talked to us as the German Jews must have talked when Hitler came into power."[29]

Baldwin's keen sense of the southern local as a zone of danger and death, especially for black men, pervades his writings of the sixties. In "Nobody Knows My Name: A Letter from the South," published in 1959, he describes being on a plane flying over "the rust-red earth of Georgia" for the first time: "I could not suppress the thought that this earth had acquired its color from the blood that had dripped down from these trees. My mind was filled with the image of a black man, younger than I, perhaps, or my own age, hanging from a tree, while white men watched him and cut his sex from him with a knife."[30] As he notes in his 1963 essay "The Artist's Struggle for Integrity," "Art is here to prove, and to help one bear, the fact that all safety is an illusion."[31] Harris, in fact, finds Baldwin's own art, and especially *Blues for Mister Charlie*, limited by his inability "to think of the South without conflict between blacks and whites . . . to see beyond racism."[32]

Blues for Mister Charlie undertakes the act of mourning for Emmett Till, Medgar Evers, and other victims of racist violence in the locality of fear and forced segregation of Plaguetown, which itself seems like a stage set of the Everses' environment in Jackson. The play is painful to read, and for white and black audiences alike, it must have been painful to watch because it emphasizes again and again the violent unnaturalness of segregation and how that unnaturalness, always made manifest spatially, itself breeds fear, bigotry, and bloodshed. Baldwin understood the relationship between the concept of "homeland"—psychic, geographic, cultural—and the borders that separate it from the rest of the world. During his 1961 Israel trip, he notes that he cannot forget that the country functions as a "homeland, however beleaguered," because "you can't walk five minutes without finding yourself at a border."[33] The play splits black and white cultural spaces, the stage becoming the location, in miniature, of the Jim Crow South. Segregation is thus concretely enforced in the stage's representation of the southern small town, with the first two acts taking place in a black church, which is divided by an aisle functioning as the division between "Whitetown" and "Blacktown." In the third act the stage becomes a segregated courtroom, further emphasizing the spatial and social chasm dividing the races in the local setting. Interestingly, Baldwin's choice to bring the show to Broadway, instead of "one of the uptown theatres where the more avant-garde LeRoi Jones and his like were working," was deliberate. "It was crucial, he said, that 'the country' should listen to 'the black man's own version of himself and of white people.'"[34]

This spatial division shows itself in terms of its characters as well. When Richard Henry, who will be murdered by Lyle Britten, returns to his hometown, he is recognized in Blacktown as belonging to the local black populace: he is greeted as the son of the minister Meridian Henry; he has his father's smile; he is welcomed back into the black community. In Whitetown, however, he is dumped into the junkyard of stereotypes where black men are rapists, "orang-outang[s] out of the jungle," "stallions," and, in the case of the biracial, "mongrel[s]."[35] In such a bifurcated locality, Richard's focused belligerence in the whitespace of Lyle and Jo Britten's store is both his effort at rebellion and his fatal error.

In the courtroom scene, during Lyle's trial for the murder of Richard, the authoritarian voice of "The State" invariably comes down on the side of the white defendant, harassing the black people giving testimony and discounting or undercutting their veracity, while Blacktown and Whitetown become choruses, shouting out contradictory messages.[36] When Jo Britten begins to testify falsely that Richard tried to assault her in the store, Whitetown chimes in: "Don't be afraid. Just tell the truth," while Blacktown yells out: "Here we go—down the river."[37] This back and forth between the segregated localities of the play on opposite sides of the stage continues throughout the court scene, stretching tensions to the breaking point as the composite portrait of "the white community of a small southern town" is seen "through its own eyes" while Baldwin portrays—as Welty does in "Where Is the Voice Coming From?"—"the wider issues involved in a racial murder [and] the terrible self-deception that racial murderers must live by."[38]

The segregation of the local in the play is further developed in the virtual segregation of its audience. Before the play closed on Broadway, Baldwin remarked, "I know what I tried to do in the play—start an argument."[39] Hernton observes: "[B]oth times I saw the play there were as many, if not more, whites in the audience than there were Negroes. One could not help but feel the negative vibrations radiating from the whites during the major portion of the evening. They seemed to squirm throughout the play and grow little in their seats; many tried to hold a straight face (face of chalk), but one could see and feel the hot charge boiling beneath their white masks." At several points in the play when the talk turns to sex, especially of the interracial variety, Hernton writes that he thought "half of the white audience might jump up and storm out of the theater." On the other hand, he writes, "Negroes seemed to be enthralled with delight and moral vindication to see for the first time the true nature of their lives, and their plight, played back to them with dignity and no beating around the bush."[40]

The jokes in the play also are designed to pit a black audience against a white one. As Carlton W. Molette describes, conversation among whites during intermission and after the play "all seemed to revolve around the fact that there was content that the blacks understood and whites did not. 'What are *they* laughing at?'—meaning the blacks in the audience—the whites kept asking each other. But the reverse situation applied as well. The white characters were frequently not understood, or not accepted as valid, by the black audience members." Molette rightly points out, though, that the play is more complex than a mere representation of a bifurcated society; yet he sees that complexity as a liability, charging that Baldwin's attempt to "explain whites to blacks and blacks to whites" probably requires "two different plays" rather than one.[41]

I would argue, instead, that Baldwin's more nuanced depiction of his characters' senses of location in Plaguetown may well stem, at least in part, from the author's experience with Medgar Evers's vision of community and the civil rights leader's method of working both against and across racial lines. Parnell James, white editor of the local newspaper "which *nobody* reads,"[42] is both friendly to the murderer and sympathetic to the plight of the local African Americans; in the end he walks alongside (if not with) the black protesters, though one has a sense of his continued ambivalence on the question of race. Meridian Henry, a black minister and widower whose wife was probably killed by a white man, and father of Richard, the murder victim, tries to maintain his equilibrium in the face of despair and insists, as Evers did in speaking about his native state of Mississippi: "I will not abandon the land—this strange land, which is my home."[43]

While Parnell's ambivalence—his unwillingness to make up his mind about what kind of home he wants and is willing to fight for—offers both frustration and possibility, Meridian's prayer offers a sense of transcendence over racism and an unwillingness to flee the local; flawed and dangerous though Plaguetown is, it is nonetheless his home. Segregated Plaguetown is a place of belief, passion, and hope as well as danger and violence, of good intentions as well as hatred and prejudice, of bridges as well as barriers. In short, the play, horrifying and tragic though it is, reflects in the black characters who remain behind—Meridian, Juanita, and the other marchers—something of Evers's long-term vision and optimism and his refusal to leave his home of Mississippi, his tragic "crossroads of circumstance," and most especially his "heart's field." As he had said in his interview with *Ebony* in 1958, "It may sound funny, but I love the South. I don't choose to live anywhere else. There's land here, where a man can raise cattle, and I'm going to do that some day. There are lakes where a man can sink a hook and fight the bass. There is room for my children to play and grow, and become good citizens—if the white man will let them."[44]

As Evers's own statement indicates and as evoked in *Blues for Mister Charlie*, the southern local is therefore complicated and messy for its black inhabitants, dense with the webs of affiliation and anxiety, hope, and despair. As rendered in Baldwin's play, the local, because of its complexity and nuance, becomes a powerful and problematic site for pondering questions of ethics and justice and, for Baldwin, the evolving role of the artist as a witness to human-inflicted trauma. In 1963, in an essay called "The Artist's Struggle for Integrity," he wrote: "The time has come, it seems to me, to recognize that the framework in which we operate weighs on us too heavily to be borne and is about to kill us. It is time to ask very hard questions and to take very rude positions. And no matter at what price."[45] This was indeed Baldwin's purpose on his southern tour—to make the local visible on the world stage, just as Evers attempted to do during his tenure as NAACP field secretary. This visibility—as well as Baldwin's incongruous placement of himself within the southern landscape of the early sixties, his saddened, prematurely lined face plastered across the covers of the nation's magazines—thrust Jim Crow's blight on the lives of black southerners into the national limelight. As an aesthetic product, *Blues for Mister Charlie* goes a step further by revealing the lure as well as the entrapment of the local for African Americans in the 1960s South—the psychological cost of being situated in a home place where you are feared and persecuted, where peace and rest are impossible.

As the first field secretary of the Mississippi NAACP and a transformational and situated leader, Medgar Evers had an intimate knowledge of the rockiness and complexity of this terrain. He was castigated by black newspaper editor Percy Greene at the very historical moment he was being criticized and lampooned by white editors of the two Jackson dailies. He knew the tensions between the NAACP and other activist organizations such as SCLC and CORE; he negotiated the interests of the local populace with the contingencies of the national organizations he served; he understood the importance of coalition, local and national, white and black. He had dreams of a better future, but he also knew his neighbors on Guynes Street—African American businessmen, doctors, and teachers—would probably rather not have had his family in their midst, bringing danger into the neighborhood.

This complexity of Evers's experience of the local is mirrored in the two faces we see behind that of the doomed Richard Henry of Baldwin's play: that of Emmett Till, the fun-seeking, brash fourteen-year-old youth with his whole life in front of him, a stranger to the racial apartheid of the local scene and the racialized shame it depended on, and that of Medgar Evers, a thirty-seven-year-old family man from a poor country background in Mississippi, a leader who knew what he was up against but insisted on his right to be at home in his home state and adopted city. Richard Henry is a complicated character who, as Emmanuel Nelson suggests, "becomes increasingly sensitive to the beauty and strength that come out of the appalling suffering of his people"; but as Harris insists, he is also "a disturbed young man" who "resorts to braggadocio to make up for what he lacks—lack of status in his current community, lack of security about his manhood." Nelson sees a pattern in the play, and in Baldwin's work in general, of a movement from suffering to empathy to community and finds that it is in Richard's "gradual identification with the collective, communal Black experience from which he had originally alienated himself that he finds his self and strength." Alternatively, Harris argues that we should not waste sympathy on him.[46]

Certainly we can see in Richard himself the tension in Baldwin's own experience of what Richard calls "the deep, black, funky South," the author's own movement between his conscientious attempts, like Evers's, to report on Jim Crow and its daily effects; his deep and well-founded fear of racial violence, a fear that would eventually cause him to leave the country; and his rage at the state of things in the place Richard describes as "the ass-hole of the world."[47] Richard wants to return home: he gives up his gun to his father; he falls in love with Juanita; he returns to old friendships. But he cannot abide the way things are: the lack of common courtesy in modes of address, the racist epithets, the sexual predation of white men that probably resulted in his mother's death, the emasculation of African American men. All of it drives him so crazy that he acts in complete disregard for his life, not naively the way young Emmett Till did but with foreknowledge of his own fate. Whether Lyle Britten would have shot Richard had he apologized is an open question, but the fact is Richard didn't/couldn't apologize because to have done so would have been to deny his own rage. For Richard that rage has a history in his mother's death; likewise, in *Blues for Mister Charlie*, Baldwin's bold strokes create a historical layering of victims of racial violence, the shadows of old crimes still visible under the faces of the newly murdered.

Solidly located in place, the play moves back and forth in time, and in the end it pivots to the future: when all is said and done, the murderer Lyle Britten will go free as his forefathers did, *but* there will be a protest march, which a white man will walk alongside, marking a tiny step toward change, an opening. This attention to time *and* place is the key to the play's power, for the spatial is layered with historical resonance, with a mystery and density that does some justice to the incremental progress achieved by those men and women who, like Medgar Evers, lived complex, textured lives of courage and engaged vulnerability, who understood and valued incremental progress. In a 1973 interview Baldwin pointed to those who had lived such lives as possessing, in retrospect, "a profound nobility, a real nobility on the part of a whole lot of black people, old and young. There is no other word for it. . . . Malcolm was noble. Martin was noble. Medgar was noble and those kinds were noble and it exposed an entire country, it exposed an entire civilization. Now we have to take it from here."[48] Interestingly, though, Baldwin, who was approaching his fiftieth birthday, was an ocean away from Guynes Street and Plaguetown when he gave this interview at his home in southern France. By then he had fled the United States in fear and disgust. He would return from time to time for book tours and teaching stints, but he would die in Saint-Paul-de-Vence, far from southern soil.

While the cosmopolitan Baldwin worked the national scene for southern civil rights in the early sixties, back in Jackson Margaret Walker and Eudora Welty, who both had reached middle age, were experiencing a vexed relationship with their home city. The two were of the same generation—Walker's dates (1915 to 1998) closely correspond to Welty's (1909 to 2001), and, although on opposite sides of the race line, both had grown up in middle-class educated families with an appreciation for books, art, and music. On the state and local scenes over the years, they won some of the same awards, and they spoke so often at the same gatherings that Welty's biographer Suzanne Marrs says they jokingly referred to themselves as "a sister act."[49] They lived only 3.6 miles apart, at least so the drive goes on today's city streets, but those miles mark, then and now, deeply divided material and cultural spaces.

Throughout her long career Walker, whose family home stood several houses down Guynes from the Everses' (the street is now called Margaret Walker Alexander Street; the house numbers 50 and the Everses' 49 on the present-day civil rights self-tour), would speak and write of Evers as a martyr and entreat African Americans to live up to his legacy. Yet Walker was far from Guynes Street on the day of Evers's death, June 12, 1963, having temporarily left her teaching post at Jackson State College and the state of Mississippi during this period, which, by her own account, was "a time of sheer terror." Unlike Tougaloo, the private black university in Jackson and the site from which much of the central Mississippi civil rights movement drew its energy, Jackson State, though attended by only black students, was controlled and funded by the all-white Mississippi Board of Education. In her memoir, *Coming of Age in Mississippi*, the Tougaloo student activist Anne Moody would scathingly refer to her sister institution as "an Uncle Tom school."[50] And Walker would say in an interview almost twenty years later:

> I found myself in an untenable position in the early sixties. My students were in revolt, and the administration was holding the line for segregation on orders of the powers that be—shall we say, the establishment. And like most of the teachers, I was called in and asked whether I was on the side of the students or on the side of the administration. And I said I couldn't take either side. If I sided with my students against the administration, I wouldn't have a job; and if I sided with the administration against the students, I wouldn't have anybody to teach, and I wouldn't be able to do that either. So I went to school. . . . I was ill in the summer of '60, in the hospital, in '61 I went out to Iowa, and I came back in the state through a hellish year, '61 and '62, but . . . the fall of '62 I was in Iowa and I stayed there three years. . . . I was gone the most violent year of all. 1963 was the most violent year.[51]

A few days before Evers's murder, Walker had traveled through Jackson after attending her son's graduation in New Orleans, staying at her house long enough to purchase a washing machine from Houston Wells, Evers's next-door neighbor, who would end up putting the civil rights leader's mortally wounded body in the back seat of Wells's station wagon and taking him to the nearby University of Mississippi hospital.[52] Back in Iowa, Walker wrote in her journal the day after the murder: "The demonstrations for Negro Rights were in full swing in Jackson and I got much material for poetry and an article — but yesterday morning came the worst news — Medgar Evers — our neighbor and NAACP Field Secretary had been shot and fatally wounded as he stepped out of his car midnight Tuesday — By 2 a.m. Wednesday he was dead — shot in the back leaving a young widow and three small children. The worst tragedy of the whole movement for equality . . . tragic, and overwhelming in its horror." In an entry from that evening, she speculates at length on the potential for revolution at that point in history and advocates "a tide of revolt" for "full rights and right now, not tomorrow."[53]

That summer of Evers's murder Welty was living with her elderly ailing mother in her family home on Pinehurst, a house the author would inhabit for seventy-six years of her life. It was (and is) a spacious Tudor-style house with lush backyard gardens on tree-lined Pinehurst Street overlooking the campus of Belhaven College to the north, though in the sixties the gardens were less than pristine because of Welty's need to care for her mother. Over many years to come, Welty would repeat the story of how she came to write "Where Is the Voice Coming From?" — its precipitous composition and frantic revisions: how, on hearing of the Evers murder on the news, she knew immediately that she had to write about it. The story itself, she has famously said, "just pushed up" and came to her out of "the strangest feeling of horror and compulsion all in one";[54] it was published in the July 6 issue of the *New Yorker* less than a month after Evers's murder. Her audacious (and, as Doris Betts points out, uncharacteristic) aesthetic move in writing the story in the first person,[55] and *as the murderer*, came out of her sense that she knew what kind of person would do such a thing, which, as it turned out, wasn't quite true, a fact that would concern her over the years to come. Welty's own narrative of the story includes her repeated accounts of its famous revisions to avoid a libel suit brought on by the story's striking similarities with the actual murder and Beckwith himself, who had by then been apprehended and charged, and also to avoid complications in his trial. In the years to come she would return again and again to discussions of the story, saying, among other things, that despite the fact that she had gotten the class of the killer wrong, "I did know the inside and I wrote from the interior, because I felt that I could. . . . What I was writing about really was that world of hate that I felt I had grown up with and I felt I could speak as someone who knew it. . . . Well, really, I just wrote from deep feeling and horror."[56]

Welty's life, like her home, was located within the relative safety of the white side of town. At the time of Evers's murder, though, she was deeply worried about the boiling racial tensions, her elderly mother's safety, and her own responsibilities as a white writer of conscience.[57] In the spring of 1963 she had insisted on having her reading and lecture at the Southern Literary Festival, which was being held at yet another institution of higher learning in Jackson, the all-white, private Millsaps College, opened to an African American audience that included faculty and students from Tougaloo, Anne Moody among them. At one point, as Marrs notes, Welty became so distraught from anonymous phone calls, threats, and the rampantly racist turn in state and local politics that she considered taking her mother and leaving the state altogether; even her doctor had "urged her to find a place where she could rest and be free of stress."[58] Welty did not heed this advice except to attend a two-week writing retreat. She was in Jackson the night Evers was assassinated.

What were Welty's and Walker's aesthetic challenges—and ethical imperatives—in the face of such a traumatic and historically significant event? More complexly, from what locations and affiliations did those challenges and imperatives emerge, and what sense of the local did they impart? Both of their writings about Evers's actions (in the case of Walker) and his death (in Welty's story) feature unforgettable voices that seem to come from somewhere deep within their home city, though on opposite sides of the race line and, certainly, diametrically opposite ethics of the characters they create. In "Where Is the Voice Coming From?" the voice of Evers's killer rasps in our ears as the assassin waits in the dark weeds across the street from his victim's house and then fixes his gun sights on his target's back as he gets out of the car. The killer pulls the trigger and watches gleefully as the civil rights leader, called Roland Summers in the story, slumps on his driveway:

> Something darker than him, like the wings of a bird, spread on his back and pulled him down. He climbed up once, like a man under bad claws, and like just blood could weigh a ton he walked with it on his back to better light. Didn't get no further than his door. And fell to stay.
>
> He was down. He was down, and a ton load of bricks on his back wouldn't have laid any heavier. There on his paved driveway, yes sir.
>
> And it wasn't till the minute before, that the mockingbird had quit singing. He'd been singing up my sassafras tree. Either he was up early, or he hadn't never gone to bed, he was like me. And the mocker he'd stayed right with me, filling the air till come the crack, till I turned loose of my load. I was like him. I was on top of the world myself. For once.
>
> I stepped to the edge of his light there, where he's laying flat. I says, "Roland? There was one way left, for me to be ahead of you and stay ahead of you, by Dad, and I just taken it. Now I'm alive and you ain't. We ain't never now, never going to be equals and you know why? One of us is dead."[59]

In interviews throughout the rest of her career, Welty, that spinner of hundreds of fictional works, would be careful to point out how "Where Is the Voice Coming From?" was different from her other stories because it was telling a true story; not only is this scene located in the actual world of Jackson's and Mississippi's racial apartheid (the victim's blackness is everywhere manifest), but it is also situated in the world of the southern, specifically the central Mississippian, natural world. The killer imagines himself as a dark bird of prey, a night hunter—perhaps an owl, or even the gatekeeper of Klan klaverns, the black-robed "Nighthawk," pulling his slain victim down.[60] The narrator also thinks of himself as the mockingbird that sings through the early morning as he waits under the sassafras tree: "I was like him. I was on top of the world myself." Of her story, Welty would say again and again: "You know, it was a *real* story" (my emphasis),[61] and certainly the natural world of plants and animals that

Welty knew so well attests to the locatedness of the story in Jackson. More broadly, her narrator keeps thinking how hot it is, and from all accounts, that June was one of the hottest at that time on record in Jackson. In the story, it is 3:45 a.m. when the narrator drives his brother-in-law's pickup truck by the local bank, where the temperature reads 92 degrees. There are trees "hanging them pones of bloom like split watermelon," probably crape myrtle.[62]

The natural world as a locale of Mississippi's history of racial trauma wasn't a new topic for Walker. She had addressed much of her poetry from the 1940s on toward what she characterized as the shocking disparity between the physical beauty of the South and the horror of racial violence; the wounds of that split seem to fracture Walker's body of poetry again and again in the gaps and ruptures of voice and image, and many of her poems insist on the enmeshment, even complicity, of nature in the South's history of racial trauma. As she put it in a 1986 interview, "The social horror and the physical beauty are constantly there, and I talk about that in everything I write—the beauty of the South and the horror of this other society."[63] Throughout her career she had written repeatedly of African Americans having a blood right to the South through their labor in the natural world. One of her most famous lines is from the poem "Delta": "We with our blood have watered these fields / and they belong to us."[64] The southern landscape, beautiful as it is, can quickly become, as it does in "October Journey," "stagnant, and green, and full of slimy things."[65] In "For Andy Goodman—Michael Schwerner—and James Chaney," written about the three civil rights workers murdered in the summer of 1964, the young men's bodies, which were hidden in an earthen dam near Philadelphia, Mississippi, are still and silently buried, indistinguishable from water, leaf, and snow. They are named and placed several times: "three faces, mirrored in the muddy streams of living," "three leaves, floating in the melted snow," "three lives / turning on the axis of our time." At midpoint the poem takes a turn into sound: "The wild call of the cardinal bird / troubles the Mississippi morning." Then larks, robins, and mockingbirds begin to sing. Finally the silent mourning dove, which has been "brood[ing] over the meadow," begins to address the murdered ones:

> Deep in a Mississippi thicket
> I hear that mourning dove
> Bird of death singing in the swamp
> Leaves of death floating in their watery grave.
>
> . . . .
>
> Mississippi bird of sorrow
> O mourning bird of death
> Sing their sorrow
> Mourn their pain
> And teach us death,
> To love and live with them again![66]

This multiple project of address, narrator to dove to the murdered young men to "us" the readers as listeners turned witnesses, testifies to the presence of the still ones and the brutality of their deaths; in the last lines of the poem, although the victims still cannot speak, their silenced lives are projected into the world by the dove's song. They are no longer hidden as their brutalized bodies were hidden by their murderers; they turn their faces to the sky, they are uncovered, located, and given voice. Their mutilated bodies address us and testify to white violence, as Medgar Evers would have, had he been alive in 1964. As he had done with young Till's and other murders, he would have determinedly alerted reporters, taken his photographs, and written his reports.

Walker's 1970 chapbook of twenty-two poems titled *Prophets for a New Day* includes many such poems. Published by Broadside Press and sold for one dollar, it featured a montage cover of the faces of African American leaders from the 1960s. The volume included elegies for slain leaders and workers in the trenches of the civil rights struggle, such as Chaney, Goodman, and Schwerner; poems that depict specific geographic sites of the movement, such as Jackson, Birmingham, and Oxford; and a group called the Prophets poems, which likened certain prominent African American figures of the period, such as Martin Luther King Jr. and Medgar Evers, to Old Testament prophets.

"Jackson, Mississippi," quoted in chapter 1, illustrates Walker's affiliation with her home. Not only is Jackson a city of "closed doors and ketchup-splattered floors," of people being hauled in garbage trucks, of "leashed and fiercely hungry dogs"; it is also a

> [c]ity with southern sun beating down raw fire
> On heads of blaring jukes
> And light-drenched streets puddle with the promise
> Of a brand-new tomorrow.

Walker ends the poem with these lines:

> Here are echoes of my laughing children
> And hungry minds of pupils to be fed.
> I give you my brimming heart, Southern City
> For my eyes are full and no tears cry
> And my throat is dusty and dry.[67]

This is a cacophonous poem, projecting multiple registers of white inhumanity; "squealers and profane voices," "ranting voices of demagogues," and a located, vocal black humanity: "blaring jukes," "laughing children," "hungry minds." In the end, the poet's voice is still, her throat "dusty and dry," projecting an address for those silenced by the billy club in this "[c]ity of tense and stricken faces"—an address of silence belied only by the fact of the poem itself. Yet, like Welty's story, which also presents in the voice of her murderous narrator, black children with American flags being loaded into paddy wagons, flying bricks and pop bottles, "a thousand cops crowding ever'where you go,"[68] the poem and the poet insist on location—in Jackson, Mississippi, these were real people in real garbage trucks or paddy wagons, also real children and real pupils, in Welty's words, "a real story." The locatable fact of their (and the poet's) existence in this place bears witness to their everyday lives—listening to music in a juke joint, raising children, teaching pupils—and their historical trauma—at the lunch counters, on the street, facing the dogs and billy clubs.

Of all the events of the early 1960s, the closest in proximity to Walker's emotional center was the assassination of Evers, so her choice of the eighth-century prophet Micah as the primary speaker in her poem about Evers may seem oddly distanced for a local civil rights leader who had been murdered in cold blood just down the block from her own home and family. In the poem "Micah: In Memory of Medgar Evers of Mississippi,"[69] published as one of Walker's prophet poems in the 1970 collection, the prophet cries out in judgment from the biblical past:

> Micah was a young man of the people
> Who came up from the streets of Mississippi
> And cried out his Vision to his people;
> Who stood fearless before the waiting throng
> Like an astronaut shooting into space.
> Micah was a man who spoke against Oppression
> Crying: Woe to you Workers of Iniquity!
> Crying: Woe to you doers of violence!
> Crying: Woe to you breakers of the peace!
> Crying: Woe to you, my enemy!
> For when I fall I shall rise in deathless dedication.
> When I stagger under the wound of your paid assassins
> I shall be whole again in deathless triumph!
> For your rich men are full of violence
> And your mayors of your cities speak lies.
> They are full of deceit.
> We do not fear them.
> They shall not enter the City of good-will.
> We shall dwell under our own vine and fig tree in peace.
> And they shall not be remembered in the Book of Life.
> Micah was a man.[70]

The Israel to which and of which the historical prophet Micah spoke was actually quite similar to Jim Crow Mississippi of the early 1960s. Chaos and violence reigned; people and property were being snatched from homes; there was no protection from marauding bands for ordinary citizens. The rich were all powerful, the poor destitute. As Klaus Koch has noted, Micah "lashes out more bluntly than any other [prophet] at this intolerable state of affairs, prophesying a devastation of the cities during which even Jerusalem will be erased from the earth."[71] Both men had their roots in the soil of their native lands. A younger contemporary of Amos, Isaiah, and Hosea, Micah grew up in a poor farming family, as did

Evers. Micah indicted, with "exceptional vigor," a social order "corrupted by the power of wealth and the exploitation of the ordinary citizen."[72] The Old Testament God addresses the Israelites through Micah and calls on them to account for cultural injustice; the prophetic voice of outrage and retribution is primary to Walker's poem.

So, out of deep biblical history, "Micah" seems to witness to the place and cultural space that produced Medgar Evers's assassination, but the poem's projection of voice and location backward into history suggests that human injustice may well proceed both temporally and spatially—from generation to generation and place to place, its progress halted only by individuals, such as Micah and Medgar Evers, who testify to its destruction. Walker's poetry, situated in 1960s Mississippi, employs an aesthetics of voice that insists on both location and projection. In *Unclaimed Experience: Trauma, Narrative, and History*, Cathy Caruth makes the assertion that the articulation of trauma may be obliquely directed through sites displaced from the wounded one or ones.[73] Walker's poems both claim the experience of cultural trauma for those who have experienced it and project that experience through time and space; her poetry records the process of leaving and returning to the place of trauma, which for her and other southern African Americans, including Evers, was home. Later in her life, many of Walker's public speeches (for example, the 1989 "On the Civil Rights Movement in Mississippi"), like Myrlie Evers-Williams's memoir *For Us, the Living*, include litanies of African Americans murdered or wounded in Mississippi and the South. Walker's heroes were Emmett Till, Evers and King, Fannie Lou Hamer and Daisy Bates, and Schwerner, Goodman, and Chaney. The wounded dead struggle to address us in many of Walker's poems. Yet these poems, grounded in time, place, and real people with real stories, also testify to the ubiquity of trauma, the wound that refuses a departure into history, that continues to cry out in loss and mourning and judgment.

For their authors, both texts—Welty's story and Walker's poem—made their own sets of demands. Both "pushed up," to use Welty's term, through other projects. Welty was working on her novel *Losing Battles* and Walker on her long-awaited collection of poetry *October Journey*. Walker's biographer, Maryemma Graham, believes that Evers's murder actually shifted Walker's attention away from *October Journey*, which was well along, to *Prophets for a New Day*. This was an ethical commitment; both writers had felt a strong sense of their responsibilities to resist the social practices that fostered racial violence. Welty's action to open up her lecture and reading at Millsaps had significant ramifications at a time when southern African Americans were putting their lives on the line to integrate public libraries and universities. On the front lines of the fight, Walker had not only written about southern racism for decades but put up civil rights activists, white as well as black, in her home.[74] In a larger sense Walker, who once said, "I knew what it was to step off the sidewalk to let a white man pass before I was ten,"[75] saw Evers's life's work as an extension of the historic struggle of all African Americans, whom she had written about most memorably in her 1941 signature poem "For My People."

But that June of 1963, Walker, as well as Welty and Baldwin, was living—in very different ways—at a significant remove from Myrlie and Medgar Evers, who, across town from Welty and across the country from Walker and Baldwin, though on the same vulnerable street with Walker's husband and two of their three children, sat holding each other at night in their barricaded living room, staying clear of the front window and at night sitting on the floor. That was "the real story" going on inside the Everses' real home, and that is a story each of these writers was only able to tell peripherally and incompletely.

This sense of incompleteness—or lack of proximity—may account for Walker's and Welty's nagging dissatisfaction concerning their own writings about Evers's life and death. In a journal entry on Saturday, June 15, the date of Evers's funeral service in Jackson, Walker states: "I have written an article that is both a tribute to Medgar Evers and an expose of the whole Mississippi story but I dare not print it now that I have written it. My family would be in danger, and there might be all kinds of reprisals. I seem to be too vulnerable, too fearful, and too cowardly."[76] The article on Evers and Mississippi has never been found, according to Graham.[77]

In the end Welty remained unsure that her story about Evers's murder, which was written, atypically, out of outrage and compulsion and in one sitting, did what it needed to do. Much like William Faulkner's postcommentary on his "magnificent failure" of a book, *The Sound and the Fury*, and Morrison's uneasy afterword to *The Bluest Eye*, Welty seemed driven as subsequent decades unfolded to write and speak of her dissatisfaction with the story, often in terms of its being inchoate, unwieldy, or unfinished. In her memoir, *One Writer's Beginnings*, she comments, "Trying for my utmost, I wrote it in the first person," but she added that she wasn't quite sure that it had been, in her words, "brought off" or that her "anger showed [her] anything about human character that [her] sympathy and rapport never had."[78] In an interview in 1978, she stated at various intervals: "I made myself do it" and "I stayed in the same mood for a long time afterwards as if I really hadn't finished the story, you know, I should have done more with it. Too late. It was pushing—I was writing *Losing Battles* at the time, it just pushed right through it."[79]

The title of the story was chosen, she said in 1984, because she "really did not know where the voice was coming from that was telling the story. It's so queer. Your material guides you and enlightens you along the way. That's how you find out what you're after. It is a mystery."[80] The sheer number of discarded titles either typed or penciled in on several drafts points to Welty's unsettled feeling about the story itself. The typescript, labeled "1st Original" by Welty and prepared for use in a 1967 volume titled *Creative Writing and Rewriting*, contains five discarded titles: in their order on the page, "It Ain't Even July Yet," "Voice from an Unknown Interior," "From the Unknown," "A Voice from a Jackson Interior," and "July 14" (the former two in holograph, the latter three in type). Possibly for the volume's editor, John Kuehl, Welty has written in parentheses "(all discarded titles)." Other titles written on subsequent drafts include "From My Room," "Where Is That Voice Coming From?" "Try and Find Who You Heard," "Find Me," "Try Finding Who You Heard," "You Don't Know the One," "Ask Me What Is My Name," "Ask Me My Daddy's Name," and "Where Is the Racket Coming From?"[81]

This plethora of discarded titles and anxious postcommentary on the story underscore Welty's uneasy sense of her own failure to locate the killer's voice.[82] His was a voice she could hear but could not place. "I tried to write from the interior of my own South,"[83] she said in 1972, and though there is little question that Welty managed to get the voice of *a* racist killer right, the question of whether she knew where that voice came from is not so clear. Her crucial mistake, and the one she mentions consistently years later, is making the killer a poor white Snopesian character jealous of Roland Summers's lawn and paved driveway rather than a man of her own class, one whose voice she might have overheard through an open window in her own neighborhood. Byron De La Beckwith was, in fact, from an old Greenwood, Mississippi, family of some standing in the community. In interviews up into the nineties Welty worried about getting Beckwith's class background wrong, and she mentions in 1972, 1992, and 1994 that she did not come to this understanding on her own but was told of her mistake by "a friend," a "someone" who said to her, "'You were wrong because you thought it was a Snopes and it was a Compson,'" a reference to Faulkner's poor white and elite families of his fictional Yoknapatawpha County, Mississippi.[84]

The draft that was used alongside the published version in the 1967 volume *Creative Writing and Rewriting* carries the title "From the Unknown."[85] In the 1972 interview just cited, Welty continued to struggle with the question of her title, saying that the published title "isn't very good, I'd like to get a better one. At the time I wrote it—it was overnight—no one knew who the murderer was, and I just meant by the title that whoever was speaking, I—the writer—knew, was in a position to know, what the murderer must be saying and why."[86] The drafts themselves contain many revisions, the obvious ones that Welty and others have said were made to eliminate identifying features of the murder and murderer for the *New Yorker* story, several of which were made after the June 26 galleys,[87] and more substantive ones as well.

It is telling, though, that in her marginal writings on the drafts, Welty is at pains to remind posterity of who Medgar Evers was. At the top of the "first original" typescript, she has written: "Real names and real people typewritten here changed to fictitious." And beside the first reference to Medgar, changed to Roland, her marginal parenthetical comment reads: "(Medgar Evers, a real victim of a crime like this.)" as if she were worried that readers of the manuscript might forget the originating event that motivated the story. And next to the deleted passage referring to Ross Barnett, governor of Mississippi, "I might even sneak old Ross in to be my lawyer, if ever should come a little trouble. How about this,

Ross? I sure as hell voted for you," Welty has written in the margin: "This was deleted from final version because Ross Barnett's firm did represent Beckwith, who turned out to be the accused killer of Medgar Evers."[88]

In short, "Where Is the Voice Coming From?" is probably the most revised and worried over of any of Welty's story drafts in the Welty Collection at the Mississippi Department of Archives and History.[89] There are no fewer than fifteen discarded titles. Clearly the story's multiple, even messy, drafts displaying her elaborate edits for both aesthetic and legal purposes point to Welty's concern that posterity understand just how worrisome this short piece of writing was to her vis-à-vis the story's legal questions, aesthetic and moral issues, and the truth claim of its witness to the "real story." She wasn't writing fiction, as she consistently, urgently reiterated throughout her life, but "about the real thing, and at the point of its happening," and out of "the strangest feeling of horror and compulsion all in one."[90] And yet, "the real thing"—the truth claim of the story had to be omitted in the two-page *New Yorker* story, which, interestingly, shares space with a drawing of a bucolic cityscape. As she herself emphasizes, both in her marginalia and her early commentary on the story, Welty had to revise her manuscript to *dislocate* Medgar Evers and Mississippi from their rightful home in her narrative, which was in the deepest sense Evers's narrative. This was a different kind of dislocation than Baldwin's Plaguetown or Walker's Jerusalem because it cloaked Evers's story rather than projected and enlarged it.

On the other hand, those same marginal notes and her subsequent commentary in interview after interview for years to come would indicate the author's concern that Evers and the horrific event of his assassination might not be remembered. In this sense the typescript revisions and marginalia, as well as Welty's repetitious and uneasy discussions of the story, testify to the historicity of the event itself, which was literally erased from the *New Yorker* story, while also being coded back into the story in sly ways (the Yum Yum Drive-In and Trailer Camp becoming, for example, the Kum Back Drive-In and Trailer Camp). Welty's sense of the irony of erasing the real, mortal, wounding of Medgar Evers, which was what made "The Voice," as she called her piece, "a real story" and not a fictional one, is thinly veiled in an interview more than thirty years later, in 1994, when she says of the *New Yorker* editors, "they didn't want coincidence anywhere. Reality was what I had just written, you know . . . but they could take no chances on any coincidence with reality."[91]

Today the testimonial significance of Welty's story might seem redundant, but in the 1960s South and decades beyond, truth claims about horrific historical events such as the Evers murder were not something to be counted on. Evers was one of many who were wounded or killed during this period throughout the South; as I noted, one of Evers's most deeply felt responsibilities was to provide a national and international witness to racially motivated killings and atrocities by providing the NAACP with information to be released to the media about murdered or wounded African Americans—those whom Myrlie Evers-Williams would later call the "unsung heroes and heroines in Mississippi that few people remember or know about."[92] In the decades to come, Welty, like Evers-Williams up to the present moment, would worry that Evers and the movement were being forgotten, as their comments cited in the first chapter of this volume attest.

So Welty wrote a "real story," as she put it, but of necessity masked in fiction, just as Walker's vociferous Old Testament prophet Micah, whose righteous ire is directed against injustice in Mississippi, becomes a mask for Medgar Evers himself. In short, both writers summon the memory of Medgar Evers at the same time their writings lay a veil across his face, perhaps like Baldwin in *Blues for Mister Charlie*, whose victim, Richard Henry, we are told in the preface, is based on Emmett Till, though summoned to life by Evers's assassination. Till and Evers share the stage in *Blues for Mister Charlie*, haunting its audiences and readers and framing in collective memory not only younger and older versions of Richard but generations of victimized African American men and youth.

All three writers, however, make their masks of Medgar Evers so transparent (Emmett for Medgar, Micah for Medgar, a fictional story for the "real story") that the masks themselves openly operate as artifice and the truth claim of the "real story" remains whole, revealing, on the one hand, Walker and Welty's shared worry that this and other stories of the civil rights struggle would be forgotten and erased from history—a very real concern for many in the volatile sixties—and on the other, Baldwin's fear that the story of white southern violence would *never* be told, in his own time or any other.

One of the memorial poems sent to Myrlie Evers after her husband's death concludes: "Medgar was a Man."[93] (We may note here the similarity of this little poem in the dusty archives and Walker's poem that ends "Micah was a man.") In Baldwin's play, Walker's poem, and Welty's story, we find Medgar the man only to lose him. But in losing him, we as twenty-first-century readers of these works may find ourselves confronting the spatial configurations that shaped his very particularly located life and death—"his heart's field"—which lay dead center at the "crossroads of circumstance" that was Jim Crow Mississippi. Wherever these authors' voices may be coming from, whatever truths they may have shielded themselves and their readers from, wherever they ended up fleeing to—France, Iowa, the white side of town—their *writings* lead us back, in memory and history, to the local, to 2332 Guynes Street and the family who lived there, right there. Although they don't go inside that house, they locate Medgar Evers and his tragic, heroic struggle in time and space.

Masked and then unmasked in these writings of the sixties, Evers's story leans forward as well as backward in history, not only sketching a frame of remembrance for pondering the lessons of the southern past but also challenging us to envision what social justice might look like in our own times and in our yet-to-be imagined futures. To meet this challenge is to imagine the contours of a longer, harder civil rights movement whose "heart's field" extends much farther than the eye can see and marks the plot lines of stories still to be told.

CHAPTER THREE

"Agitators" and Aesthetics

JACKSON'S NEWSPAPERS AND THE BATTLE FOR COLLECTIVE MEMORY

> The newspaper pages have nothing to say,
> They either tell lies or they hide it all away,
> Day after day after day . . .
> — MALVINA REYNOLDS, "What's Going On Down There"[1]

Flying down to Jackson and preparing to land at Jackson-Evers International Airport in the spring of 2007, I was asked by the man in the seat next to me what I was coming to Mississippi for. He was white and appeared to be in his mid-thirties; he lived in a community outside the city called Clinton. Over the course of the hour-long flight, he had worried aloud about the state of my soul—was I saved or not?—and the teaching of evolution in the schools, what it was doing to young minds. He said he liked to hunt.

When I answered his question by saying I was working on a book about the assassination of Medgar Evers and the way we remember him through literature and song, he replied with no hesitation whatsoever, "Oh, don't you know? His own people did that to him. *Outside agitators*. Don't let nobody tell you different." Fueled by Myrlie Evers's analysis in her memoir of the "ancient mythology of outside agitators and innocent, happy local Negroes . . . woven deeply into Southern beliefs about Negroes, that had salved white consciences for generations,"[2] I argued indignantly to the contrary, chastising him in my best schoolteacher fashion for not knowing his history, to which he retorted, "Well, let me tell *you* something: there's two sides to every story. Don't believe everything you hear down here."

Medgar Evers was murdered between press runs. He died shortly after 1 a.m. on Wednesday, June 12, 1963, and there was no mention of his death in Jackson's morning newspaper, the *Clarion-Ledger*; like the other two morning papers in the state, it had finished printing the next day's edition when news of Evers's assassination became public.[3] What the *Clarion-Ledger*'s readers saw instead when they opened up their papers over coffee that morning was a picture of a deflated George Wallace stepping aside from the door of Foster Auditorium at the University of Alabama after he was confronted with federal troops, an act that allowed two African Americans entry to a campus he'd vowed to keep them out of. Television and radio broke the Medgar Evers story, and by the afternoon of the day of Evers's assassination, the actual news of his death had already fallen into the dark hole of the past in the local white print media. The afternoon *Daily News* on June 12 led with the follow-up story: the police investigation and responses from local, state, and national officials. Even knowing the two white-owned Jackson daily newspapers had "spearheaded a campaign to maintain 100 percent segregation throughout the state," we might attribute this gap in the coverage of Evers's death to the demands of the news cycle or to the fact that, except on their editorial pages, Mississippi newspapers in general had ignored Evers up to his May 20, 1963, television rebuttal to the Jackson mayor's speech.[4] Yet other daily afternoon and morning newspapers across the country were leading with the Evers assassination through June 13, despite the fact that it was a busy news day; the night before, President Kennedy had addressed the nation about civil rights, and Wallace had acquiesced to federal troops. The banner headline in the *New York Times* on the morning of June 13 read: "NAACP Leader Slain in Jackson; Protests Mount."

In contrast to this sleight of hand regarding Evers's death as a news item in the *Clarion-Ledger* and *Daily News*, Byron De La Beckwith's arrest seems, in retrospect, oddly tipped toward the local newspaper cycle, although his capture in the Mississippi Delta town of Greenwood, which took place at 11 p.m. on Saturday night, occurred less than an hour and a half earlier than had his shooting of Evers in Jackson ten days before. Moreover, Sunday newspapers, by their very bulk, are considerably larger and more preplanned than weekday editions. Nevertheless, on Sunday morning, June 23, the fertilizer salesman's arrest became banner headlines in the combined *Clarion-Ledger* and *Daily News*—a serendipitous coincidence, if indeed it was coincidence, for the Citizens' Council–backed paper to prove to its substantive Sunday morning readership that justice could be served in Mississippi, despite the fact that it wasn't local police but FBI agents, armed with fingerprint evidence and a federal warrant, who had taken Beckwith, also a Council member, into custody. The next day, June 24, two photographs of the nattily dressed Beckwith sans handcuffs appeared on the front page of the *Clarion-Ledger* on either side of another large picture of the rifle used to shoot Evers. In addition, the paper showed a Marine Corps photo of a younger Beckwith on a jump page and an elaborate sidebar about his old southern family and rare book collection.

Until the arrest of Beckwith, local print media coverage of the Evers murder had primarily focused on worries about the effects of the event on national perceptions of Jackson; white unease with the volatile and massive displays of mourning in the black community; platitudes and untruths by state and local officials (all white, of course); and the purported search for the killer, who Governor Ross Barnett had speculated was, as my flying companion would have it, an "outside agitator." Indeed, when Beckwith was arrested, the June 24 headlines of the *Clarion-Ledger* read, "Californian Is Charged with Murder of Evers," despite the fact that Beckwith had lived in Mississippi since he was five years old and came from an old Mississippi Delta family, and that the day before, when the story first appeared, the paper's headline was "FBI Nabs Greenwood Man in Evers Murder."

As discussed in the first chapter of this book, the two Jackson daily newspapers had been much more rabidly segregationist in their news coverage of civil rights issues than most other Mississippi newspapers, which was saying something; and the Hederman family, which controlled both publications, worked hand in glove with the Mississippi Sovereignty Commission and Citizens' Council. When James Meredith, who, with crucial support from Evers, entered the University of Mississippi under court order on September 30, 1962, editorials in the *Clarion-Ledger* further polarized the races and intensified opposition to desegregation.[5] A perusal of the columns running in these papers shows that, in the *Jackson Daily News*, editor Jimmy Ward used his front-page column "Covering the Crossroads" to frame the civil rights struggle in dripping sarcasm and racially inflected ridicule, and Charles M. Hills's column in the *Clarion-Ledger* passed along racist vitriol and humor, ridiculing, among other African Americans, black women in prisons.[6] Many African Americans read the two white-owned dailies. When Bill Minor, a reporter for New Orleans's *Times-Picayune*, interviewed parents of black protestors, they told him how much Ward's columns had hurt them, "that Jimmy's words did more to hurt them than anything else. . . . He was brutal in his comments, and he even referred to those blacks as 'chimpanzees parading down Main Street' [terminology echoed in James Baldwin's *Blues for Mister Charlie*] as they fought for the right to vote."[7]

The newspapers' layouts reinforced this vitriol visually. Both columns ran alongside laudatory pictures and stories of attractive white children and young adults—Boy Scouts, beauty queens, gardeners—on the one hand and stories of rapes and other violence by black men on the other, often complete with mug shots. The result was a bifurcated aesthetic that featured a score of positive and negative images that made blacks seem ugly and violent monsters or "tom-tom"–beating savages and whites beautiful or manly productive members of society.[8] In addition, as John R. Tisdale notes, "Tom Ethridge's 'Mississippi Notebook' column in the *Clarion-Ledger* routinely attacked Evers, the civil rights movement, and editors who did not agree with his arch-segregationist opinion." These and other forms of "news" and opinions were disseminated to the two white papers' statewide combined readership of more than ninety thousand in a period when newspapers remained the primary source of local, national, and world news.[9] In 1963 Minor, whose column "Eyes on Mississippi" appeared weekly in the *Times-Picayune*, called the *Clarion-Ledger* "the most morally bankrupt newspaper in the United States." As Jerry Mitchell, the present-day award-winning *Clarion-Ledger* reporter, said in 2007, "The paper campaigned to preserve segregation, no matter the costs . . . prompting some in the African-American community to call the publication 'The Klan-Ledger.' A day after Martin Luther King's famous 'I Have a Dream' Speech in 1963, the headline in the *Clarion-Ledger* read, 'Trash Taken Out in Washington.'"[10] In recent years, Mitchell's prize-winning investigative reporting has helped put four Klansmen, including Beckwith, behind bars.

The third newspaper in Jackson, the weekly African American—owned *Jackson Advocate*, edited by black conservative Percy Greene, also came down on the side of segregation. Greene's editorials were written in the vein of Booker T. Washington, stating that "separate but equal facilities 'are a far better answer than racial tension, confusion and hatred engendered by integration attempts.'"[11] Greene also criticized and ridiculed civil rights organizations and their leaders, both local, such as Evers, who actually was seen as representing outside interests in the form of the NAACP, and "outside agitators" such as Dr. Martin Luther King Jr.[12] As a number of civil rights organizations became more successful in launching black protest campaigns in the state, including not only the NAACP and SCLC but also CORE, the Student Nonviolent Coordinating Committee (SNCC), and the Urban League (UL), Greene remained staunchly aloof from and disapproving of their efforts. As his biographer, Julius Thompson, notes, from the time Evers took the rein of the NAACP effort in Mississippi in late 1954, Greene contended that the field secretary's work "sought to carry out 'the policies of the NAACP' to 'crush any Negro who got in their way, especially one who voiced any criticism or opposition to their program or methods.'"[13]

More shocking, Greene served as an informer for the Mississippi Sovereignty Commission and, in fact, provided the Commission with information on Evers himself. Over the course of the decade, Greene received more than $3,500 from the Sovereignty Commission and, in fact, was paid $750 to publish a supplement for the Commission.[14] Greene's position as an editor mirrored that of some of the African American establishment in the state. As Tisdale notes, "In many cases, middle-class African Americans earned economic independence with help from whites, or relied on whites to buy their products or services. If the protests upset the balance, those in the middle class might lose their economic and social status."[15]

When Evers was shot, the weekly issue of the *Advocate* ran the banner headline "State NAACP Secretary Is Shot to Death," but the Evers story is less than prominent on the front page, which is taken up with a large picture of a black model in a Cleopatra-type pose and a story about her, the combination of which occupies three times the space as the story of Evers's murder. Greene never wrote an editorial about Evers's murder. Although Greene supported the goal of voter enfranchisement for African Americans, he believed that the economic boycotts of white businesses launched by local activists, and supported by Evers and NAACP bonds money, hurt rather than helped blacks. In an editorial from April 16, 1960, he chastised Evers for drawing a ten-thousand-dollar salary while other African Americans stood to lose their jobs if whites decided to counter the boycott and fire their black employees.[16] Greene believed that Mississippi's African Americans should focus on attainable goals and work with white people to achieve them: on June 22, 1963, his editorial was titled "Time for Negroes to Start Being Americans."[17]

What has not been analyzed or even remarked on is the revolutionary black aesthetic that emerged from the pages of the *Advocate*. It was by far the most international of the Jackson newspapers, and many of the articles in it related to the rebellions and shifting political regimes in Africa. As in the white newspapers, the editors ran many pictures of attractive women, but in the *Advocate* these were not only African American and African women but often women who had distinguished themselves nationally or internationally. Black men, women, and children were offered positive reflections of themselves in a prism of Afrocentric models who came directly from the mother country and from other national and international venues rather than from the local or state scene. In foregrounding the African revolutionary figures and forces, the *Advocate* called on a cultural memory of strong and revolutionary African heritage for its southern black readership, which, counter to the paper's stated editorial stance, might well have been drawn on for rebellion on the local and regional scene.

Greene's refusal, as editor of the state's leading African American newspaper, to disseminate the civil rights protest message or even give the movement fair coverage caused Evers himself to get in the newspaper business and form the *Mississippi Free Press* in 1961. In his memoir of the Jackson movement, John R. Salter, a white professor at Tougaloo and a

leader in local sit-in and boycott efforts in the early sixties, characterizes the "little weekly" *Free Press* as largely the "brainchild" of Evers and
several others, old and young, black and white, in Jackson and Canton,
twenty or so miles away.[18] A four-page tabloid at its inception, printed
with serious repercussions in Holmes County by Hazel Brannon Smith,
editor of the *Lexington Advertiser*, and distributed in Jackson to a weekly
circulation ranging from two to three thousand in the early sixties,[19] the
Free Press was the only newspaper in the Jackson reading area that included unvarnished news of civil rights efforts throughout the state and
nation as well as on the local scene. Everyone associated with the paper's
printing and distribution was harassed—by police, the Citizens' Council,
the Sovereignty Commission, the KKK, and other official and unofficial
arms of the white supremacist power structure in Jackson. Smith's office was firebombed and crosses were burned at her home.[20] Salter himself and his wife were followed and harassed after publishing articles in
the paper.[21]

This cursory discussion of the Jackson newspapers makes obvious the
fact that they were far from neutral in reporting on the local and statewide civil rights struggles in the spring of 1963 and the death of Medgar
Evers that June; moreover, their publishers saw their own papers as
transferring competing ideologies around racial justice to their own
readers and future generations, for example, to my thirty-something
man from Clinton who wasn't even born in 1963 but has obviously inher-
ited a cultural memory of people called "outside agitators," a buzzword in
the local white southern newspapers of the sixties such as the *Clarion-
Ledger*.[22] From the unbridled racism of the Hederman family and its two
white supremacist dailies to Greene's conservatism and pessimism about
the goals of the movement alongside his elevation of an Afrocentric aesthetic and value system, and finally to the progressive social optimism,
often balanced by outrage, of the fledgling *Free Press*, these papers served
as "acts of transfer" in their competing attempts to solidify what Raiford
and Romano have called "consensus memory" of the civil rights movement.[23] And they did so in a time when people got a far greater percentage
of their news from print media than we do today. As I noted earlier, the
impact of newspapers in the Jackson area was all the more pronounced
because national and local news of racial prejudice and civil rights ac-

tivities was blacked out by local television stations or worse; when a local newscaster referred on the air to the Birmingham jail being "half full of niggers now," the *Mississippi Free Press* was the only newspaper in the Jackson area to report the slur and force an apology.[24]

These papers functioned not only as acts of transfer of cultural knowledge and memory in terms of what they reported but as complicated visual texts whose very constructions—layouts, pictures, headlines—aestheticized the cultural messages they sought to impart. They therefore serve for us today not just as historical records but as complex, material intersections between competing ideologies and visual representation. In newspaper work, layout and design are almost always done on the spot and in haste, but usually editors approve these visual representations of the news (such would have been especially true during the most volatile few weeks of racial unrest in Jackson's history to date); the actual placement of stories on the page in Jackson's newspapers of Evers's time reflects these news organizations' political stances. It is not a stretch to say that most of the reporting and editorial staffs of these newspapers knew that they were in a significant historical moment and that the publishers of their papers were trying to shape not only the events of the present but also cultural memory for future generations. The complicated form of what, in an admitted stretch, I call "aesthetics" poses fascinating questions about how such "texts" construct a remembered past long after these newspapers were tossed in the trash by their readers.

Thus the Jackson papers of the early 1960s were not only archival transmitters of "knowledge"; they also visually performed what they construed as knowledge, with wire service (in the case of the white-owned papers and the *Advocate*) and local desk copy being manipulated to express implied political messages through its proximity to certain kinds of photos, its placement on the page, and the size and placement of headlines. Although they are "texts" and certainly archival, these newspapers served a performative function in their own times, not in the sense of Diana Taylor's definition of performance of "live, embodied actions," which she sets in contrast to written texts in her distinction between "the archive" and "the repertoire," but in the fact that, in their own time and for their own readers, the staffs of each paper manipulated black and white bodies *as* texts. In doing so they produced, for good or ill, a form of "embodied knowledge" that would create for future generations a complex web of memory around the subject of race and racial history.[25]

These local newspapers were, of course, only a small part of the weaving of a larger web of cultural memory, and also of a cultural form of "post-memory," if my white man from Clinton, Mississippi, may again serve as example. In her book *Family Frames*, Marianne Hirsch describes the workings of "post-memory," or memory that has been embraced and enhanced by a younger generation from ancestors through the medium of photographs. These "family frames"—in Hirsch's analysis, part of the memory of trauma and loss produced by the Holocaust—are still part of the present; they are part of family history and readily available to new generations as post-memory, along with the stories and family histories that go with them.

Unlike Hirsch's "family frames," the photographs and the stories in these Jackson newspapers, especially in terms of their visual impact on whole pages, are nearly inaccessible to readers of today as they reside in an archive that can be retrieved only through microfilm in a library. Issues of the *Advocate* are missing because the paper was firebombed three times, most recently in January 1998, when arsonists did a hundred thousand dollars in damages.[26] The beleaguered *Mississippi Free Press* is especially difficult to study. The few copies available in either paper or microfilm are tucked away in odd places.[27] Moreover, any study of these newspapers as texts with aesthetic components requires that they be printed in pieces from microfilm and taped together. It is almost impossible to reproduce good visual images of the photographs and drawings in them.

In a sense, then, we might see these newspapers as *lieux de mémoire*, archival sites of collective memory,[28] but sites that themselves remain for us today hidden from view, although their traces—a phrase here, an allusion there, perhaps a striking picture or story, but mostly deep-seated theories and beliefs about race and the civil rights movement—remain strongly present in southern and American cultural memory.

How might archival materials that are not readily displayed for future generations be studied as sources of post-memory? In another, less often cited discussion of familial memory and how it is transmitted generationally, Nicholas Abraham and Maria Torok suggest that certain traumas in a family may be passed down from generation to generation at a subconscious level without ever being fully articulated or acknowledged.[29] Such traumatic events take on a phantasmic quality, haunting a family's collective psyche long after those who experienced them have died. As sociologist Avery Gordon has pointed out, though, haunting is not just individual or familial but rather "a constituent element of modern social life"—so much so that "[t]o study social life one must confront the ghostly aspects of it."[30] Gordon turns to literary texts to identify historical hauntings of the cultural psyche. It is much more difficult and ultimately impossible to trace the ghostly residue left by a picture or story in a newspaper, a racial slur in a column, or even, as in the case of Evers's picture, a glaring absence of representation. Who knows what effect a slur or absence might have on the man, woman, or child who detects it either consciously or unconsciously and how the traces of that reading effect might manifest through generational and cultural transfers of memory and history? This chapter, in fact, is a story of details and how they fit together to create embodied texts. I suggest, though I can't prove it, that the ghostly residue of those texts remains with contemporary southerners, black and white, who never have seen them or heard about them, like the smudge a newspaper can leave on the hands of the one who reads it, which then becomes transferred to another through a handshake or a touch.

In further exploring the question of memory, it bears noting that implicit to Raiford and Romano's and Jacqueline Dowd Hall's worries about how the civil rights movement is misrepresented or appropriated in the twenty-first century, which I discussed in the first chapter, is their shared assumption that the movement is viewed and expressed as a positive event in our present-day world, even and especially by those who misrepresent or appropriate it. However, events such as those in Jackson itself, where James Craig Anderson, forty-eight, a black gay family man, was robbed, beaten, and then run over in 2011 by a group of white teenagers because he was African American, powerfully illustrate the fact that racially motivated violence remains deeply embedded in the cultural crevices of the U.S. South (as well as the country at large), despite claims to the contrary.[31] In examining the Hederman-owned newspapers and their rampant racism, I want to suggest that post-memory might be created in one generation of white southerners and passed on, not through the original textual artifacts themselves, whose traces remain visible only to the scholar, but through complex lingering performances of those artifacts and their representations of race. Such performances of racism become phantomlike, embedding themselves in cultural memory; they haunt our present and make the necessity of the call for an ongoing civil rights movement all too painfully apparent. Yet to retrieve them whole is all but impossible. They are more forgotten than remembered, but still they continue to flit through our present as they migrate to the future.

The story of each of these newspapers, however, is even more complicated. They or their predecessors have created their respective memories of their own particular histories in a process that has been more about the erasure of history than the remembering of it. Although the two white Jackson newspapers, under new management, have shed their segregationist images from the Hederman era and in fact been instrumental, along with reporter Jerry Mitchell, in bringing old murder cases to light,[32] their virulently racist past has never been fully owned. Upon Jimmy Ward's retirement in 1984, the *Daily News* editorial page, while acknowledging his stance on segregation, blandly stated: "Jimmy Ward's place in Mississippi history we leave to Mississippi historians. To them he will be another figure in Mississippi's turbulent past."[33] Not one of the Hedermans attended a 1987 symposium at the University of Mississippi, "Covering the South: A National Symposium on the Media and the Civil Rights Movement"; the Hedermans also refused an interview with Tisdale for his 1996 dissertation, "Medgar Evers and the Mississippi Press."[34] In 2011 the website for the papers, which were purchased and consolidated by the Gannett media chain in 1982, offers a "History of *The Clarion-Ledger*" that cloaks its organizational narrative of the paper's civil rights coverage with the resounding understatement: "Over the years, *The Clarion-Ledger* and *Jackson Daily News* took many firm stands on issues."[35]

Meanwhile, the *Jackson Advocate* has recast its lackluster history during the early years of the Mississippi movement. On its website in 2009 it was presented as "the voice of black Mississippians" and "Mississippi's oldest African American newspaper," which has, since its beginning in 1938, "continually published groundbreaking articles on the civil rights movement, including the fight for the right to vote and to desegregate schools and other public institutions." A photograph of Percy Greene as founder was prominently displayed alongside the present publisher, Charles Tisdale, and associate publisher, Alice Tisdale; the site even provided a link to the NAACP, Greene's arch-nemesis during the 1960s. Over the past five years, according to the present-day site, the newspaper has received awards from many African American groups, including the Mississippi Legislative Black Caucus, the Nation of Islam, the SCLC, and the Black Trade Unionists. In 2011 the site no longer described the newspaper's history, although the phrase "the voice of black Mississippians" appeared as a subtitle to the paper on the online masthead.[36]

In another kind of revision, the liberation story of the *Mississippi Free Press* has been retrieved and deployed by a contemporary namesake, the *Jackson Free Press* (*JFP*), which was founded as an alternative weekly in 2002 and "named after the *Mississippi Free Press*, a civil rights movement newspaper started by a multiracial coalition including Medgar Evers [and] R. L. T. Smith, and printed by white newspaper publisher Hazel Brannon Smith."[37] The twenty-first-century newspaper reached back into the civil rights period when, in 2005, editor Donna Ladd broke the story that reputed Klansman James Ford Seale, who had been reported dead by his family, was alive and well in Roxie, Mississippi. As a result of Ladd's investigative reporting, Seale and an accomplice were subsequently charged in the 1964 murders of two nineteen-year-old black hitchhikers, Henry Dee and Charles Moore, who were beaten and drowned. In 2006 Ladd received an investigative reporting award from the Association of Alternative Newsweeklies for her stories about the Dee-Moore case and related Klan activity in and around Natchez in the 1960s; *JFP*, as the paper is called, has an active blog covering progressive issues.[38]

Three of these four newspapers, then, have recast themselves for their twenty-first-century readers by disremembering their own histories at the moment in history when Medgar Evers lost his life in the struggle for social justice. They have erased, laundered, and refurbished their own pasts, and ironically, their willful forgetting of what they once were has come at a moment in history when print culture in general and newspapers in particular have lost much of their importance in a profoundly visual world. Yet, despite their own forgetting, they have left a residue of collective memory that remains embedded in the contested history of Mississippi's racial strife in the 1960s and the life and death of one man, Medgar Evers, in his historical moment of alternative political imagination. The print in these old newspapers has blurred to the point of illegibility, but the traces of their messages remain. Those traces evince the racially inflected politics around the question of what is remembered and what is forgotten, a politics with aesthetic properties that have been overlooked.[39]

THE *CLARION-LEDGER* AND THE *JACKSON DAILY NEWS*: RACISM AND EMBODIMENT

On the day of Evers's death, *Clarion-Ledger* columnist Charles M. Hills accused President Kennedy of "ordering and supporting invasions of the State of the Union, thus disrupting domestic tranquility at every turn." In his diatribe against the president, Hills approvingly quoted from a speech in which Mississippi state legislator Jesse Shanks said that white Mississippi's "enemies—the communists, socialists, pseudo-liberals, pinkos, do-gooders and one-worlders . . . are seeking not equality but demanding preferential treatment attuned to the beating tempo of 'aboriginal tom-toms' and the chanting lyrics of 'bush jargon' as parodies upon our most sacred religious hymns."[40] In an issue that pictured Wallace giving in to federal troops at the door of the university he had vowed to keep segregated, Hills's emphasis on the so-called savagery of African Americans was a theme that both the morning and afternoon Jackson papers manipulated throughout the civil rights movement, but most especially during the tension-filled days leading up to and following Evers's death. Two days after Evers was shot, on June 14, Hills reinforced this representation of violent African Americans in his "Affairs of the State" column, where he suggested, first, that President Kennedy's speeches incited the killing, and second, that Evers was killed by "his own people" (a phrase echoed by the man on my flight) under the influence of those incendiary speeches. Evers himself is never mentioned by name but simply called "a negro," and the tone of this section of the column, titled "Blame," is both tongue in cheek and bitingly racist:

A negro was shot to death from ambush here the other night.

As Gov. Ross Barnett says, it was a dastardly act.

For instance, it is being said that a paid assassin might have done the job.

There are rumors that the man was expendable.

And, the people of the nation, even to the Congress, and, the President, are shocked. . . .

Race friction is cropping up all over the nation, while the Kennedys talk and aid and abet.

Two white men were shot in Maryland almost simultaneously with the Jackson killing. . . .

The blame . . . where do you think?[41]

This fear of uncontrollable black violence against whites was a theme that both local white-owned newspapers manipulated around coverage of Evers's death. In contrast, on June 13, in a front-page lead story on Evers's murder, the *New York Times* directly confronts white fear: "Whites in this strongly segregationist community publicly expressed shock. But privately they showed more concern over the possibility of Negro retaliation."[42] The June 14 *Times* story, reporting on demonstrations the day following Evers's death, gave graphic descriptions of police brutality, running a front-page picture of Tougaloo's John Salter getting arrested after being clubbed into submission from a blow to the head. The *Times* also reported, "Six Negroes were struck or choked by police nightsticks drawn across their throats. Others were snatched or pushed from the porch of a Negro home," and when black ministers went to Mayor Thompson to protest police violence, he said he knew nothing about it.[43]

Rather than reporting on police brutality, however, the stories, layout and design, and omissions on the front pages of the *Clarion-Ledger* and the *Daily News* reveal a visual representation that creates embodied texts of black savagery and violence. In the *Clarion-Ledger*, the term "race agitators," used several times in headlines, is equated with violence against whites. On the day of Evers's Jackson funeral, June 15, the city gathered itself for a planned demonstration, which fizzled when the U.S. Supreme Court upheld a chancery court injunction banning racial demonstrations.

The newspaper's top two front-page stories that day reported on a "get tough policy" in Virginia against "race agitators" and the Supreme Court decision, with the headline "Agitators Are Warned of U.S. Court Decision." Headlines for the two stories, which ran at the top of the page, were flanked by a three-column photo of nineteen-year-old Rosalie Smith, an African American from Boston, lunging with a knife at a white patrolman in a dramatic tableau of black-on-white urban violence. Smith, according to the caption, "had already slashed a 65-year-old man sitting in an auto nearby."[44] The picture was titled "Carving Knife vs. Nightstick." Smith's motives remain a mystery since no story accompanies the picture, but its implication is quite clear: African Americans, even young women, are vicious, lawless creatures.

On the afternoon of that same day, on which services for Evers were held at 11 a.m., the *Daily News* front page presented its readers with a three-column photo of ten white smiling finalists in the National College Queen contest—the only photograph on the front page and captioned "Why Boys Go to Coed Schools." These beaming symbols of young white womanhood preside over a front page of black violence and mayhem. The lead headline, "Youth Wounded by Sniper Bullet," accompanies the primary story of a nineteen-year-old white man who had been hit by a "sniper bullet" as he rode down Lynch Street, one of the major streets in the black area of the city. The young man wasn't seriously hurt, but the story elaborates on the fact that he, like Evers, had been shot in the back. In the days to follow, the two shootings and the reward money would be conjoined. The subhead "Negro Students Hurl Missiles at Autos" offers the secondary topic of the lead story, which describes students at Jackson State University throwing rocks and "gasoline bombs" out of their windows. These two events happened, the story reports, as "Negroes poured into town to attend funeral services for integration leader Medgar Evers." The time and other details of the funeral aren't mentioned until the eleventh paragraph of the story, and the fact that 1,011 people had been jailed in the past three weeks for demonstrating is left until its last sentence.

The two dailies used national wire service stories, but they were heavily edited and presented with incendiary headlines, a practice obvious in three more wire service stories of actual or threatened black-on-white violence on the June 15 *Daily News* front page. From Cleveland: "Rape Enrages Ohio Whites," the story of six black youths who allegedly stabbed an eighteen-year-old white man and raped his fifteen-year-old female companion. From Detroit: "Negro Hoodlums Beat and Slash Detroit Father," in which another group of black teenagers is arrested for stabbing a white auto plant worker who was picking up his children at school. From Cambridge, Maryland: "Guardsmen Quell Negro Marchers," a story that proved its headline false by reporting that demonstrators disbanded after being told by an NAACP official, "We have women out here. We have children out here. Please go home." The front page also features a column by Jimmy Ward, who makes fun of James Meredith's discussion of racial problems at a recent press conference and ends by saying, "Just a little education at a Mississippi school works remarkable miracles inside the skull of a negro. Maybe this integration isn't so bad after all."[45]

On the *Daily News* editorial page of the same day, another photo, this one showing a white demonstrator for fair housing being carried out of the Ohio capitol, is used to ridicule what the caption calls "An Era Known as the Sittin' Sixties," and the caption describes the picture as "one more photograph of foolishness. Our Jackson 'models' have been photographed so often we take you to Columbus, Ohio, for a change of scenery." The editorial itself manipulates this theme of what it calls "Sittin' Season" from a standpoint of ridicule to one of fear by characterizing racial activism as a Frankenstein's monster, and saying that the Kennedy administration has "gotten a big hungry bear by the tail" and "they'd better find some way to turn that bear loose" if they didn't want to be "gobbled up."[46] Much of the rest of the editorial page is filled with columns and letters to the editor that are ripe with racist vitriol.

The racially inflected interplay between black violence and white innocence illustrated in the June 15 papers continues unabated through the days and weeks to come. On Sunday, June 23, the day after Beckwith's arrest, a three-column front-page picture of two white Boy Scouts and one white Girl Scout flanks the headline "Bar Vigorously Raps Civil Rights Program." One of the few pictures of an African American depicts a photograph of a black janitor sweeping the street in Philadelphia after refusing to stay off his job during an organized boycott protesting Evers's death; the three-column photo features the caption "It Wasn't a

Clean Sweep."[47] On June 13, the first morning issue of the *Clarion Ledger* that responded to Evers's death, there is no picture of the civil rights leader on the front page, but rather a four-column photo of a white youth: "eighteen-year-old Steve Young, the artistically talented son of the Harold Youngs of 2153 Southwood, seen at work with water colors." "His Brush Brings Pictures Life" is the ironic caption, which itself sits directly over the headline of a front-page editorial titled "Slaying Here Misrepresents White Attitude As Agitators Do Colored." The front-page editorial offers a meager one-thousand-dollar reward for information about the killer, blames ever-threatening "outside agitators" for foment-ing the tensions that led to Evers's death, and expresses the hope that "all our citizens, both white and colored, immediately will return to the work of building a law-abiding, progressive city." At the bottom of the page is a two-column shot of a black man squatting in the field where police found the rifle used to kill Evers. On the jump page, atop a continued story of protest marches, is a one-column picture of a scowling Evers.[48]

The two newspapers' biased coverage of Evers's death relied on omis-sion as well as editorial and visual juxtaposition. A case in point is Evers's burial in Arlington Cemetery on June 19, an event that is folded into a front-page puff piece on Mayor Thompson's efforts at racial reconcilia-tion (forced upon him by President Kennedy), the frontispiece of which was the hiring of the city's first black policeman, who just happened to be the mayor's golf caddy. Although both the *Washington Post* and the *New York Times* carried prominent photographs on pages four and eighteen, respectively, of the American flag being held over Evers's coffin by six white soldiers and equally prominent stories of Evers's burial with full military honors, there is no picture of the flag or the burial service—both tableaus sure to connote heroism, patriotism, and tragedy—in the morn-ing *Clarion-Ledger*. Instead, directly above the front-page story, titled "City Continues Work for Racial Solution," which buries a description of the Evers interment four paragraphs in, is, incongruously, a four-column picture of seventy-nine-year-old Choctaw chief Sam Hitchitee in full headdress. The caption, "The Pride of the Choctaws," describes "Sam" as "a colorful attraction" at a dude ranch between Hattiesburg and Meridian who "has never had a single dose of medicine in all these years."[49] Not only is Evers's burial in what many white southerners felt was a white cemetery obscured by a lack of coverage; his death at thirty-seven as a result of his activism is placed in stark contrast to the long and healthy life of this model Native American, whose racialized performance amuses (white) tourists. In contrast, the headlines in the *Post* ("Evers Gets Hero's Burial in Arlington") and *Times* ("Evers Is Interred at Arlington; His Fight for Freedom Extolled") bespoke the civil rights leader's heroic status as a freedom fighter abroad as well as at home. The *Post* story details his service history as follows: "Evers served in the Army from 1943 to 1946 and received two battle stars for his part in the Normandy invasion and the campaign in France. He was a technician 5th class at the time of his discharge from the famed 'Red Ball Express' unit of the Quartermaster Corps."[50] Also unlike the Jackson newspapers, both the *Times* and *Post* quote eulogies from the service, describe Myrlie Evers breaking down when "We Shall Overcome" was sung, and take note of the dignitaries at Arlington and Myrlie Evers's later visit with President Kennedy. The large majority of Jacksonians and other readers in the state's largest newspaper's circulation district, though, didn't have access to the *Times* or *Post*; they didn't read these stories or see the flag folded over Evers's casket by white soldiers in uniform or the tears in Myrlie Evers's eyes.

THE *JACKSON ADVOCATE* AND THE PARADOX OF ACCOMMODATIONIST AFROCENTRISM

The *Jackson Advocate* story of Evers's death sits under two other stories on the June 15 front page: the commencement address, given by a Dr. S. M. Nabrit, at Howard University in Washington, D.C., and the secret military trials for officers in the Haitian army who tried to "escape the wrath of dictator-president [François] Duvalier." The type size for the two-column headline, "Medgar Evers Slain by Bullet from Sniper's Rifle," is only slightly larger than the stories above it; the banner headline, "State NAACP Secretary Is Shot to Death," sits above the masthead and is the same size. The masthead itself is flanked by two boxes with the following messages inside: "Patronize Our Advertisers—Their Advertising in this paper shows that they appreciate your trade," an interesting admonition given the ongoing black boycott of white businesses, many of which advertised in the *Advocate*, and in slightly larger type, "Good Conduct

Will Always Gain You Respect. Watch your public conduct." In short, the *Advocate* urges its readers to patronize white businesses at a time of black boycott—most of the newspaper's considerable advertising came from white businesses—and to behave themselves in front of white people.[51]

There is no photograph of Evers. The story of his murder is a scant two and a half paragraphs on the front page, with a jump to page eight and five more paragraphs. Evers's accomplishments are summed up in the last paragraph: "Evers, a 37-year-old Veteran of the Second World War is a graduate of Alcorn College, and leaves behind him to mourn his slaying a wife and three young children."[52] Along with the arresting three-column photo of the reclining Cleopatra-like model to the left of the Evers story on the front page ("New York Career Girl–Model Sparks Africana Image") and a story of a black marching band to the right of it are headshots of Dr. Benjamin Mays, president of Morehouse College, and Trevor Armbrister, associate editor of the *Saturday Evening Post*. Ambrister had just returned from Haiti and was predicting its downfall. The busy front page bristles with an astonishing twenty-four local, state, national, and international news stories with datelines that range from New York to San Diego; Salisbury, Southern Rhodesia, to Itta Bena, Mississippi; Elisabethville, Congo, to Tuscaloosa, Alabama. Amid this sea of news and next to the large photo of the model, the brief Evers story, lacking any information about his Jackson or Arlington funerals, floats insignificantly. Despite the fact that the *Advocate* had had two full days to accumulate material on the Evers assassination—a wealth of hours in news time—the paper says more about Haiti and Duvalier than about Evers or his death. The front page thus runs the requisite banner headline announcing the murder but almost erases the story itself; certainly it erases Evers the man and his accomplishments from the story of his assassination.

Percy Greene's editorial in the June 15 issue similarly slights Evers, who appears in a subordinate phrase in the last of five paragraphs devoted to urging blacks and whites to work together without the help of outsiders or organizations:

> In light of the current events in Jackson, including the slaying of Medgar Evers, we think the time has come for the responsible white and Negro citizens of the state to find the courage and spirit to link

ourselves together as Mississippians and as American citizens to begin working towards a new era of inter-racial progress and good will;
acting not because of the proddings of any kind of civil rights organization; or because of any kind of threatened or actual demonstrations; but because of a new vision of the future, a new kind of magna-
nimity, and a new purpose toward interracial cooperation.[53]

The editorial thus ignores injustice and violence, dismisses Evers's life's
work, offers dire warnings of another post-Reconstruction era for southern blacks if they don't work with white locals, and cautions against rely-
ing on President Kennedy.

Even as the June 15 issue diminishes Evers and his assassination, however, it elevates certain black individuals and groups, from the marching
band from Itta Bena to the Howard University commencement speaker.
Dr. Benjamin Mays of Morehouse University not only earns a picture but
also a story because he was one of a four-member group who would offi-
cially represent the United States at the funeral of Pope John XXIII. Nada
Hendricks, the model who gets twice the front-page space as Evers, is
variously described as "a study of woman in all of her glorious personi-
fication," "a sparkling, vivacious young woman," and "indefatigable." The
front page of the next issue, on June 22, likewise features pictures of four
notable black individuals, though still no picture of Evers or his flag-
draped coffin at Arlington.

The June 22 issue is kinder to Evers. The headline under the masthead
reads "Medgar Evers Laid to Rest Among Nation's Heroes," underneath a
larger headline on top of the masthead that reads "Pres. Kennedy Talks to
Mayor Thompson," and above "Supreme Court Sounds Death Knell Street
Demonstrations." The story of Evers's burial at Arlington is particularly
interesting in terms of visual representation. The headlines read: "Rowdy
Demonstrations Mar the Solemn Funeral Rites for Medgar Evers Here
Saturday; Police Quell Demonstrations; Many Notables Attend Rites."
Directly underneath the two-column headlines, where one might expect
pictures of Evers and his burial, which were peppered throughout the national media,[54] is a headshot of a man from Detroit named George Young,
who was recently named Acting Special Assistant for Employee Relations
for the Post Office in the Chicago region, "the second Negro to serve at

this high level in the Department's regional set-up." Scattered across the front page are three other photos, the largest a two-column headshot of Mrs. Yolanda H. Chambers, who had been selected as a vice president for a major department store chain, and the other two of black men who had been named to other business posts.[55] Although there are no fewer than five Evers-related stories that begin on the front page, the visual effect of the page emphasizes the accomplishments of black individuals who work within their respective white-dominated businesses and government organizations, not the tragedy of Evers's death. The lack of a picture of Evers in both of the two weekly issues following his death is made notable also by the fact that the *Advocate* did not stint on photos, which sometimes extended to four-column shots—for example, one on page six of the July 22 issue of a group of black and white men at a Coca-Cola conference in Washington, D.C.

The lead story of Evers's funeral and burial, however, is detailed and speaks positively of his accomplishments. His body "will rest among some of the outstanding heroes of the nation." He is described as a veteran and "the leader of the drive for Negro civil rights in Mississippi where he heroically presented the case for Negro rights at every opportunity." Flanked by ads on the jump page and still without a photo of Evers, the story continues, listing notable individuals who attended his funeral and quoting the eulogy of Roy Wilkins of the NAACP, who described Evers as "a martyr in the crusade for human liberty," and declaring, "If he could live in Mississippi and not hate, so shall we, though we shall ever stoutly contend for the kind of life his children and all other must enjoy in this rich land." As for the "rowdy demonstrations," these were instigated by white marchers after the police-protected "solemn procession" from the Masonic Temple, where the services were held, back to the funeral home, a fact made questionable by another story on page six, which names the twenty individuals arrested and fined in the postfuneral demonstration. Of those twenty, only four are identified as white. Instead of pictures of the demonstration or arrests, the Coca-Cola conference photo sits next to the brief story. The narrative of white-instigated (read "outside agitators") demonstrations is echoed by the June 16 combined Sunday issue of the *Clarion-Ledger* and *Daily News*, which features the lead headline "Funeral March Ends in White Agitation."

Greene's June 22 editorial, "Time for Negroes to Start Being Americans," is flanked by two statements on Evers's "apparent murder." The first is by W. M. Mann, president of the conservative Jackson Chamber of Commerce, who calls for preserving law and order.[56] The second comes from Richard O. Gerow, bishop of the Catholic diocese of Natchez-Jackson, who optimistically asks that "legitimate grievances of the Negro population" be recognized and that "the clouds of hate and fear may be pierced by the light of justice and fraternal love." The editorial discusses problems in New York's Harlem schools and argues that black schools should be "defended and protected from discrimination in the allocation and distribution of public money for education, and other purposes designed to raise the standard of American citizenship." The piece *urges* African Americans to insist on their place as Americans with rights to a separate but equal education and states that the movement toward integration has damaged the prospect of equalizing educational institutions for blacks. The editorial ends by warning its readers about "a continuing crisis in race relations in this country that will have increasing harsh effects on the progress and well beings of Negroes."[57] Despite, then, the coverage of Evers's funeral and burial and a variety of other stories connected to Evers—for example, the naming of Charles Evers as the new Mississippi field secretary, the Jackson police's slow efforts to trace the rifle that killed Evers, and a wire service story on the troublesome effects of Evers's murder on civil rights progress—the visual representation of the Evers story in the June 22 issue matches the accommodationist tone of Greene's Booker T. Washington–style editorial.

Perhaps, though, the most astonishing piece in the *Advocate*'s June 22 issue is James Bundles's column "Up and Down Farish Street," which humorously quotes one of the "Farish Street brothers" complaining about the constant discussions of "the Race Question" coming from everyone from his wife to his preacher: "he didn't want it served to him for breakfast dinner and supper. He said it looked like to him that people had forgotten things like, baseball and picnics and fishing and fun and laughter." In a small separate item toward the bottom of the same column, Bundles writes: "Our Sympathy Goes Out . . . to the family of Medgar Evers . . . just returned from his burial in Arlington National Cemetery . . . the resting place of heroes. Med and I didn't always agree on everything but we were pretty good buddies . . . and the whole town misses him already" (ellipses original). The complaints about "the Race Question" were apparently a warm-up for the next week's column, in which Bundles attributes his message to "this fellow, who runs a little business up in North Jackson." This "fellow" criticizes the black boycott of white merchants and says, "a lot of them people leading the boycotts and telling all the brothers and sisters not to trade with them other people . . . is slipping around trading with them other people themselves." Bundles ends the column with his signature "Me? I was just listening." The tone of Bundles's columns, the use of black dialect, and his humorous, archconservative stance are strangely reminiscent, in fact, of the virulently racist humor of Jimmy Ward in the Hedermans' *Daily News*.

The story of Beckwith's arrest is almost completely buried on the front page of the *Advocate*'s June 29 issue, which features three lead headlines urging a halt to public demonstrations. Above the masthead is "Baptist Urge Halt in Demonstrations," and below in slightly smaller type, "Nation's Only Negro Daily Newspaper Joins President Kennedy in Call to Stop All Public Demonstrations." A smaller headline directly under these reads: "Rev. Martin Luther King Ignores President Call to Stop Demonstrations While Congress Considers Civil Rights Legislation" with a picture of King adjacent, interestingly, in the very spot where Evers's picture would logically have been in relation to the previous two weeks' stories of his murder. The largest picture on the front page features two black Jackson garbage collectors smiling broadly as they receive pins from white officials for their respective forty- and twenty-year service records.

The page is again cluttered with stories—twenty-three in all—and the space allotted the Beckwith story ("Accused Slayer of Medgar Evers Awaits Action / Hinds [County] Grand Jury") is minuscule—one paragraph and an additional four lines—in comparison to more fulsome stories such as "United Giver Fund Says 'Thank You,'" "Race Relations Workers to Meet at Fisk University This Week," "African Cardinal Helps Elect New Catholic Pope," and, most prominently, "Joe Lewis Land First Jackson Negro Policeman," the latter about Mayor Allen Thompson appointing his caddy at Jackson Country Club to the post. The coverage given to Beckwith's arrest seems particularly diminutive alongside coverage for Sunday, June 23, by both the combined *Clarion-Ledger* and *Daily News*, which made it the lead story, and the *Mississippi Free Press*, which had screaming headlines of the news. Both issues ran prominent pictures of Beckwith on the front pages. This pattern continues throughout the *Advocate*'s coverage of the Beckwith trial. The July 13 issue, for example, has the banner headline "Byron de la Beckwith Pleads Not Guilty" and a paragraph-and-a-half story sans photo on the front page, but the reader's attention is directed away from both headline and story by a large and riveting picture in the top center of the page of a bearded man in a white, long dress coat holding a book. The caption reads: "COMING TO THE UNITED STATES: His Imperial Majesty Haile Selassie I, Emperor of Ethiopia, The Lion of Judah, who traces his ancestry to King Solomon and the Queen of Sheba, and beyond to CUSH, 6000 years before Christ, is planning to make another of his periodic visits to the United States early this fall."

In all, Percy Greene's *Advocate* was as complex and contradictory as the man himself; it is important to note that he started his paper at the end of the 1930s, with the Great Depression at his heels and fascism on the march across Europe. As Caryl A. Cooper points out, Greene's long career spanned the decades: he was born in 1897, served two tours of duty in World War I, and was denied entry to the bar in 1926 because of an altercation with a white man. He believed in black suffrage and in the 1940s became "an influential spokesman for African Americans in his state, to the degree that a columnist of the *Daily News* threatened a lynching."[58] But with the *Brown v. Board of Education* ruling in 1954, he, like some members of the black southern middle class, feared integration would doom racial pride and solidarity, as well as put black teachers out of work. As his conservative stance hardened, he moved from being a respected member of the black community to an affiliate of the white power structure, including the state Sovereignty Commission. Yet, as Cooper says, "Even when judging his actions within the context of his times, Greene's actions defy understanding."[59] Thompson speculates that Greene transferred the racist propaganda he grew up with into self-hatred: "Perhaps he wished to be white too, but knowing he could never reach this goal, he chose to idolize and imitate his heroes."[60] This is perhaps why he may have displaced any desire for the elevation of black people to the national and international scenes, supporting the movement of a number of African states to gain independence from Europe while maintaining the necessity of interracial partnerships to Africa's future.[61] The *Advocate*'s notable lack of coverage of Medgar Evers's death, in the form of either text or visual representation, reflects and refracts that complexity, and itself has a history. As Cooper points out, earlier murders of African Americans in the state, those of Emmett Till, Rev. George W. Lee, and Lamar Smith in the 1950s, had received little attention in the *Advocate*.[62]

The aesthetic components of Greene's newspaper call for more extensive study because they make visible the paradox of an accommodationism that, on the one hand, elevated black accomplishment and physical beauty at all levels, from garbage collection to international leadership, from beauty queens to African kings, and in all places, local and global. What Greene didn't want to see, or see depicted in Evers's life and death, was the tightening vise of terror and violence that bound his own home and had, sadly and ironically, killed his own spirit. The murder of Evers testified to everything Greene had closed his eyes to. Beckwith's act, in all its present horror and deep history, made painfully visible, in the blood of the fallen civil rights leader, the violently enforced repression of all southern African Americans. Like the white men Greene worked for, the newspaper editor needed to blot out that stain, to render it invisible, for to see it would belie the positivist message of the *Advocate* that black men and women from garbage collectors to kings and queens would be respected and treated well if they behaved themselves and played by the rules of white supremacy.

THE *MISSISSIPPI FREE PRESS* AND EVERS'S LONG FALL

> Medgar, when you fell, you fell forward, covering the full
> six feet and two inches of your body. You carried us that
> far down the road to freedom. We will never have to
> retrace those steps.
> — AARON HENRY, "Dear Medgar,"
> *Mississippi Free Press*, June 13, 1964

One very tangible piece of heritage left by Medgar Evers was his *Mississippi Free Press*.[63] In a 1992 interview with James Tisdale, the Reverend Edwin

King, former chaplain at Tougaloo and civil rights organizer, made the following observation: "We used to think, if we could just tell the truth to America, it would be different. And then we discovered it's very hard to tell the truth when the organs through which the truth is supposed to be told are citizens of that America who don't believe it."[64] Evers, whose work as NAACP field secretary had included in no small part the national dissemination of truths about racial violence and mayhem that would otherwise have remained buried in the byways of rural Mississippi, was acutely aware of the fact that "truth" was contested terrain in the local and statewide media. He and others founded the *Free Press* to tell what he believed to be the truth about what was really going on in the state. Over the course of its twelve-year run (1961–73), the little weekly explicitly urged its readers to register and vote, work for civil rights in various capacities, and support labor and unionize. An early editorial in the paper diplomatically called this truth "point of view" and argued that a newspaper is not an unbiased observer of events but instead "must take a point of view" in order to "best fulfill its part in the democratic process."[65] Although the other papers in Jackson obviously presented distinctly biased points of view regarding the civil rights movement, the *Free Press* was the only one that was forthright in owning up to offering its own version of "truth," a position that the column elaborated in the same editorial statement:

> A newspaper can take a point of view in several different ways. First, it has the choice of which stories to report and may leave out those with which it does not agree. Second, an editor can report an incident in such a way that it will support his own opinions. He does this by leaving out minor facts which might oppose his notions; and by choosing the words in which he describes the incident. For instance, one newspaper might describe a man as a "leading citizen," while another would call him a "notorious agitator." And, third, the best and most usual way for a newspaper to take a point of view is through its editorial and columns.

The argument that follows is that once readers understand that no news source is unbiased—certainly an unarguable point in the Jackson circulation area in the early sixties—they probably will want to support the paper that best represents what they believe, "even if this means taking a stand in the face of opposition."[66]

This editorial's relativist approach to the question of truth in local news reporting of the civil rights movement undergirds the urgent political mission of the *Mississippi Free Press* and its editors' and publishers' belief in an ultimate truth concerning the moral necessity of freedom from racial discrimination and white-on-black violence. As Aaron Henry, state NAACP president and one of Evers's closest friends and associates, wrote in a five-column letter to the slain civil rights leader in the July 13, 1964, issue, which commemorated the first anniversary of his death:

> Medgar Evers often said, "It is all but impossible to read or hear the truth in Mississippi.". . . Much could be done for Mississippi, he responded, if radio, television and the press were free to present facts.
>
> In his pursuit of an outlet for free expression and truth, he induced local leaders to join him in the creation of a newspaper designed to fill that need. It was he who selected the name, FREE PRESS.[67]

The weekly *Free Press* differs starkly from the white-owned daily newspapers and Greene's weekly *Advocate* in appearance as well as in content. Compared to the two white-owned dailies and Percy Greene's *Advocate*, the *Free Press* was a tabloid half the size of the other papers. It contained fewer pages (four to eight over the course of its twelve years) and featured fewer, much smaller pictures, mostly headshots, and fewer sidebars, giving it the look of an inauspicious newsletter. Advertisements were scarce and very small; they were for black funeral homes, restaurants, beauty shops, furniture stores, and other local establishments with black-area addresses such as Lynch, Pearl, and Farish Streets. The only media outlet in the Jackson area that offered unvarnished news of and advocacy for civil rights and labor unions, the *Free Press* evinces little editorial attention to layout and design, pictures, sidebar formats, and other aesthetic components.

Unlike the *Clarion-Ledger* and the *Daily News*, which manipulated aesthetics to create racist narratives of white innocence and black violence, and the weekly *Advocate*, which offered photographs and designs that created a transnational Afrocentric aesthetic, the diminutive *Free Press* focused in its early years before and after Evers's death on presentation of as much information as possible about crimes against African Americans and the advancement of civil rights and unionization. Its five-column pages were crammed full of stories of court decisions, police brutality, lynchings and beatings, and meeting and marching plans. Pictures were often of the dead, wounded, or arrested.[68] In the June 15 issue that reported Evers's death, for example, the screaming front-page headlines read: "Evers Murdered; Civil Rights Leader Shot in Back; NAACP's 'Man in Mississippi' Dies in Struggle for Freedom: Jackson Community Shaken by Tragic Loss: Trembles with Anger." On a page half the size of those of the other local papers, the masthead headline is in larger type than the Evers headline in the *Advocate* of the same date, and it appears even larger vis-à-vis the page. Below Evers's picture and story is a picture of civil rights leader Fannie Lou Hamer, who, along with two other women, was beaten all over her body by police in Winona, Mississippi, for using a white waiting room in the Trailways bus station. Four other Mississippi civil rights stories, in addition to the Evers and Hamer stories, crowd the first page: a white minister, Dr. Selah, resigns from Jackson's largest white Methodist church when Negroes are turned away from services; thirteen black ministers are arrested in Jackson for marching to protest Evers's murder (information in stark contrast to the *Advocate*'s story of the demonstration as being the product of outside agitation fueled by whites); the mayor of Clarksdale, Mississippi, refuses to meet with African American leaders to discuss desegregation; and Cleve McDowell, the second black man to enroll in the University of Mississippi Law School after James Meredith, is successfully registered after plans for white rioting were squelched. Of these, only the McDowell story makes the front page of the *Advocate*. Dominated by the shattering lead headline of Evers's death, the front-page stories and their headlines seem pieced together in the *Free Press* with little attention to visuals — no Cleopatra-like models here.

The issue's editorial casts blame for Evers's "tragic and wasteful murder" on "incredible poverty and ignorance," undergirded by "the selfish and corrupt government of the state." The editorial ends in a passionate tribute: "This man worked throughout his life for what he knew was right for the people of his race and all people who were injured by the affairs of the state. He gave his life in that effort. The only proper credit to the memory of his life and work is to take to heart the philosophy which he has symbolized."[69]

In some issues of the *Free Press*, though, photographs tell a powerful story of trauma. For example, the first-anniversary issue commemorating Evers's death features directly above a newly designed masthead a full five-column family photograph of a somber Myrlie Evers and her children holding memorabilia from Evers's life. The caption above the picture reads: "Young Mother, Young children—No Husband, No Father; What Price Freedom; The Medgar Evers Family; one year after the murder."[70] In the haunting photo the two Evers sons, Darrell, eleven, and James, four, stare directly into the camera. Darrell, whose tearful face had appeared on the front of the June 28, 1963, issue of *Life* as he was being comforted by his mother at his father's funeral, looks vacantly into the camera, his face appearing old and wizened. As he stands beside his mother with his arm protectively around her shoulder, Darrell's mouth is grimly set. He bears a startling resemblance to a photograph of a grim-faced James Baldwin taken during his tour of the South when he had traveled with Medgar Evers eighteen months before and published in a feature story on Baldwin's visit to the South in the May 17, 1963, issue of *Life*, which focused on civil rights. To the readers of the *Free Press*, the photograph would have been all the more poignant given the fact that the preceding April, Beckwith had been released from jail after two mistrials because of hung juries and greeted in his hometown of Greenwood with "Welcome Home DeLa" signs and Confederate flags. Prosecutor William Waller had decided not to pursue a third trial without new evidence.[71] From the photograph and the tenor of the remainder of the issue, the message is that there had been no closure around Evers's death and that the familial and collective mourning following Evers's death remained painfully unmitigated by justice.

More than any other issue of the *Free Press*, and certainly of any other local newspaper, this first-anniversary issue of Evers's murder presents a study in mourning. Intensifying the effects of the front page's grim Evers family portrait of a young widow and her three young children, the editorial page's picture of Evers, Aaron Henry's "Dear Medgar" tribute, and a brief account of Evers's founding of the newspaper on page five is a poem titled "Medgar Wylie," Evers's middle name. A small picture of Verna

Bailey, a smiling girl with braids who appears to be about ten, flanks the poem, which is, according to an introductory note, a parody of "a poem of Edgar Allan Poe," "Annabel Lee." The last stanza of Verna Bailey's poem begins:

> For the stars never beam,
> Without bringing me dreams
> Of the wonderful Medgar Wylie
> And the speakers never rise,
> But I feel the Bright eyes
> Of the wonderful Medgar Wylie.[72]

A year earlier, in contrast to the three other Jackson papers' scant coverage of Evers's last rites and burial, which focused on the ill-advised destructiveness of the ensuing demonstrations, the *Free Press* had separated the stories of the burial and the demonstrations on its June 22, 1963, front page, giving full coverage to the burial itself and offering a separate story of the local protests. The headline "THOUSANDS MOURN EVERS; Slain Leader Buried in Arlington Cemetery" topped a story about the funeral in Jackson, Evers's burial at Arlington, and condolence letters from President Kennedy and pictures of dignitaries attending the funeral. On the jump page, the story of the spontaneous demonstration after the funeral gets some attention, but the main story of the demonstrations is on the front page and focuses on police brutality. For example, the police brutality story tells of arrests topping one thousand, police clubbing demonstrators and bystanders, and women and children being beaten with clubs and put in "sweat boxes."[73] In a visual move that directly counters the white papers' aestheticization of whiteness and visual representations of black violence, the *Free Press* issue, like many of its other issues, offers a two-column front-page picture of white police with bullhorns directly above the police brutality story. The police photo overshadows a small photo of Representative Charles Diggs of Detroit, undersecretary to the UN, and Ralph Bunche, both prominent African Americans, who attended Evers's funeral. The juxtaposition of the two photos—one of the brutal local policeman, and the other of the two black dignitaries who paid their last respects to Evers—is a bold aesthetic move offering the implicit contrast not only between racist policemen and the respectful black men, but also between the state of race relations on the local versus the national and global scenes.

The visual presentation of the Beckwith arrest story differs markedly from that of the white newspapers and the *Advocate*. Both the *Free Press* and the *Advocate* published on Saturdays; the June 29 issue of the *Free Press* featured a top-of-the-page, two-column headshot of a smiling Beckwith in a tie looking directly into the camera as if taunting his viewers.[74] The almost smirking Beckwith presides over a front page that bristles with other stories of white-on-black violence. The image of the smiling white murderer challenges the notion of impartial justice, a challenge raised in the subject matter of the rest of the news stories. The huge lead headline reads: "KILLER SUSPECT CHARGED; Byron de La Beckwith Held in Evers Murder; Citizens Council Member to Face Grand Jury."

Directly under the story of Beckwith's arrest is an "exclusive interview" with state NAACP president Aaron Henry, in which he states that he has "no real optimism for justice in view of justice in the past" in Mississippi.[75] This distrust of justice is borne out in the July 6 and 13 issues, in which the *Free Press* ran a series about miscarriages of justice in Mississippi concerning white men who had killed African Americans and were not punished for the crimes. In the July 13 issue, the second of these two articles is placed directly below a brief story on Beckwith's arraignment, which ends with the resoundingly ironic sentence: "In Greenwood, 14 business and professional men were appointed directors of a fund set up to help pay for Beckwith's legal expenses."[76] The front page of the July 13 issue also contains a prominent story of another tragic miscarriage of justice that had been closely followed among proponents of civil rights: Clyde Kennard's death from cancer. Kennard, a former student at the University of Chicago, who in 1959 had attempted three times to enter the University of Southern Mississippi, was convicted of a trumped-up charge of receiving twenty-five dollars' worth of stolen chicken feed. He was sentenced to seven years of hard labor in Parchman Penitentiary, where he fell ill from what turned out to be colon cancer. He was denied treatment and release from prison until Evers took up his case in the national media. After widespread publicity and pressure, and after it became clear that he was dying, Kennard was pardoned by Governor Ross Barnett, whose law firm would in the coming months mount Beckwith's defense. Through several different strands, then, the Kennard story was closely tied to the issue of justice in the Evers case.

In the *Free Press* the Beckwith story continues through the two mistrials as an ongoing chronicle of a justice system gone missing. On January 25, 1964, a story bearing the sardonic headline *"After Long Delay* Beckwith Trial Begins; Conviction Doubtful" (emphasis original) reads: "The accused Byron de la Beckwith is white, and if his trial follows the usual pattern, the jury will find him innocent on that fact alone. . . . To the minds of many, the outcome of the trial is a foregone conclusion — Beckwith will be released, and since he is the only suspect in the murder assassination, the slayer of Medgar Evers will not be brought to justice."[77] After Evers's murderer was released on ten thousand dollars bond following a second mistrial, the smiling Beckwith picture reemerges on the front page of the newspaper's April 25, 1964, issue under the headline "Beckwith Home Free; Posts $10,000 Bond." The story, directly under the picture, which is now located at the bottom of a front page with no other pictures on it, begins with the bitterly ironic statement: "Yes, they let him go. And now he is home free. Greenwood, Mississippi put out signs to welcome home hero Byron de La Beckwith, who was released on $10,000 bond last week after 10 months in jail and two mistrials." The Beckwith story continues in this vein, dripping in sarcasm: "Following his release, the very obliging Sheriff of Hinds County, and one of his deputies, let Beckwith lie face down on the floor in the back seat of an unmarked car which was waiting at the side of the courthouse. The kindly Sheriff sped his famous prisoner to his hometown of Greenwood. At home, the signs and other expressions of sympathy brought tears to Beckwith's eyes."[78] For the *Free Press* and the community it represented, then, the story of Medgar Evers's murder ended in Beckwith's smirk and white Greenwood's welcome mat for a returning hero. It was a deeply bitter end, and that bitterness came at a time when the coalitions that Evers had worked so hard to build had mostly fallen away. In retrospect, the photograph of the smiling Beckwith seems to stand in for more than just a lack of justice in Evers's murder. It also seems to evoke a more pervasive despair brought about by the continuing killings in the South, especially the Birmingham church bombing that had resulted in the deaths of four young girls in September 1963, as well as the assassination that November of President Kennedy.

The visual representation of bitterness and disillusionment—the head-shot of a grinning murderer who eluded justice for the second time that spring—must have evoked for the *Free Press*'s local readership a depth of despair and outrage that had little parallel.

It is therefore interesting that the newspaper chose to subordinate that picture by placing it at the bottom of a front page whose main story was not Beckwith's release at all but rather that of a black woman who was cursed at and insulted by a white bus driver when she didn't have the correct change. There is no photo of the woman; Beckwith's picture is the only photograph on the front page. The headline to the lead story, "'No More Bus Insults; We're Going to Walk'; Woman Reports Nasty Driver; Mass Meeting Votes to Stay Off," offers, alongside the Beckwith picture and story, a resounding note of rebellion. The story itself relates that the woman who was mistreated told her story to a large crowd gathered at Pearl Street Church, and that following her report,

> Rev. R.L.T. Smith, himself a civil rights organizer and one of the cofounders with Evers of the *Free Press*, asked the crowd, "Are we going to let our women be treated this way? What are we going to do?"
>
> "WE'RE GOING TO WALK," shouted back the crowd.
>
> "Who's going to walk?" asked Rev. Smith. "Whoever wants to walk to work until our women are treated with decency and courtesy, STAND UP."
>
> The entire capacity crowd jumped to its feet.
>
> Before the mass meeting ended, the Jackson Movement had resolved to walk to work and home again until two demands are met.
>
> 1. All drivers show courtesy and respect to everyone.
>
> And
>
> 2. Negro drivers be hired.[79]

Toward the bottom right of the page, directly across from Beckwith's headshot, the bus story ends by pulling together the narrative strands of the aborted Evers murder trial and the woman's mistreatment at the hands of the driver. The term "trial" is expanded beyond the legal, as "hung jury" likewise conveys the miasmic inaction of city officials: "This city is getting used to having trials. Now there seems to be a new one. The question: Will bus drivers be able to continue to be discourteous to Negro women? Will there be another hung jury?"[80] The reader's eye ends at the smirking face of Beckwith, on April 25, 1964, a free man, a portrait of a killer thrown down as a gauntlet for the paper's local readership, bespeaking the continuing lack of justice, progress, and decency ten months after he had shot Evers in the back and walked free. One can only wonder how that portrait, decades later, still may haunt the terrain of memory, even though only the traces of that smile may reside in its readers' actual memories of those days, or, through the continuing slippage of time, in its post-memory hauntings of a whole new generation.

When Aaron Henry spoke of Evers's long fall forward, he meant that the fallen leader had moved the cause just that much farther down the long and rocky road of social justice. We may think also of Evers's fall forward as a long civil rights movement journeying into the future. Although his death and the cause he died for were greatly diminished, not only through misinformation and lack of information but also through aesthetic manipulation in the pages of three of these newspapers, his legacy of activism continued to live in the *Mississippi Free Press* until 1973, and by the time the paper folded, much of what he had fought and died for had been achieved. Mississippi was a better place and itself falling forward into a future Medgar Evers could only dream of in his own time.

But even as Evers's work, made manifest in the *Free Press*, still pivots toward an egalitarian future, these other Jackson newspapers cast long, menacing shadows into the past. And if, in parts of Evers's home city and state, "outside agitators" are alive and well in racially inflected collective memory, the Hederman and Greene publications have had no small part in their longevity.

IN MEMORIAM

MEDGAR WILEY EVERS
July 2, 1925 — June 12, 1963

Left: A program from one of the many memorial services for Medgar Evers. Courtesy of the Medgar Wiley and Myrlie Beasley Evers Papers, Mississippi Department of Archives and History, and Myrlie Evers-Williams. *Below:* NAACP field secretary Medgar Evers interviewing Mrs. Beulah Melton, twenty-nine, and her four children, following the murder of her husband, Clinton Melton, on December 3, 1955. Mrs. Melton herself would die in an accident soon after. The author wishes to thank the National Association for the Advancement of Colored People Records for authorizing the use of this image.

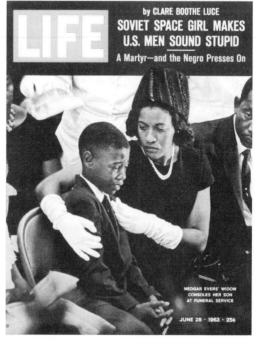

Above: Medgar Evers at his desk around 1960 in Jackson, Mississippi. Photo courtesy of Michael Ochs Archive / Getty Images. *Right:* June 28, 1963, cover of *Life* magazine showing Myrlie Evers comforting her son Darrell Kenyatta at the funeral of murdered civil rights activist Medgar Evers. Photo by John Loengard / Time & Life Pictures / Getty Images.

Above: Front page of Jackson's *Clarion-Ledger* announcing the arrest of Byron De La Beckwith. The *Clarion-Ledger*, which, along with the afternoon *Jackson Daily News*, was owned by the Hedermans, who, like Beckwith, were members of the White Citizens' Council of Mississippi. *Opposite top: Mississippi Free Press* headlines announcing Beckwith's arrest. The small weekly was started by Medgar Evers and other activists to disseminate news of civil rights activities in the state and on the local scene. *Opposite bottom:* Banner headline announcing Medgar Evers's murder in the *Jackson Advocate*, though the story of his death is buried. The *Advocate* was owned by conservative black newspaper editor Percy Greene, who was staunchly opposed to Evers's and the NAACP's efforts in Mississippi.

Mississippi

FREE PRESS

"The Truth Shall Make You Free"

Vol. 2, No. 29   18   Jackson, Mississippi — Saturday, June 29, 1963   10c Per Copy

Killer Suspect Charged

Byron de La Beckwith charged with murder of Medgar Evers.

Byron de La Beckwith Held In Evers Murder
Citizens Council Member To Face Grand Jury

Police have charged Byron de La Beckwith of Greenwood with the ambush slaying of Medgar Evers. FBI agents arrested the accused killer in Greenwood last Saturday evening and brought him to Jackson Sunday morning where local police prepared the murder charge.

An intensive search which began the night of the shooting, June 11, led police to Beckwith. A local officer found a 30-06 rifle in a vacant lot near Evers' home.

Fingerprints

Police traced the gun's telescopic sight to a gun dealer in Grenada and then to Beckwith. The FBI matched a fingerprint on the sight with prints in Beckwith's Marine Corps record.

When Beckwith learned that the FBI was watching his home, he arranged through his attorney, Hardy Lott, to turn himself in. The FBI charged him with violating an individual's civil rights but dropped the charge Monday when Jackson police accused him of murder.

Concessions Relieve Tension; Efforts Expand In Jackson

Concessions from the Mayor of Jackson and intensified voter registration and selective buying campaigns highlighted a week of easing tensions.

Thursday afternoon, Mayor Allen Thompson swore in the first Negro policeman in the history of the city.

Mayor Thompson told Negro leaders that the policeman, Iva-Vell Sand, a body (sic) would be assigned to a Negro district in town, but that he would have full powers along with other members of the force.

Policeman Only A Start...

Henry On Beckwith: 'Court Won't Indict'

In an exclusive interview with the FREE PRESS about the ... Beckwith, State NAACP president Aaron Henry said he had "no real optimism for justice in ... of justice by the ... in Mississippi."

Henry said, however, that he still hoped that race "down not affect just punishment, if Beckwith is guilty."

Henry, who calls himself "one of the best friends" of Evers...

Grand Jury

Beckwith made before the committee Judge James Spencer Tuesday afternoon where he pleaded not guilty to the charge of murder. However, the court decided from a trial what evidence against him to send his murder...

People Jailed As Campaigns Grow In Itta Bena, Greenwood

ȘTATE NAACP SECRETARY IS SHOT TO DEATH

Jackson Advocate

Volume XVII—Number 31   Jackson, Mississippi, Saturday, June 15, 1963   PRICE TEN CENTS

PRESIDENT PRESENTS NEGRO CAUSE TO NATION

TWO NEGRO STUDENTS ENROLLED AT UNIVERSITY OF ALABAMA

New York Career Girl-Model Sparks Africana Image

Howard Grads Called Upon To Offer Knowledge To New Nations

Dr. S. M. Nabrit Of Texas Southern Delivers Address

Washington, D. C., June — The 1963 graduating class of Howard University was called upon to help in the solution of world problems by offering its knowledge and ability to the newly emerging nations.

The appeal came from Dr. Samuel S. Nabrit, president of Texas Southern University, who was the principal speaker at Howard's 95th Commencement. During the exercises degrees were conferred upon some 565 graduates...

Haiti Starts Secret Trials For Plotters Against Pres. Duvalier

Joy Reigns Over U. S. Resuming Official Relations

Port Au Prince, Haiti, June 1 — The Haitian Government has started secret military trials of civilian and military refugees in hiding, charged with plotting to overthrow the regime of President Francois Duvalier.

It is understood that the officials arrested...

MVC Marching Band Scores In Indianapolis 500 Festival Parade

Band Draws High Praise From Press And Spectators

Itta Bena, Miss. — The Mississippi Vocational College 101 piece Marching Band did itself proud at the "500" Festival Parade and on the 100 mile Track at Indianapolis, May 28th and 29th.

As T-hour o'clock a.m. the MVC Marching Band played "one-twelve Fanfare" on Pennsylvania Street at the Platform...

President Kennedy's Speech Called Strongest On Behalf Of Negro Rights In Presidential History

SEE MIXED POLITICAL REACTION

Washington, D. C. — President John F. Kennedy, in a speech broadcast over the nation's entire radio and television network, presented the cause of Negro rights to the nation early Tuesday evening.

In plain courtesy the speech was called the strongest on behalf of the Negro citizens of the country in the history of the presidency.

The speech was delivered during the dramatic continuation of Governor Wallace and Federal authority at the University of Alabama.

(Continued On Page Eight)

Negro Among U. S. Delegates To Pope's Rites

MEDGAR EVERS SLAIN BY BULLET FROM SNIPER'S RIFLE

The State Secretary of the National Association for the Advancement of Colored People, Medgar Evers, was shot to death early Wednesday Morning, as he entered his home on Guynes Street upon returning from a Civil Rights rally.

Evers was shot in the back with a high powered rifle. The bullet passed through his body and spent itself inside the home where it was found on a table in the kitchen. According to investigating authorities, Mr. Evers died shortly after the shooting at the University Hospital.

Local police authorities made off the full detective force upon the investigation immediately after...

(Continued On Page Eight)

See New Civil Rights Proposals Facing Rough Going In Congress

Washington, D. C. June 16 — The administration confidence in Thursday all its plan to secure a broad program...

(Continued on Page Eight)

Negro Enrolled   **President Urge Business Leaders**

Above: Singer Bob Dylan performing his song about the murder of Medgar Evers, "Only a Pawn in Their Game," at a rally in Greenwood, Mississippi, on July 2, 1963. Camera shot by Ed Emshwiller from the film *Don't Look Back* by D. A. Pennebaker. Courtesy of Ashes & Sand / Pennebaker Hegedus Films. *Right:* Topical musician Phil Ochs, who, with Bob Gibson, wrote the ballad "Too Many Martyrs," also called "Ballad of Medgar Evers." Michael Ochs Archives / Getty Images.

★ ★ **DICK WEISSMAN** ★ ★

THE THINGS THAT TROUBLE MY MIND

HE HAD A LONG CHAIN ON · NEVER COMIN' BACK · PORTLAND TOWN · WARTIME BLUES
A HARD RAIN'S A-GONNA FALL · GOIN' AWAY, DON'T YOU WANTA GO · PRETTY BOY FLOYD
EAST VIRGINIA BLUES · LULLABY · THE HARVEST SONG · TROUBLED · THEY STILL GO DOWN

Top: Singer-songwriter Nina Simone performing at the piano on the BBC's *David Frost Show*, London, on December 8, 1968. Simone's song "Mississippi Goddam" was written as a response to the murder of Evers and was performed with her at the piano. Photo by Michael Putland / Getty Images. *Bottom:* Album cover of *The Things That Trouble My Mind*, recorded by folksinger and songwriter Dick Weissman, who wrote and performed "Lullaby (for Medgar Evers)," which was recorded on this album and covered by Judy Collins.

Left: James Baldwin, author of the play *Blues for Mister Charlie*, which is dedicated to the memory of Medgar Evers. Photo taken in 1964 by Jean-Regis Rouston / Roger Viollet / Getty Images. *Below:* Jackson, Mississippi, writers Eudora Welty (left) and Margaret Walker (right) in their later years. Photo by Rick Guy of the *Clarion-Ledger*, a Jackson, Mississippi, newspaper.

I says to my wife, "Just reach and turn it off, And be quiet. You don't need to set and look at a black nigger face no longer than you want to or listen to what you don't want to hear. It's a free country."

That's how I give myself the idea.

I says, I could find where that nigger lives without a bit of trouble.

And I ain't saying it might not be pretty close to where I live. The other hand, there could be other reasons for knowing a place in the dark. It's where you all go for the thing you want most when you want it. Ain't that right?

The First National Branch Bank sign tells you in lights all night long, even, what time it is, and how hot. When it was midnight, and 92, that was me going by.

So leave Five Points at the Rotisserie ("Come As You Are," ha ha), and ride out Delta Drive, past Jackson Surplus & Salvage, not much beyond the Yum Yum Steak House and the Trailer Camp, not as far as where the signs commence to say Live Bait, Used Parts, Fireworks, Peaches, and Sister Roberts Reader & Advisor, stop before you hit the city limits, and duck back sharp towards the railroad. And his street's paved.

First page from the "1st Original" of Eudora Welty's "Where Is the Voice Coming From?" Her heavily edited story, first published on July 6, 1963, in the *New Yorker*, is about the murder of Medgar Evers. Replica of the manuscript page provided by the Mississippi Department of Archives and History. Reprinted by permission of Russell & Volkening as agents for the author. Copyright 1963 by Eudora Welty.

Above: The Medgar Evers Museum, formerly the Everses' home, featured in the 1997 film *Ghosts of Mississippi* after being refurbished into its original state. Evers was shot in the back as he unloaded a stack of T-shirts from his car in his driveway and tried to drag himself to the door, which had been placed on the side of the house for safety reasons. The house is now under the auspices of Tougaloo University. Photo by author. *Right:* Display of Evers memorabilia in the Medgar Evers Museum. Photo by author.

Above: Curator of the Medgar Evers Museum Minnie Watson of Tougaloo University in the living room of the Medgar Evers Museum. The shot that killed Evers came through the front window of the living room and lodged in the kitchen. Photo by author with permission from Minnie Watson. *Below:* Replicas of the Evers boys' beds in the Medgar Evers Museum situated on the floor of their bedroom for safety. Photo by author.

Top left: New York City–based contemporary hip-hop duo Dälek (Will Brooks, left, and Alap Momin, right), who wrote and perform the song "Who Medgar Evers Was." Photo by Hervé Baudat, courtesy of Dälek. *Top right:* Chattanooga, Tennessee, singer-songwriter Kathy Veazey, who penned "I'm Alive" after an unsettling chance encounter with Evers's assassin Byron De La Beckwith. Photo by John Rawlston. *Bottom:* Frank X Walker, author of *Turn Me Loose: The Unghosting of Medgar Evers*, a collection of poetry inspired by Medgar Evers's life and death.

Christening ceremony of the USNS Medgar Evers in San Diego, California, on November 12, 2011. Myrlie Evers-Williams smashes the champagne bottle into the piece of metal attached to the side of the USNS Medgar Evers for its christening ceremony at the General Dynamics NASSCO. Behind her is her and Evers's son Van Evers and at the left is their daughter Reena Evers-Everette. Photo by Charlie Neuman / *San Diego Union-Tribune* / ZUMAPress.com.

Above: An "Obama Platform for Change" event held on July 29, 2008, on the campus of Medgar Evers College in Brooklyn, New York. Photo by mstearne, available online at http://www.flickr.com/photos /39304906@N00/2714718389/. *Left:* Wood-carved portrait of Medgar Evers by contemporary Jackson, Mississippi, folk artist Carl Dixon. Courtesy of Carl Dixon.

CHAPTER FOUR

"It wears, it tears at the root of your heart"

MEDGAR EVERS AND
THE CIVIL RIGHTS MEMOIR

In a return to the literature of mourning and remembrance that emerged from Evers's life and death, this chapter on memoir poses questions about testimony as it shapes collective memory and history. Testimony that serves as evidence in courts of law and as partial evidence in the making of history emerges from the act of remembering. How, then, is memory, thus evidence, thus what we call history, shaped by trauma? How is memory located in the material world, the local comings and goings of what Eudora Welty called "the heart's field"?[1] Complicating and extending these questions, a work of memoir is closely aligned with the process of self-development and self-expression, the making of a kind of self on the page that both partakes of and exceeds the person doing the writing. This autobiographical process becomes entangled in contradiction when the very existence of the self—one's own humanity—is called into question, as it inevitably is in the institutionalization and violent enforcement of discriminatory practices. In such cases, as philosopher Kelly Oliver says, "[s]ubjectivity requires a responsible witness. The process of witnessing is both necessary to subjectivity and part of the process of working-through the trauma of oppression necessary to personal and political transformation."[2] In other words, memoir presents testimony that witnesses not only to specific events of the past but also to the sense of selfhood of the person remembering those events.

These processes of witnessing to and working through conditions of extreme trauma and oppression are at the heart of the memoirs of Anne Moody, who was active in the Mississippi movement during her college years, and Myrlie Evers-Williams, who worked and lived alongside her husband's more public activism. Both women—the first a gifted college student from a poor country background and wise beyond her years, and the other, a brilliant young woman with a quick wit and an aptitude for music, a wife and mother whose worries about her husband's and family's welfare were at times overwhelming—wrote out of the compulsion to offer testimony about a time of terror and fragmentation, of courage and unity. Yet, as Oliver suggests, while "the act of witnessing itself can help restore self-respect and a sense of one's self as an agent or a self . . . the paradoxical nature of bearing witness to your own oppression makes it difficult and painful to testify" and forces recollection of the special pain of the experience of being made into an object. "The experience of testifying to one's oppression repeats that objectification even while it restores subjectivity."[3] This "special pain" becomes part of the fabric of these two memoirs—surfacing again and again as Evers-Williams tells of ironing mountains of shirts on the morning before her husband was killed because she was too nervous to do anything else, shirts he told her he wouldn't be needing, and as Moody writes of the intense anxiety of being a visible target of violence, of being pelted with ketchup at the Woolworth's lunch counter, of being afraid to walk down the street or drive dark roads in the countryside, of being so fearful she couldn't think straight. As Moody said in an interview twenty years after her Mississippi civil rights work in the early 1960s: "it wears, it tears at the root of your heart" because "that's the way it was . . . it really was like that."[4]

Both memoirs—Moody's 1968 *Coming of Age in Mississippi* and Myrlie Evers-Williams's first memoir, the 1967 *For Us, the Living*, written with William Peters—are forms of what Brett Ashley Kaplan calls "aesthetic mourning."[5] Both bear witness to the grueling day-to-day hardships and terrors of civil rights work for women, work that resulted in Moody's breakdown and Myrlie Evers-Williams's devastating loss of her beloved husband. Both narratives are located in what Welty called "the heart's field," Myrlie Evers-Williams in her violated home and Moody in her violated sense of agency. There is an urgency in these two memoirs that manifests what Shoshana Felman describes as "a performative *engagement* between consciousness and history, a struggling act of readjustment between the integrative scope of words and the unintegrated impact of events."[6] To complicate that engagement further, Evers-Williams's and Moody's autobiographical acts of history making occurred at a time when (white) historians and archivists in the South were writing and collecting white, not black, history; the memoirs of these two African American women therefore confronted several layers of validation and were in danger of erasure on several fronts. As historian Fitzhugh Brundage notes, "The larger message of the public history movement in the South was unmistakable: while the black past had no relevance for public life, white history was fundamental to it."[7]

Those double markers that Welty set in defining the complexity of location—"the heart's field" and "the crossroads of circumstance"—are very much at odds in the lives and texts of these two women; circumstance invades the heart's field and tries to destroy the woman who inhabits its crossroads of circumstance. That repeated and forced dislocation of the black woman from her rightful place leaves indelible marks on the pages of these two memoirs. Writing about the persona of memoir, Thomas Larsen makes the observation that "memoir allows the authentic self to lift the mask . . . beget the authentic self to come forward, to assume the mantle: expose the inauthentic. . . . The unmasking is a liberating act."[8] But masks, as illustrated in my discussions of Baldwin, Walker, and Welty, have multiple permutations, both literal and figurative, and lead to vexing questions: What if masking is necessary for survival at the same time its removal is necessary for freedom? What if masks are violently removed by external forces, the forces of "circumstance"? How does the memoirist write about the complexities, the exigencies, of masks and unmasking against the backdrop of African American and southern history? How does she testify to the fear that accompanies exposure and at the same time write in a politically efficacious way about freeing oneself from the historical necessity of living behind the mask? These were dilemmas—aesthetic and ethical—that confronted Moody and Evers-Williams in constructing their memoirs.

In *For Us, the Living* Evers-Williams worries about the exposure of her husband and children, yet she also found herself targeted on more than one occasion. Shortly before her husband's murder, her car, which was parked in the carport, was set on fire by a homemade firebomb; she was home alone with the children and had to extinguish the car fire with a garden hose to keep the gas tank from exploding. On the last night of his life, an exhausted Medgar ordered her to get off the sofa under the front window and sit on the floor of their living room so she herself couldn't be picked off as a target. She recalls that, clinging to her husband in that moment, "I first felt all through me then that we were lost, and wordless tears were the only possible response."[9] After his death, she will trace the path of the bullet that killed him and smashed through the living room window and realize that, had she been sitting in that particular spot that night, she too would have been killed with the same bullet that took her husband's life.

While both Moody's and Evers-Williams's memoirs record their authors' courageous battles to break the grip of Jim Crow in Mississippi in the early 1960s, there is also a sense in which those struggles seem to move into the future as both women, writing in the mid- to late sixties, question what that future will hold for African Americans. This question hovers around the fear of public exposure borne out by John Kennedy's assassination in November 1963 and Martin Luther King's death in 1968, the same year as the publication of Moody's *Coming of Age in Mississippi*. At the same time, both memoirs have the effect of urging others to embrace exposure as the cost of freedom. Angela Hudson describes Moody as suffering from a "racial melancholia" much like an open wound, one that requires a form of autobiographical self-exposure that leads to the exposure of social injustice.[10] Evers-Williams's grief is more pronounced and specific; she mourns Medgar Evers the husband and father.[11] Yet Evers-Williams also risks self-exposure for the sake of remembrance; she wants her husband to be remembered as a leader; she wants his life and death to count. Her book rallies civil rights activists to continue their uphill battle in the South. This tension that tunnels through these two memoirs around the anxiety, and necessity, of exposure finds its focus in representations of Medgar Evers, who early on in his career as a social activist had laid down the mask and in doing so put himself within the telescopic sights of Byron De La Beckwith's rifle.

In a speech to 3,500 people jammed into the Masonic Temple in the record heat of the night of June 7, less than a week before his assassination, Medgar Evers said: "I love my children . . . and I love my wife with all my heart. And I would die, and die gladly, if that would make a better life for them."[12] Evers-Williams recalls that, on hearing her husband's words, she shrank from his willingness to die for the cause he believed in. She writes: "It was a price I didn't want to pay. . . . Of all the thousands of people who heard him say what he said that night at the rally, I guess I was the only one who really didn't understand. I loved him too much for that kind of understanding."[13] Moody, on the other hand, sees in a Klan flyer the potential consequences of her own exposure mirrored in the X's across the faces of Evers and others pictured on the flyer. And while both women survived those times, both of their memoirs close with lists of the deaths of those who were exposed as "troublemakers" and then killed. Moody's and Evers-Williams's memories—the fault lines of their locations in the world—thus place them as wanderers in a literal and metaphoric graveyard. This is a frightening place especially for Evers's young widow, who was barely thirty when her husband was killed and who understood that, despite an almost overwhelming desire to kill herself after her husband's death, she needed to take care of her children and keep her husband's dreams alive in the world. She would go on to have an astonishing career as an activist, community worker, and writer.

I will turn first to Moody's *Coming of Age in Mississippi*, which has as its bedrock purpose the urgent need to witness to "the way it was." In a 1985 interview, she describes herself as "shell-shocked" from her experience in the Mississippi movement, "half out of my mind. Crazy, almost."[14] After she hastily left her home state of Mississippi soon after Evers's assassination, civil rights activists introduced her to Jackie Robinson, who had by then retired from baseball and was also working i[ ] He urged her to write a memoir about her experiences, b[ ] that point; the memories were still too raw. The book, [s]

interviewer, would have "come out with too much hatred."[15] After breaking down during several of her speeches in the Northeast, she withdrew from speaking engagements and went to work at Cornell University as a civil rights projects coordinator. Then, two years later, in 1965, she contacted Robinson, who put her in touch with his editor. She wrote *Coming of Age* between 1965 and 1967. She tells her story in all its rawness, though she was pressured on a number of fronts to make it more palatable to a mainstream audience.[16]

Moody's memoir relates the pivotal effect of Medgar Evers on her early activism. She was born Essie Mae Moody and grew up in Centreville, Mississippi. During high school she had worked as a domestic servant to help her mother put food on the table for nine children. She was desperate to get a decent education, so she worked as a waitress in New Orleans to make money for school and then attended the tiny, poorly managed Natchez College, a junior college for African Americans, on a basketball scholarship. Her idea of activism was a student boycott to protest the poor quality of the cafeteria food, specifically, maggots in the grits. When she finally managed to get to Tougaloo College, outside of Jackson, in 1962, she was always strapped for money, running from her traditional upbringing and her mother's admonitions to remain in the church and not interfere in affairs of race. She joined the college chapter of the NAACP and heard a "big hearty" speech and a call to demonstrate by Evers, followed by another the next evening. In *Coming of Age in Mississippi*, she writes that by the end of that first rally, "all the students were ready to tear Jackson to pieces." Partly as a result of these pep talks, she became so involved in the movement that at mid-semester she barely had a one-point average. An excellent student who had planned on becoming a doctor, she writes: "I started concentrating more on my work—with little success. It seemed as though everything was going wrong."[17] Yet she also maintains that "something happened to me as I got more and more involved in the Movement. It no longer seemed important to prove anything. I had found something outside myself that gave meaning to my life."[18]

Moody writes that during the summer between her junior and senior years, when she worked on voter registration in the Mississippi Delta as part of an effort by the Student Nonviolent Coordinating Committee (SNCC), she could feel herself "beginning to change. For the first time

I began to think something would be done about whites killing, beating, and misusing Negroes. I knew I was going to be a part of whatever happened."[19] Such statements illustrate the power of Moody's narrative, a story torn by her struggle to make a better life for herself and other southern African Americans. Always defiant and assertive, she became even more determined to make a difference in Mississippi; at one point during that summer she and another young woman tried to integrate the white waiting room at the Trailways bus stop in Jackson, both of them barely escaping being beaten up or worse.

The experience of learning about Emmett Till's 1955 murder connects her to Evers at a much earlier age. When Evers, who had just taken the post of NAACP field secretary in November 1954 and had already investigated the murders of two local voting rights leaders, George Lee and Lamar Smith, heard about young Till's kidnapping and the discovery of his body in August 1955, he examined the mutilated body and filed reports to the NAACP. Along with other NAACP officials, who disguised themselves as fieldworkers to investigate the crime, he tried to convince members of the black community to become legal witnesses. As his wife reports in *For Us, the Living*:

> When Emmett Till's body was found, Medgar and Amzie Moore, an NAACP leader from Cleveland, Mississippi, set off from our house one morning with Ruby Hurley, down from Birmingham, to investigate. All of them were dressed in overalls and beat-up shoes, with Mrs. Hurley wearing a red bandanna over her head. To complete the disguise, Amzie had borrowed a car with license plates from a Delta county. Watching them leave, knowing the tension and hate that gripped the Delta, I lived through the day in a daze of fear until their safe return that night.[20]

Charles Evers says of his brother: "Medgar wanted to shame all America with the story of Emmett Till. He wanted to make the civil rights struggle a mass movement." As NAACP field organizer Howard Spencer, who helped Evers with the Till investigation, declared in a 1968 interview, "Had it not been for Medgar Evers . . . it would have been another 'case' that's been forgot. The Emmett Till case was the beginning of the Montgomery bus boycott. It was the beginning of a lot of incidents in the South that began to make the Negro aware of the fact that he would *have* to get out and expose himself to these racists — to these people that were gonna kill him."[21]

Like James Baldwin, Medgar Evers, and African Americans across the nation, Moody never forgot young Till's murder, but for even more personal reasons. Exactly his age of fourteen and poised on the brink of high school, she felt his death acutely as an initiation into the vicissitudes of racial violence, its unpredictability, volatility, and inevitability. She recalls asking her mother about the murder, having heard about it from some classmates on the way home from school; her mother, who continually warned her against disturbing the racial status quo, replied, "That boy's a lot better off in heaven than he is here."[22] At that time young Anne was working as a domestic servant, and her mother instructed her to pretend to her white employer that she didn't know anything about the murder. When her employer, "one of the meanest white women in town," used Till's death to threaten her, Moody recalls:

> I went home shaking like a leaf on a tree. For the first time out of all her trying, Mrs. Burke had made me feel like rotten garbage. Many times she had tried to instill fear within me and subdue me and had given up. But when she talked about Emmett Till there was something in her voice that sent chills and fear all over me.
>
> Before Emmett Till's murder, I had known the fear of hunger, hell, and the Devil. But now there was a new fear known to me — the fear of being killed just because I was black. This was the worst of my fears. I knew once I got food, the fear of starving to death would leave. I also was told that if I were a good girl, I wouldn't have to fear the Devil or hell. But I didn't know what one had to do or not do as a Negro not to be killed. Probably just being a Negro period was enough, I thought.[23]

Moody never forgot that moment of sheer terror. Thirty years later, on February 19, 1985, she gave an interview to Debra Spencer at the Mississippi Department of Archives and History, which, along with an (apparently lost) interview with writer-activist Thomas Dent in New Orleans the following day, seems to be her last interview of public record. In this halting and haunting interview, she answers Spencer's first question about whether any one specific event had made her feel she should become active in her resistance to Jim Crow practices: "Well, I think when you get to the point in the book when I finally—when Emmett Till was murdered, right?—and we were exactly like the same age, and up until Emmett Till's death, I think, these things were not real to me, and I became more aware of the fact that it happened to not only adult black men, but children, my own age. And it just was the whole injustice of it happening to such a young fifteen year old. It was like . . ." (ellipsis original with nothing following).[24]

After working for SNCC during the summer of 1962, Moody, at that point in her senior year of college, threw herself into the movement, first with the Woolworth and bus station sit-ins, and later the voter registration effort in Canton, Mississippi, just north of Jackson. When Evers was killed, she was so outraged that she and a friend went over to Jackson State University, Margaret Walker's place of employment, and ended up getting kicked off campus by the president himself after the two of them ran from classroom to classroom announcing the mass march in protest of Evers's death and urging students to boycott classes. She recalls reading the biased account of the murder in the rabidly racist afternoon paper, the *Jackson Daily News*, and feeling, quite strongly: "I had to get out of this confusion. The only way I could do it was to go to jail. Jail was the only place I could think in."[25] She proceeded to do just that by participating in a demonstration protesting Evers's death and found herself locked in a paddy wagon with the windows rolled up on that hundred-degree day and being taken to the fairgrounds to be locked up in the livestock pens. She recalls that the driver pulled up to the fairgrounds, rolled up the windows of the paddy wagon, turned up the heater, and left the students inside for what seemed like an eternity. After finally being taken to the pens inside, she, like Evers and other civil rights leaders, imagines herself "in Nazi Germany, the policemen Nazi soldiers. They couldn't have been any rougher than these cops. Yet, this was America, 'the land of the free and the home of the brave.'"[26] The food served to them was cooked in a garbage can, and by the time Moody and the others were released three days later, she had lost fifteen pounds and was weak with nausea.

One moment in Moody's memoir positions her in close proximity to her hero. In this chilling moment after Evers's death, a friend in Jackson showed her a Klan blacklist with her own picture on it, alongside one of

Evers that had been crossed out. At this point in her narrative, Moody was on the verge of a complete breakdown. She was working in the frustrating and dangerous voter registration effort in Canton and living unprotected from both locals and police harassment with a group of young women in what was called Freedom House, the windows blacked out and broken. She was being harassed by a sinister cop, taking large quantities of sleeping pills but still unable to sleep, and experiencing choking sensations and blackouts. She writes: "It had gotten to the point where my weight was going down to nothing. I was just skin and bones. My nerves were torn to shreds and I was losing my hair."[27] When she saw the pictures on the Klan blacklist, she realized that most of the people on it were either dead, including Evers and Emmett Till, or had left the state, including John Salter, her white professor; Joan Trumpauer, a fellow student, also white, who had influenced her to get into the movement; James Meredith, who had integrated the University of Mississippi; and a minister who suddenly had taken up missionary work in Africa. A few days later, Moody reports,

I was walking around in a daze. I didn't only feel choked up, as I had been feeling for two weeks, I felt I was carrying the weight of the world on my shoulders. It was too much of a burden for me. . . . I felt like a robot, and worked like one, too. . . .

Later that evening I tried to go for a walk and my feet felt as if heavy iron bars were attached to them. I could barely move them. I got a block away from the Freedom House and turned around. I went back and sat on the steps. It was there on the steps of the Freedom House that I decided to leave the project for a while. I sat there trying to analyze what was going on, and discovered that I couldn't even think any more. It was like my brains had gone to sleep on me or frozen.[28]

When asked in the 1985 interview whether many people who worked in the movement had suffered "battle fatigue," Moody answered in what is transcribed as halting speech: "Yeah—you know you got that I think from my reading last night, but actually when I—I think a lot of people—you don't know the effect that it has on—on you, I mean mentally. It wears, it tears at the root of your heart."[29]

At the end of her narrative, Moody feels "very old." She is on a bus to Washington with other Mississippi African Americans who will be testifying at the Council of Federated Organizations hearings about the conditions in the state. As the jubilant group on the crowded bus sings "We Shall Overcome," Moody looks at the passing Mississippi landscape and thinks: "Images of all that had happened kept crossing my mind: the Taplin burning, the Birmingham church bombing, Medgar Evers' murder, the blood gushing out of McKinley's head, and all the other murders. . . . I could feel the tears welling up in my eyes." As the song swells around her, she thinks: "I wonder. I really wonder."[30] And the memoir ends here.

As did Moody's work in her home state of Mississippi. After landing in Washington, she gave passionate and well-received speeches there and in New York, but as she puts it in the 1985 interview, "I was shell-shocked—I mean I was half out of my mind." After several months of breaking down in tears during her talks, she took the job at Cornell University and, after the passage of two years, began to write the book in which her life and passion, as well as her vulnerability, would be reflected back to her alongside Medgar Evers's, just as their pictures appeared together on the Klan flyer, his Xed-out face mirrored and inscribed in hers. Yet that closeness for Moody was unbearable, its outcome erasure, the X across the face. She fled Mississippi to run for her life. She wrote that unbearable story, not just Evers's but her own; and more than twenty years later she would turn back to the local to explain to her white interviewer: "[Y]ou wouldn't have understood the depth of my anger. I had to present it in that way by showing you *this* little girl, growing up in this *particular* house, you see what I mean, encountering these *certain* experiences, and how she gradually became what she became" (my emphasis).[31]

So, perhaps in part through the demands of the genre of memoir and in part through her desire to speak to a broad readership, Moody brings to an aesthetics of historical transformation and political alterity the methodology of framing in the local—*this* little girl in this *particular* house with those *certain* experiences—her embodied knowledge of terror: headaches, insomnia, weight loss, and constant trembling, as well as her remembered history: the monkey faces and raised fists in the bus station, the ketchup smears from the Woolworth's lunch counter, the dead friends and relations. This specificity and locatedness both mark "the crossroads of circumstance" of her story and give it its continuing power. Like Baldwin, Walker, and Welty, then, Moody mourns the death of Medgar Evers, but beyond that she also mourns the loss of his inheritor: that hopeful young woman who could sing "We Shall Overcome" without wondering whether it was true. The one who hadn't yet felt the violent unmasking power of the X across the face. The one whose loss drives *Coming of Age in Mississippi*, and locates it in "the heart's field" of a longer and harder civil rights struggle.

Moody's book, which would become a best seller and be translated many times over, memorializes Medgar Evers's all-too-brief moment in history, the struggles of the late fifties and early sixties whose blood price has never truly been reckoned. At the same time, Moody testifies to a violent erasure of identity, the X on the face; she writes that self back into being, testifying to its resilience as well as its vulnerability. But the damage was done, and some of it irrevocable. Moody didn't return to Mississippi until eleven years later, and then only to visit her good friend in the movement, C. O. Chinn, who was in prison. Two years after that she returned to visit her mother on her deathbed. When, in 1985, several universities brought her back south to do readings and lectures, she left abruptly and unexpectedly.[32] The only other book she ever published was a 1975 short story collection called *Mr. Death: Four Stories*, a slim volume with an apt title and grotesque story lines and characters. "Mr. Death" claims a cross-section of the rural southern population: black children who get run over in the road, die from self-inflicted gunshots, or get eaten by dogs; old white people who burn alive. There are nightmarish images of fragmentation, bloody organs, a girl who looks and acts like a cow.[33]

In Moody's 1985 interview she gave, in explicit detail, the plot summaries of *nine* other memoirs and works of fiction that she said she had in process, several of them, she asserted, complete at the time. She mentioned them all by title and expressed excitement about each and every one, saying in fact that, except for the matter of chapter length, she would have read from one of them at her reading the day before at Tougaloo: the book she called *Farewell to Too Sweet*, which was about her mother and was one of her two sequels to *Coming of Age*. Today, a quarter century later, not a single one has been published, and Anne Moody's silence resonates through the decades.

Like Moody, who left the South on that Greyhound bus and never returned except for brief periods, Myrlie Evers-Williams had a firsthand acquaintance with the local, the underbelly of her home state. About halfway through her 1967 memoir, *For Us, the Living*, as she recounts events of the fifties and very early sixties, presenting a spatial metaphor of violence—a map of Mississippi—she writes:

> I remember the names of the victims of those years of terror, unfamiliar at first, then burned into memory by the repetition of the cold, brutal facts of death and torture. I remember the towns whose violence drew Medgar, towns whose names came to stand in my mind for a murder, the rape of a Negro schoolgirl by white men, the beating of a Negro woman by white police.
>
> A map of Mississippi was a reminder not of geography, but of atrocities, of rivers that hid broken bodies, of towns and cities ruled by the enemy. No spot was safe, no road without its traps, and Medgar was a constantly moving target. . . .
>
> If the years were stamped with the names of the murdered, the months were inked with those of the beaten and maimed. Affidavits testifying to the routine cruelty of white Mississippians toward Negroes piled up in Medgar's files. Each represented an hour, a day, a week of Medgar's life in a surrealist version of Hell.[34]

This map bears the weight of southern history, the burden of a time of vigilante violence and institutionalized apartheid that was still ongoing and even more intense when *For Us, the Living* was published in 1967. In her memoir, the first of two she would produce, Evers-Williams describes her husband at the forefront of the battle—fending off police harassment, bailing hundreds of children out of fairgrounds livestock pens, taking down statements, ferreting out evidence, and keeping bail money flowing in from the NAACP. She describes a growing sense of foreboding and fear during this time: "It seemed impossible now that he could survive each day."[35]

For Us, the Living also conveys an urgency around the issue of collective memory. It is important to both Moody and Evers-Williams that the details are all there: the X across the faces, the headaches, the ironed shirts that would go unworn, bullet holes, blood on the driveway. Evers-Williams still believes that mapping the past can serve a testimonial function. In an interview in 2010, she said that she finds "an insensitivity to the history of race relations sad" and troubling. Besides raising her children, her driving purpose in life has been keeping her first husband's memory alive, saying, "I've devoted my life to rearing our three children and keeping Medgar's memory alive. I believed that if I didn't do everything in my power to keep his memory alive, do whatever I could do, he would be forgotten in one year — one year."[36]

As in Moody's memoir, and perhaps even more so, the book provides a strong sense of a woman's voice. Seven years younger than her husband and married before she could finish college, Myrlie Evers was thrust into unexpectedly frightening situations that left her aghast early on in their marriage. For example, when Evers announced his intention of seeking admission to the University of Mississippi in 1954, a few months before the U.S. Supreme Court's *Brown v. Board of Education* ruling, she recalls:

> I thought he had lost his mind.
> My first reaction, when I finally grasped the implication of what he proposed to do, was one of complete devastation. It was like a personal attack on me by the man I loved most of all people in the world. I felt isolated, lost, alone, let down by the man who had sworn to love and protect me. I could not have felt worse if he had left me a note that he was leaving me. What I heard was that he was leaving me and Darrell [the couple's oldest son], abandoning us, going off on his own on some wild mission that could only end in disaster. What I heard was the wrenching, tearing, uprooting of my marriage.[37]

For Us, the Living looks back to the past and forward to the future. Evers-Williams wanted her husband to be remembered as a leader whose life's work and ultimate sacrifice jolted the nation and the South into action, a man who made an enormous difference in history; she wanted her personal memories of this public man to mold collective American memory. She also seemed to see her memoir as transforming collective memory into social action well into the future. In terms of both purposes, then, a more public, black uplift narrative—like many African American autobiographies at the end of the nineteenth and beginning of the twentieth centuries—would have served. But that is not what we get, not by a long shot. Hers is an intimate story, told by a wife and mother of the 1950s and 1960s who worried incessantly about her family, whose own sense of self seems to become subsumed as her story becomes enmeshed in her husband's commitment to social change. Further, although her analysis of the sexual and gendered politics of race is astute, this is a book firmly located in the traditional domestic sphere of the fifties and early sixties.

Thusly situated, Evers-Williams's story rings true;[38] it makes us see Medgar Evers as a man with quirks, vulnerabilities, passions. Toward the end of her story, she says that in the months following Evers's death she remembered him as "almost perfect. It was only later, slowly," she writes, "that I could bring myself to recall moments that had not been so pleasant, that I could return to the reality that both he and I had had faults and that our marriage had not been without problems."[39] In the end, money problems compounded the tension in the house. Evers, who worked as a life insurance salesman before he became NAACP field secretary, had allowed his own life insurance policy to lapse.[40] Two nights before his death, as he confessed this fact to his wife, he broke down and cried. She remembers: "We clung to each other as though it were our only hope, and in my heart I felt that time was running out. There was no anger, no bitterness, not even a sense of having been robbed of what other people took for granted. There was just a bottomless depth of hopelessness, of hurt, of despair. I think I first felt all through me then that we were lost, and wordless tears were the only possible response." The next morning, though, a Monday, the everyday world of the domestic reasserted itself; it was, Evers-Williams writes, "another day to get through." From an outside perspective that morning, the family life of the young couple, as rendered in the memoir, might have seemed perfect. The two older children ran off to play, and Evers threw a miniature football with his youngest son, Van, but paused to examine his prize plum tree and call out to his wife through the window, "Myrlie, I think we're going to have our best year ever for plums." She writes, "I went out then and told him that he had worked hard enough on that tree to deserve a good year, and we walked around the back yard together."[41] The power of Evers-Williams's memoir lies in such specifically located moments in the Evers household, heart-breaking in their poignancy and bitter irony.

The Everses' closeness that day was hard won. Early on in her story, Evers-Williams focuses more on how her husband's passion for social justice grew out of his work as an insurance salesman in the early days of their marriage, as well as on her early skepticism about his emerging political commitment. Going from community to community, he witnessed the acute poverty and dire living conditions of his people. A returning soldier, he had seen the devastation of European fascism, which, as noted earlier, made Jim Crow seem like a close cousin to Hitler. His young wife had resisted many of his efforts at social activism and fought him at every turn. About a third of the way through her memoir, Evers-Williams writes that she, like Moody, had "grown up in a family that never discussed race, that never complained about discrimination."[42] She had planned on having a quiet life with her prospective husband and family. However, she describes a turning point in her attitude toward Evers's activism: how she, at her mother's urging, over the course of two days came to terms with her own resistance to her husband's insistence on breaking down racial barriers. She writes that she realized suddenly that "what attracted me most about Medgar were the very qualities of courage and fearlessness of which my mother spoke with such warmth and admiration. I knew that what had always made him stand out from almost all the other men I had known was the fact that he was indisputably a man. And that, at least, was the beginning of understanding, for Southern Negroes are not supposed to behave like men. They are often in mortal danger when they do."[43] Evers-Williams then spends at least ten pages analyzing the emasculation of African American men in the South from slavery times to her present. While being denied the right to make a decent living for their families and protect women from sexual predation by white men, they had been made the brunt of the white man's "almost obsessive fear about the sexual safety of his own women," while "[i]t is the white man throughout Southern history who has played the role of rapist. . . . At base, [there was] a guilty fear of retaliation." This gendered racial politics and the "terrible impotence" it demanded, Evers-Williams explains, deeply affected her husband on several occasions. She tells how he became enraged when African American women were accosted or raped.[44]

She realizes, moreover, that white male supremacy had also deeply molded her experiences as a black girl. Walking was particularly danger-ous for black women. She recalls two incidents, one in which her mother was accosted as she and Evers-Williams's stepfather were walking. When her stepfather was unable to hold off a carload of white men, forcing him and her mother to run to a white family's home, the two white police-men who were called were annoyed and asked insulting questions. When Myrlie herself was fourteen and was walking home with her Aunt Myrlie, they were both accosted by a white man in a car. "In time," she writes, "I came to understand, as all Southern Negro girls do, what that experience had meant, but it was not until the night at my mother's house, as we sat for hours discussing such things, that I really felt the fullness of the hor-ror those experiences had for Negro men."[45] At the cusp of Evers's official plunge into the movement in 1954, then, she came to an intellectual and emotional understanding of his commitment to racial equality and his willingness to fling aside the mask and be true to himself as a black man. She realized that she admired his courage. At that point, though, she had no comprehension of the emotional toll that commitment would exact on both of them and their future children.

As she relates the stories from their next decade, Evers-Williams speaks to her and her husband's ability to live at "the edge of disaster," to fend off the threatening or pleading phone calls, to manage the mo-ment when there was no control over what could happen. Preparing her children for stray bullets and firebombs, instructing them to sit on the floor while watching television, to drop to the floor and crawl to the bath-room at the first sign of danger, reminded her of how schools were pre-paring students to crawl under their desks in preparation for a nuclear strike.[46] In such an environment, exhaustion and fear meld, and when Evers made a television appearance at the end of May 1963, his wife feared that "[t]housands of Mississippi whites who had never seen a pic-ture of him would now be seeing Medgar on television. . . . When it was over, he would be recognized everywhere: at a stop light in the city, on a lonely road in the Delta, in the light from the fuel pump at a gas station."[47] Although the reasoned, thoughtful speech was well received and had some positive effects in Jackson, Evers lost his anonymity, making the vise of hatred tighten around him and his family. Evers himself became overwrought and sleepless in the pressure cooker they found themselves in, so much so that one night, when he heard a noise, he took the rifle he kept loaded by the bed and almost shot Darrell, who had gotten up to use the bathroom.[48] His wife remembers, in an odd echo of Moody's recollection of her own debilitated mental state: "He had aged ten years in the past two months."[49]

Throughout the danger and uncertainty, Evers-Williams tried to look to the future needs of her family. After Byron De La Beckwith's bullet had torn through her husband's body, leaving, as Margaret Walker's son related, "blood everywhere," and her neighbors raced him to emergency care where he would expire shortly thereafter, she packed Medgar's toothbrush and pajamas for the hospital.[50] Early the next morning her friends found her scrubbing her husband's blood off the driveway so that her children wouldn't see it.[51] His death, though, moved her into a state of extended shock in which she was able to give her children only minimal care and emotional support. She writes: "The whole first year without Medgar was a living nightmare. I searched my memory for every tiny detail, every precious moment we had shared. I lived in the past; the present was nothing; the future didn't exist."[52] It is more than thirty-five years later, with the publication of her second memoir, *Watch Me Fly*, published in 1999, that the details of this time will emerge: within a month of her husband's death she had miscarried their fourth child, leaving her thankful she didn't have an infant to consider; she stockpiled a stash of pills in her lingerie drawer in hopes of having enough to kill herself; she had made plans for her sister-in-law to care for the children after her death, admitting, "I was at the bottom of a deep, dark pit, struggling to climb out, and life kept battering me downward. But the public could not know. The strong widow image had to prevail."[53] It is decades later, then, after a distinguished career culminating in her position as chair of the NAACP, that Evers-Williams takes off her own mask of the "strong widow" to uncover the chasm of her own suffering.

In most of *For Us, the Living*, Medgar Evers's sense of his people's right to human dignity and the drama of his life's work take center stage. Much of the strength of this memoir lies in relating his public struggle for justice to the private anguish that went on inside the small, green suburban house at 2332 Guynes Street, the house that would become a tourist attraction in the months after his death.[54] After describing her husband's death, though, Evers-Williams begins to tell her own story, the story that clearly was left unfinished until *Watch Me Fly* appeared decades later. A hint of that story comes in angry spurts as she writes about white hypocrisy in Jimmy Ward's column in the *Jackson Daily News*, a persistent *Life* magazine photographer, roving parties of sightseers in her front yard, threatening phone calls and hate letters, and the funeral and burial arrangements for her husband planned by the NAACP, including the purchase of a dress for her to wear to his funeral—none of which she approved.[55] After giving a speech at a mass meeting at Pearl Street Baptist Church the night after Evers's death, she turns and walks out the door. As she goes to the car, she hears the people begin to sing, but unlike Moody at the close of her memoir, who listens to the song "We Shall Overcome" and questions whether her people will ever overcome, Evers-Williams says that at the moment she left the church, "I [didn't] know what they sang because I had no heart to listen any more and I closed my ears and my mind and my thoughts."[56]

Like *Coming of Age in Mississippi*, *For Us, the Living* ends with a list of the dead. While Moody mourns the dead as she listens to strains of "We Shall Overcome" and her bus takes her through "the passing Mississippi landscape,"[57] Evers-Williams simply lists the names of the victims of racial violence and the situations of their murders in a section titled "In Memoriam" at the back of her book. The section begins with the caption "These Americans, too, were murdered in recent years in pursuit of the cause of civil rights."[58] Preceding this listing, the final chapter of the memoir closes with an image of disease, the deadly disease of racism that "kills and infects and wounds and cripples individuals [and] can also kill initiative, infect political systems, wound legal institutions, cripple the conscience of a nation."[59] And so, despite its optimistic title and a final gesture to a future that would "make Mississippi the place that Medgar dreamed it could be,"[60] *For Us, the Living* closes in a graveyard of those killed by the disease that brought down Medgar Evers. For his widow in 1967, mourning the fallen and working through the trauma of grief are the work of a future as yet undetermined.

Sociologist Kai Erickson has observed that trauma can both create community and damage it, sometimes irreparably.[61] Moody's and Evers's memoirs, published only a few years after Evers's death, reveal the initial damage the assassination caused to the movement in Mississippi, but in their own times these books of the 1960s served as rallying calls to that damaged and traumatized community and became standard-bearers of a national movement for racial justice that was gathering strength and confidence.[62] In this regard, they expose the personal cost of living under white institutions of violently enforced oppression and rally their contemporaries to overturn, in the late 1960s, these systems of white oppression in the South that denied the commensurate humanity of African Americans. They thus form part of a constellation of writing around Evers's life and death that continues to witness not only to the trauma of working in the movement but also to the very process of witnessing itself—in their case, to their shared sense of identity and voice as southern African American women in the midst of violence and chaos.[63]

A witness to such stories requires a listener, someone who hears testimony and accepts it as true. This listener, or in the case of memoir this reader, must respond both to the veracity of the memoirist who witnesses and to the sense of erasure the memoirist has experienced in traumatically oppressive situations. This reader is confronted with the necessity of what Oliver calls "response-ability," and that "response-ability" must fold into an ethical commitment to justice.[64] Thus "response-ability"—that is, the ability to respond to and confirm such life narratives as those that Anne Moody and Myrlie Evers-Williams relate—leads to an ethical obligation. Both Moody and Evers-Williams demand this ethical obligation from their readers.

It is interesting, then, that Willie Morris, as a white Mississippian of the Everses' generation, wrote the 1995 introduction to a new University Press of Mississippi edition of *For Us, the Living* three years before his own memoir about the Evers story was published. He writes in the introduction that he considers *For Us, the Living* "one of the finest of our American memoirs" and praises "its human dimensions, its everlasting themes: courage, sacrifice, grief, loyalty, and love, Old Testament in their intensity."[65] Might we then think of Morris as a white writer whose sense of "response-ability" led to a desire to confirm Evers-Williams's own story, one he felt continued, on the cusp of the twenty-first century, to touch whites and blacks alike with its "honesty and dignity"?[66]

Certainly memoirs by white southern writers, such as Morris's flamboyantly titled *The Ghosts of Medgar Evers: A Tale of Race, Murder, Mississippi, and Hollywood*, serve a testimonial function. So do other creative nonfiction texts in which white writers from the South wrestle with the meaning of the Medgar Evers story, as in the case of Reed Massengill's *Portrait of a Racist: The Man Who Killed Medgar Evers*, which ponders the engorged racism of the author's former uncle-in-law, Byron De La Beckwith.[67] Yet Morris's and Massengill's books—and arguably Welty's "Where Is the Voice Coming From?"—offer up another kind of witness, not to the vicissitudes of being black in the 1960s South but to the guilt and anxiety of being cloaked in a southern whiteness that won't wash off, a whiteness that is both frightening and monstrous, that is itself a stain. Instead of erasing the self, whiteness in the implicit and explicit violence of a racist society and history comes to define subjectivity; the white southern memoirist of conscience must thus attempt to write himself *out of* the history of southern white racism and create another kind of self, a "response-able" one.

In contrast to Moody's terrifying affiliation with the X on Evers's face in the Klan flier and most especially Evers-Williams's heart-wrenching experience of her husband's death, Morris approaches the Evers murder thirdhand. He never met Evers and, like James Baldwin, was living in New York at the time of the civil rights leader's death. Morris's 1998 memoir is about the making and reception of the film *Ghosts of Mississippi*, which has as its subject neither Evers's life nor even his death but rather the third trial and 1994 conviction of Beckwith. Morris, a sixth-generation native of the Mississippi Delta and an urbane writer most known in southern literature circles for his memoir *North toward Home*, which was published, like Evers-Williams's first memoir, in 1967, was a consultant on the film in the mid-1990s. He hobnobbed with the director, cast, and crew, and much of his book offers gossip, anecdotes, and technical information about filmmaking.

The Ghosts of Medgar Evers is indeed ghostly, and Mississippi is a place haunted by the past. Morris knows how to set a scene; he is also drawn to place and, by his own account, was invaluable to the film's director, Rob Reiner, because, as a native Mississippian, he could send crews to the right locations for specific scenes. He directed the film crew to the most haunted places in Mississippi and then describes them for his readers, such as an area in the southwest corner of the state:

> To me there is no more haunted, complex terrain in America than the countryside between Port Gibson and the river. In this spooky, seductive earth, the southwest corner of Mississippi, resides the colonial, territorial, Confederate, and American history of this beguiling and tortured state. . . . The woods are dark and profuse with creeping vines, snakes, and the ubiquitous Spanish moss. The hills and entangled embankments are precipitous, the older roadways deep tunnels of green, and the river is never far away. The land is full of ghosts.[68]

Of his home state, Morris asks: "What is it that would still be here after Hollywood departed? Black and white people trying to live together on this common soil. Heroes and villains. Suffering and pain. Human history and memory."[69] In an early Faulknerian description of the Mississippi Delta landscape, he sees not as Moody does at the end of her book, the images of those who have been murdered, but black people's laboring bodies both beautiful and doomed, "bent low before the cotton in the ancient ritual, ebony silhouettes in the sunshine. They stand and wave, as if the car itself is a magnet that ripples among the flesh." He describes "unpainted shacks," "barefooted children in ragged clothes," "naked infants in grassless yards," and "hybrid dogs under the arching chinaberries," and he ends a thickly descriptive paragraph thusly: "A strange sense of doom seems to hover over the land itself."[70] He positions himself largely in the "panoply of white in the undulating gloaming" of the cotton fields in the late afternoon of early fall and writes:

It makes you feel big and important in such a moment—at least those who never worked these fields—to know that the ancient Egyptians grew this same cotton, and that it has been with us since hieroglyphics. . . . This incredible Delta land consumed and shaped me, irrevocably and forever, as a child—it was not in my mind then, only in my pores—and as a man and a writer I find it dwells in my being. I love it beyond all measure, and I fear it too, as I always did. It is the very power of this land itself that makes you both love and fear it. It is what I am, and always will be till I die.[71]

Morris connects the labor of rural African Americans to Evers's own family history: "In the town, almost every house had its black maid, who for fifteen cents an hour left her own dwelling early in the morning and did not return until late afternoon—cooking, laundering, mopping, sweeping as Medgar Evers's mother had done."[72] Evers himself and the racial history his death embodies, Morris argues, will always haunt Mississippi. He ends his memoir by writing:

Medgar Evers had known this ground in his deepest being, how crucified it had been by slavery, peonage, and affliction, how tragic and ineluctable and abiding it was. He had fought with all he had in him against the cruelties of this land, yet a part of him had passionately loved it. It was his final and supreme contradiction, the contradiction that made him real. This was *his* land, and it was mine also. His ghost still envelops this land, too, just as it does all the people and places and happenings in this story—including, of course, the man who wrote it.[73]

This idea that Morris himself, a white progressive Mississippian, is haunted by Medgar Evers's ghost is compelling and suggestive, and it seems specifically located in place, both literally and in the idea of Mississippi as a state of mind. Is Morris feeling the way Eudora Welty did when she sat down and just had to write "Where Is the Voice Coming From?" because she felt she knew something about location, the place she came from and the people it fostered? Or because, in both of their cases (and by the time both of them wrote about Evers's death they were both famous writers), there was something they felt deep down they *didn't* know about the place they inhabited? Something that caused Welty to create a Snope-sian poor white killer instead of an upper-middle-class Mississippian like herself?

There is something uneasy, and a bit uncertain, that calls attention to itself in Morris's memoir. Yes, he knows every nook and cranny in the state, but does he know what Welty called "the heart's field" of his place? More to the point: does he know *his* location in that place, in that story? By his own account, he grew up as a middle-class white boy who was all too aware of the daily violence against black people. He is deeply sorrow-ful about Mississippi's violent history, but like Evers himself, he loves his home state.

What is particularly arresting about Morris's memoir is the way his narrative hovers uneasily at the site of Evers's death—his home and driveway, the place of his murder and the place his blood flowed. Several scenes in the book focus on the driveway, including the filming of the murder scene in the driveway of Evers's refurbished home. Morris tells the story of how the scene was put together and shot many times, us-ing bags of fake blood, how Charles Evers, Medgar's brother, and the neighbors stood by and watched. In the end the scene seemed so lifelike, Morris writes, that "[r]eality was being created, not an illusion. It was in-credibly powerful and *gratifying* [my emphasis]. I want to tell you, what I experienced that night of the filming didn't have anything to do with moviemaking anymore. But by the same token it had *everything* [Morris's emphasis] to do with moviemaking."[74] I want to pause, uneasily, at the word "gratifying" and ask, gratifying to whom and toward what end? Is this an aesthetic or ethical gratification Morris experiences? While Moody is confronted with Evers's and her own images on the Klan flier and recoils in horror and fear, Morris instead chooses to put on Evers's martyrdom as a kind of hair shirt over his white skin. The film he de-scribes at such great length becomes the aesthetic vehicle that enables that cathartic, self-focused moment of encounter with Medgar Evers's pain and his blood. Ironically, however, as I noted earlier, the film it-self has been severely criticized for its focus on the white district attor-ney Bobby DeLaughter instead of on Evers and his family, and especially on Myrlie Evers-Williams's decades of seeking justice for her husband's death.

Morris visited the scene of Evers's murder several times. That moment of filming was presaged by another scene in the memoir when Morris and his wife, JoAnne, take the film's producer, Fred Zollo, on a "dark windless midnight" visit to the Evers house. It was the night of Beckwith's guilty verdict in 1994. Morris notes that it was "about the same hour as the killing in 1963." The Evers house was eerily boarded up (this was before the movie crew restored it) and everything was shadowy and still. Morris's prose becomes a ritualistic litany as he describes the scene of Evers's collapse: "This was the door through which his wife and children rushed to him and shouted, 'Daddy, get up!' This was where he tried to crawl toward his wife's arms. This was the concrete over which his blood flowed."[75]

Morris then turns to the passage of time:

> In the preternatural quiet I pondered anew how the passing of time itself had been the fabric and sinew of these recent events, witnesses who were young then grown into the fullness of their years, memory itself ripened and culminating. Medgar Evers, who as a young man had attained martyrdom that would soon heighten with the making of a Hollywood movie, would have been seventy years old at the time of the final verdict; his children now were his age then. Everyone, myself among them, was older.
>
> Beckwith was older too.[76]

In the rhetorical logic of this passage, Evers's martyrdom, his blood, becomes layered onto Morris's own history, and Morris's history becomes layered onto Beckwith's. This palimpsestic description is reminiscent of the passage in Welty's story: "Something darker than him, like the wings of a bird, spread on his back and pulled him down. He climbed up once, like a man under bad claws, and like just blood could weigh a ton he walked with it on his back to better light."[77] Medgar Evers's ghost, Morris writes, "reigns" over the history he lived and the history that surged forward in his violently enforced absence from it: "It reigns over the making of the movie itself, because even though he was not a major part of it, his ghost resides indwellingly in its heart, spirit, and soul."[78]

In a sense, then, Morris's story isn't about a movie at all but rather about a white Mississippi man who as a boy watched other white males harass and hurt black boys and men, who still feels the shame of that history and seeks a way to become "response-able" to it and to move that "response-ability" into the future. But that search gets sidetracked in a circular, aesthetic response to bloodshed, an acting out rather than a working through of a trauma not his but one that he remains fascinated by and strangely drawn to years later. In the end Morris is pulled in, like the tourists in the days following Evers's murder who drove slowly by his house to gawk and click their cameras. While Moody and Evers-Williams fled the site of Evers's bloodshed (the latter gathering a bucket of soap-suds to try to scour it off the driveway), Morris, three decades later, hovers at that *lieu de mémoire*,[79] that site of memory: Medgar Evers's driveway. It seeps into Morris's own life story, leaving an indelible stain.

The stories of Medgar Evers all three of these memoirists tell are stories of place: Mississippi, Jackson, Guynes Street, an overgrown vacant lot, a Woolworth's lunch counter. A driveway. As a conclusion to this chapter, let me reiterate what I have said earlier: that the literature of human-inflicted trauma is always local. Traumatic events happen specifically and particularly *somewhere*: a place, a geographic location. They have an abiding relationship to the ground on which they occur; if they were not so situated, their claims to truth might be invalidated. Yet human-caused traumatic events are also global, both in terms of time and space. They do not remain in just *one* place. They and the human suffering they evoke proceed from site to site, generation to generation, century to century. The dead claim a voice through the memory of the living, who tell stories that are both located in place and set free to wander the world, planting the seeds of social justice and moral "response-ability" in the present and future. These stories, those of the living and the dead, tend the heart's field of southern and American history, sowing—and reaping—a difficult harvest.

CHAPTER FIVE

Music and Medgar Evers

THE HEARTBEAT OF MEMORY

Memory, like the heart, beats beyond our capacity to
control it, a lifeline between past and future.
— DIANA TAYLOR, *The Archive and the Repertoire:
Performing Cultural Memory in the Americas*

This chapter considers how songs past and present have remembered and
memorialized Medgar Evers and how music, like language and visual representation, inflects and drives memory. Whether issuing from one voice
or many, song has always been a conduit of memory, and the bonds—and
beats—that link song and memory go back to the most ancient lyric expressions, in which the sounding rhythm of words embeds their messages in mind and body simultaneously. The simple repetition of a refrain
ensures that these words will be passed on, even as their meaning can be
recast and recreated in ensuing performances and reception. Song is also
somatic, its rhythms pervading the body; swaying, clapping, strumming a
lyre or guitar, the movement of feet in dance and procession—all serve to
implant memory. From Orphic hymns to indigenous chants, from biblical psalms to slave songs and performed word poetry, song sustains repetition and remembrance. Diana Taylor's comparison between memory
and the heart is apt, then, because such a comparison rests on embodiment and location as key components of memory. Just as Medgar Evers's
activism and death had its "heart's field"[1] in the state of Mississippi in the
late fifties and early sixties, auditory memory is powerfully and irrevocably linked to bodies and their location in the world.

In the sixties, songs about Evers spanned topical and protest music and freedom songs, although the roots of these songs are densely entangled. The civil rights movement itself rode in on a wave of freedom songs that were deeply rooted in the distinctively oral traditions of African and African American cultures, and those traditions absorbed such Anglo-American musical forms as the ballad, forming complicated hybrid music that became the foundation and inspiration for activism. The battle hymn of the movement, "We Shall Overcome," for example, can be traced back to the slave song "No More Peck of Corn" or "Many Thousand Gone" sung on the slave coast of South Carolina, but as Dick Weissman points out, a version of "We Shall Overcome" was used in a 1945 strike by black food and tobacco workers. The first music director of the Highlander Center in Tennessee, Zelphia Horton, made some changes in the song and taught it to Pete Seeger, who in turn taught it to Guy Carawan, who—along with guitarist Frank Hamilton—produced the version that spread throughout the movement, the United States, and the world.[2]

The rhythms of such songs helped sustain the long, treacherous marches for freedom, often by accompanying and supporting processionals. Freedom songs differed from protest and topical music of the sixties in this connection to embodiment and African American history. As with the historical work songs of slavery and spirituals, freedom songs became infused in the bodies of those who marched, creating momentum for the walk toward grave danger and making walking itself an agent of memory. In *"When the Spirit Says Sing!": The Role of Freedom Songs in the Civil Rights Movement*, Kerran Sanger shows how the significance of the freedom songs lay not only in their ability to stir emotions and to inspire but also in their capacity to propel individuals and communities to take action, to lay their bodies on the line. Sanger's study explains how music has a "kinesthetic appeal [that] promotes a physiological and psychological response." The freedom songs thus meshed with and supported the actual physical, embodied actions of activists who "were involved by their physical presence and by the act of protest—whether it was marching, sitting-in, or swaying with the music of song." These songs may be viewed not only as providing spiritual and mental strength for those participating in the struggle but also as constituting the rhythmic and corporeal motion that underlay and gave rise to the physical and social action of the movement. For example, Sanger notes the prevalence of singing freedom songs in jails, remarking that while "many other forms of direct action were denied the activists . . . [through] singing, they were able to find a positive rhetorical place between passivity and acts of violence."[3]

Carawan, from his perspective at the Highlander Folk School, has noted the many other situations in which freedom songs were useful, even critical, and observed that they were "sung to bolster spirits, to gain new courage and to increase the sense of unity. The singing sometimes disarms jail guards, policemen, bystanders and mob participants of their hostilities." Bernice Johnson Reagon of the original SNCC Freedom Singers observes that "by the end of the Freedom Rides, the songs of the Sit-ins, bus and jail experiences were considered essential for organizing. No mass meeting could be successfully carried off without songs."[4]

In the March 20, 1964, issue of *Broadside* magazine, the nexus of sixties topical and protest music,[5] Julius Lester, in an article titled "Freedom Songs in the North," defines freedom songs by saying, "To paraphrase the definition of a minister, freedom songs should comfort the disturbed and disturb the comfortable." Lester, whose primary concern was whether singers of freedom songs (mostly white and from the Northeast) were maintaining the spirit and essence of the music, devotes part of his article to the particular aesthetic and affective aspects of freedom songs: "Freedom songs have a definite 'sound.' They also have a very definite fabric. The 'sound' of a freedom song can only communicate to the ear and set the foot tapping in rhythm. It is the fabric, which spirals from within the singer and his tradition outward, to spin itself around and into the listener." This sound, Lester writes, is directly related to the black liberation struggles. Consequently, he describes freedom songs as ones in which "live the blood and body of every Negro who has wept and laughed, suffered and exulted at life in America." Yet, while the songs were an outgrowth of African American history, Lester also acknowledges: "Being a Negro is not a necessary prerequisite for singing freedom songs. Being willing to understand the Negro and his history is. It is here that the fabric of freedom songs is found."[6]

Whoever sang them, the freedom songs were indeed the beating heart of the civil rights revolution and if not the primary way, at least one of the primary ways it is remembered. Anne Moody's and Myrlie Evers's momentary turns away from the song "We Shall Overcome," which I described in the preceding chapter, are telling markers of their intense personal suffering and despair.[7]

Because memory is grounded and embodied, Taylor argues, we need to pay attention to the way cultural memory is passed along by performance — "live, embodied actions" performed for live audiences. And because musical performances can and do career through time and space like comets, morphing into other performances that do the same, songs cause us to consider history, both the actual events that originally precipitated what were called topical songs and the history of specific songs themselves. The songs of the 1960s about Evers, with the possible exception of Bob Dylan's 1963 "Only a Pawn in Their Game," are seldom heard today, but their traces reverberate. The songs of our own times offer echoes and improvisations of those earlier performances so that the heart of Evers's memory beats on in songs of the present, which take their inspiration and rhythms from songs of the past. We can hear Dylan's bursts of internal rhyme from "Only a Pawn" — "From the poverty shacks, he looks from the cracks to the tracks" — in what Ali Neff calls the "hip-hop hypermasculinity" of contemporary Jackson rapper David Banner, or in the words of the 2009 song "Who Medgar Evers Was" by the underground, experiential hip-hop group Dälek.[8] The topical 1960s ballads about Evers find their way into the ironic tone coupled with traditional stanza forms of Kathy Veazey and Soul Consolidation's 1995 song "I'm Alive." Thus Medgar Evers — his life and death — inhabited the music of his own time but also has moved through the ensuing years into the twenty-first century. As in Baldwin's *Blues for Mr. Charlie*, Morris's *The Ghosts of Medgar Evers*, and Welty's "Where Is the Voice Coming From?" it is primarily, though not exclusively, Evers's death rather than his life that initiates and drives the 1960s music about him, from Dylan's analysis of the manipulation of poor whites by the rich to the SNCC Freedom Singers' mournful "The Ballad of Medgar Evers," although Matthew Jones's ballad, written for the SNCC Freedom Singers, also spends time on Evers's fight "for freedom all of his life."[9]

Four songs specifically about Evers's death were widely performed in the early 1960s, soon after Evers's death: Bob Dylan's "Only a Pawn in Their Game," Phil Ochs and Bob Gibson's "Too Many Martyrs (Ballad of

Medgar Evers)," Matthew Jones and the Freedom Singers' "The Ballad of
Medgar Evers," and Dick Weissman's "Lullaby (for Medgar Evers)," written and first performed and recorded as "Lullaby" by Weissman, then
as "Medgar Evers Lullaby" by Judy Collins.[10] These songs were intended
to, and did, evoke grief and outrage, graphically illustrating the need for
social activism in the South. Unlike contemporary groups such as Dälek,
they did not probe the question of memory, nor were they primarily designed for the purpose of remembrance. They were songs of rage and sorrow; they were calls to action.

All of these songwriters and performers were part of the surge of folk
music of the early sixties, and all the songs had been written and performed by the spring of 1964, less than a year after Evers's death. Ochs
and Dylan sang their songs about Evers at the pivotal Newport Folk
Festival in July 1963. Both Dylan's and Ochs's songs were published in
Broadside magazine, which published lyrics, music, articles, and reviews
related to popular folk/topical artists, as were songs of other popular musicians of the movement, such as Nina Simone and Malvina Reynolds.[11]
Simone's "Mississippi Goddam" is especially interesting because of its
roots in the murders of Evers and the Sixteenth Street Baptist Church
girls in Birmingham and the wide circulation of the song, though Evers is
not mentioned by name in the lyrics.

Of these four groups of songwriters and performers whose songs directly refer to Evers by name, only Matt Jones and the Freedom Singers
were African American and on-the-ground activists. Jones drew on the
cultural memory of multiple African American song traditions, including
the black ballad, to produce "The Ballad of Medgar Evers," which moves
through several layers of folk and African American song traditions and
sounds more like a spiritual or hymn than a traditional folk ballad.[12]
Jones was also the only southerner among these songwriters. Ochs's and
Weissman's songs derive from British ballad traditions; Weissman pushes
ironically at the tradition of the lullaby, which has an interesting history
in the subgenre of the traditional murder ballad.[13] Ballads, unlike lyrics,
stress action and narrative, and Ochs's, Jones's, and Weissman's songs
include detail, action, and a narrative trajectory, although Jones's ballad
is more circuitous.[14] Jones's and Ochs's songs also draw on the murder
ballad in their detail and moral tone; Dylan's "Only a Pawn" depends less

on narrative than on analysis, but it, like the murder ballads, pronounces the villain doomed to infamy as "only a pawn," if not to full punishment for his crime.

Traditional murder ballads have a deep history in American music. Of English, Scottish, Irish, and Scandinavian origin, they appeared, as Olive Woolley Burt notes, on "old penny sheets [called broadsides] that used to be peddled at the foot of the gallows on execution day."[15] The verses, which were sung as well as written down, retold the crime in detail (sometimes in the voice of the murderer) and pointed to the moral that murder led to the gallows, in retrospect a grim irony in Evers's murder case, given the fact that Beckwith not only escaped execution but lived out most of his natural life because of two hung juries. Moreover, Burt indicates, some lullabies were either murder ballads or derived from them.[16] Burt's study of the murder ballads, published in 1958, precedes the bloody sixties and maintains that, because ballad makers were generally white, they were "little inclined" to sing about murders "perpetrated upon people whose pigmentation differed from theirs," a fact that the songs of Dylan, Ochs, and Weissman would, a few years hence, belie. While her treatment of murder ballads relating to African American music traditions is sparse, Burt argues that "John Brown's Body" may be considered a murder ballad and a "true folk song," as well as the folk song "Stackalee," known also as "Stagolee" in African American folk traditions.[17] Like the ballad form in general and the murder ballad in particular, all of the four Evers songs of the sixties, several with varying lyrics (also a characteristic of the murder ballad), tell stories that lead to moral premises.

The most famous of these and also the song with the earliest known public performance, Dylan's "Only a Pawn in Their Game," is the "Where Is the Voice Coming From?" of the song world and a precursor for Frank X Walker's astute poetic analyses of the psychological moorings of Byron De La Beckwith's rabid racism. Like Welty's story on the 1960s literary scene, it is the most cerebral of the topical songs about Evers, focusing on the killer and calling the listener to contemplate the political, economic, and psychological sources of racist violence. Like the literature about Evers, "Only a Pawn"—or at least its first performance—has close connections to Evers's local scene in Mississippi. Dylan, in fact, brought the song onto Byron De La Beckwith's home turf of Greenwood, the stubbornly

Jim Crow river town whose residents would hold a parade the following year when Evers's killer was released and sent back home after two hung juries. On July 6, 1963, a little more than three weeks after Evers's assassination and the very day the *New Yorker* issue containing Welty's story hit newsstands across the nation, the twenty-one-year-old Dylan, then a rising star on the folk music scene, arrived in Greenwood, Mississippi, to support a SNCC voter registration drive. Activists were struggling, fearful for their lives; the morale following Evers's death and other forms of white-on-black violence had hit rock bottom and people were dead tired. As Mike Marqusee notes, civil rights workers in Greenwood and the surrounding area had been brutally assaulted and arrested, state officials had blocked federal food supplies to the poor black population in the Delta to starve people into submission, and the faltering movement badly needed a shot in the arm.[18]

This was Dylan's first visit to Mississippi in particular or the South in general. Actor-singer Theodore Bikel had paid the young singer's plane fare in the belief that Dylan should get a firsthand view of the civil rights struggle on the ground. Like Baldwin on New Year's Day 1963, they flew from New York. Bikel relates: "We flew all night, changing planes in Atlanta, waiting there two hours, then changing again. Most of the way down, Bob was writing little notes on envelopes. . . . [H]e didn't really talk too much. . . . There was something churning inside him all the time, something quite deep. It seemed more a personal thing with him to be going down into the Deep South. He moved from the universal to the personal, while most artists and writers tend to move from the person to the universal."[19]

Arriving at the Jackson airport, Dylan was confronted by Jim Crow for the first time. He was visibly upset to see segregated water fountains and restrooms and asked Bikel what he thought would occur if he drank from the fountain marked "Colored Only." In Greenwood he was inspired by the black sharecroppers and young activists he met as he, like Baldwin on his clandestine trip into the Mississippi backwoods with Evers seven months earlier, briefly shared their danger and difficulties.[20] He and Bikel were met by two white civil rights workers and driven to Greenwood. That night they slept in a church loft, and the next morning they lay flat in the car as they were driven to the rally in order not to be seen in the same car as African Americans, a certain cause for arrest. A large contingency of activists and performers awaited Dylan in Mississippi: Julian Bond, Bernice Johnson Reagon and the Freedom Singers, James Forman, and Pete Seeger, among others, along with reporters and a TV film crew. Writing a report for *Broadside*, Seeger reported: "I was three days in Greenwood this July lending some small support to the Negro voter-registration drive down there. Sang in a small Baptist church, at a large NAACP meeting, and out in an open field. The last was a songfest attended by Theodore Bikel, Bob Dylan, and several hundred of the most enthusiastic freedom fighters and singers one could imagine. All ages."[21]

At dusk on July 6, after a postponement because of the intense July heat, Dylan, Seeger, Bikel, and the Freedom Singers hopped up onto the back of a truck about two miles outside of Greenwood and began to play and sing in a cotton field for around three hundred local African Americans, mostly farmers; young white activists; and reporters and film crew. Police and Klan members watched from surrounding cars.[22] Dylan was reported to be humble in his comments to the farmers, saying, according to Bikel, that "he hadn't met a colored person till he was nine years old, and he apologized that he had so little to offer."[23] According to Johnson Reagon, "The Greenwood people didn't know that Pete, Theo, and Bobby were well known. They were just happy to be getting support. But they really liked Dylan down there in cotton country."[24]

As it grew dark, Dylan joined hands with the other performers and sang "We Shall Overcome"; he later made a donation to SNCC.[25] He leaned forward and refused to smile for the news cameras while singing the song, although singer Maria Muldaur reported that when he had sung it for her in a Greenwich Village coffeehouse, he laughed after finishing. She recalled, "That song made me aware of things I never thought about before. But when it was finished, he just laughed. He *laughed*."[26] The coffeehouse incident, which provides a foreshadowing of Dylan's eventual withdrawal from the protest music scene, occurred in the early sixties, but it is not clear whether it happened before or after the Greenwood performance.

In his capacity as NAACP field secretary, Evers had visited the Greenwood area many times, and many of the activists at the performance knew him personally, so when Dylan sang, for the first time, "Only a Pawn in Their Game," the song touched a chord in the local audience. As Marqusee says,

"By all accounts, the topicality of the song gripped the audience — some of whom would have seen Evers himself in recent months. Even more, the political analysis exercised a strong appeal. . . . In contrast to the moralistic and utopian rhetoric favored by the movement at this time, Dylan's song argued that racist violence was the product of manipulation and an unjust social system."[27] The July 7 *New York Times* story also notes that "one of the more popular songs presented by a local singer was one dedicated to Medgar W. Evers." Clearly Dylan was not yet famous; the *Times* story not only incorrectly spells the young singer's name but also makes him a Mississippian.[28] Despite the performance, though, the concert did the Greenwood voter registration drive little good: "On election day, white voters outnumbered blacks by 33 to 1 — in a county where the black population was twice that of the white."[29]

Soon after Dylan performed "Only a Pawn" at the voter registration drive in Greenwood, he sang the song publicly for the second time as an honored guest at a glitzy Columbia Records sales conference in Puerto Rico, where it didn't go over well with the southern contingency, some of whom walked out.[30] Dylan's third performance of "Only a Pawn" — on that occasion titled "The Death of Medgar Evers" — at the March for Jobs and Freedom in Washington six weeks after his Greenwood performance also encountered mixed reactions amid questions about the role of white performers in the civil rights struggle.[31] The march drew "the greatest mass mobilization of African Americans ever seen" — between two and three hundred thousand, many from the South — and tens of thousands of white demonstrators. When the young Dylan took the microphone to sing at the foot of the Washington Monument, he was following some big names: Joan Baez, Odetta, and Peter, Paul, and Mary.[32] As Marqusee points out, Dylan's first song, "When the Ship Comes In," promised liberation, but "Only a Pawn," "driven forward by a contained rage,"[33] was more cynical, focusing not on Evers himself but on the man who killed him, a man (mistakenly, as it would turn out) who is hoodwinked by politicians and privileged whites who dangle the bone of racism to keep him in his place. Dylan's song argues:

> . . . the poor white remains
> On the caboose of the train

> But it ain't him to blame
> He's only a pawn in their game.

Evers's killer is thus only the mindless triggerman for the white up-
per class. Unlike the murderers in Welty's story and Baldwin's play, the
shooter isn't individualized; he is "Like a dog on a chain / He ain't got no
name." The beginning of the song makes the killer nothing more than a
sum of body parts, set in motion as if he were a puppet:

> A bullet from the back of a bush took Medgar Evers' blood.
> A finger fired the trigger to his name.
> A handle hid out in the dark
> A hand set the spark
> Two eyes took the aim.

So, while Medgar Evers is lowered into his grave "as a king," his assassin's "epitaph plain" will be "Only a pawn in their game." It is interesting,
then, that the young Jewish Minnesotan, again like Welty the upper-crust
white southern writer, got the class of the killer wrong. Christopher Ricks
notes that "Dylan's art does not traffic in clichés, but it travels far and
near by the vehicle of cliché."[34] For Dylan, who would soon rebel against
being classified as a protest singer and songwriter after producing a diz-
zying array of songs about racial injustice and violence, this might have
been a matter of rubbing up a bit too closely to cliché and stereotype.[35]
Certainly "Only a Pawn," like the political analyses of Welty's story and
Myrlie Evers's memoir of the sixties and Frank X Walker's poems of the
twenty-first century, astutely scrutinizes how class oppression fuels racial prejudice and injustice, but in the song's assessment of Evers's murder, it fails to account for the deeper mystery: how a middle-class man of
an old Greenwood family—a man who had some resources, a man who
belonged to the upper-crust Episcopal church, a Compson instead of a
Snopes—could pull that trigger.

Betsy Bowden says that the best of Dylan's protest music "can make a responsive listener take action outside the song, to change what is wrong."[36]
"Only a Pawn in Their Game" is and is not such a song. Performances of
the song reveal that Dylan's words are crisply enunciated even though the
melody of the song is forgettable. The emphasis on lyrics makes the prob-

lem of social manipulation crystal clear, but the song offers no solution or course of action. The problem posed seems too large and amorphous to attack. Unlike much of Dylan's protest music, whose power derives from its grating energy and its gritty realism, "Only a Pawn" fosters not so much rage but a disquietude occasioned not only by the terrible injustice of Evers's death but by the middle- to upper-class white establishment of the Jim Crow South—its White Citizens' Councils, its state-funded, state-operated spy agencies, though it's not clear how much Dylan knew about these organizations. In this sense, at least, it echoes Medgar Evers's own analysis of race and class and the reason many of his goals as NAACP field secretary were economic; for example, he recognized that the local black boycott of white merchants would have major effects, which it did in his own time and continued to do for months after his death. As Evers knew all too well, power depends on who holds the purse strings, and, as in the case of Dylan's lyrics, those who do are able to control those who don't:

> The deputy sheriffs, the soldiers, the governors get paid,
> And the marshals and cops get the same,
> But the poor white man's used in the hands of them all like a tool.

Dylan could trace the hierarchy of power that made the poor white man "a tool" and "a pawn" who's "taught how to walk in a pack / Shoot in the back." His song, though, memorializes not so much Evers or his kingly burial but this fictional white killer who, like Welty's narrator, remains behind the screen of the real story of Evers's real murderer. There are no answers that lead us to the psychology of this man; they blow in the wind. Nonetheless, Evers might have approved of "Only a Pawn" because it traces the complex trajectory of oppressive relationships that he spent his adult life attempting to untangle and challenge. Evers was a complex, careful thinker; all of his adult life, he had tried to outsmart the white man and had observed firsthand the manipulation of poor southern whites by their more economically advantaged brothers and sisters. Simply by being who he was, he had shaken and partly broken the web of white power that Dylan's song describes, but in that song he too becomes only a pawn.

Phil Ochs's "topical, or 'finger-pointing,' songs" are often used by

Dylan enthusiasts (I believe wrongly) as foils for Dylan's music. Bowden, for instance, characterizes Ochs as "a skillful craftsman working within the musical and sociological context of Greenwich Village in the early 1960s, a context that Dylan's songs have outlasted and indeed transformed." In *Performed Literature: Words and Music by Bob Dylan*, Bowden contrasts Ochs's "The Ballad of Oxford, Mississippi" to Dylan's "Oxford Town," both published by *Broadside* in late 1962, by pronouncing Ochs's song "inflammatory journalism, set to music and interwoven with poetic imagery—images of cold and heat, red and yellow, and finally, ironically, the white heat that evil racists will suffer in hell."[37] Ochs was actually quite proud of and insistent upon his commitment to writing about injustice in the world; his was a music deeply committed to issues of social justice, a commitment that, unlike Dylan's, was long-term and deeply felt until the onset of severe mental illness, alcoholism, and death by his own hand at age thirty-five. He performed at numerous civil rights rallies and later organized large-scale, coordinated anti–Vietnam War events. His second manager, Arthur Gorson, had close ties with progressive groups such as SNCC.[38]

Ochs preferred to be called a topical singer instead of a folk singer. As his *New York Times* obituary notes, "By the time he broke into professional playing cabarets in Greenwich Village, he had a repertory of more than 60 songs, virtually all of which had a social punch line or question. . . . [His] lyrics quickly began to supersede his reputation as a singer."[39] Ochs seemed proud of his musical attachment to real people and real places, despite derogatory comments from his sometimes-friend Dylan, whom he deeply admired. In a remarkably articulate interview in 1976, shortly before his suicide, he reports Dylan's words to him: "He used to say, Phil, you're a journalist—you shouldn't write" and adds that his songs had always been "semi-journalistic" and that he was "always a quarter journalist" who believed that standing back and assessing particular events had engendered his creative spirit.[40]

Ochs's vocal responses to disturbing events such as the rioting in Oxford when James Meredith was enrolled at the University of Mississippi ("The Ballad of Oxford, Mississippi") and countless acts of brutality, especially the 1964 murders of James Chaney, Andrew Goodman, and Michael

Schwerner ("Here's to the State of Mississippi"), as well as Evers's murder, bespeak his acute interest in the affairs of Evers's 1960s Mississippi. About a year after Evers's death, Ochs spent a week in Mississippi as a member of a group of singers who performed and met with local activists on a tour of towns with the Council of Federated Organizations' 1964 "Mississippi Caravan of Music." Mississippi was as shocking to Ochs as it had been for Baldwin in January 1963 and for Dylan shortly after Evers's death; he arrived just as the news broke that the bodies of the three civil rights workers had been uncovered in swampland. Ochs, in fact, became convinced that someone would shoot him while he was performing his controversial songs, a fear that would haunt him for the rest of his career.[41] But he made good use of his time in Evers's home state and seemed to see himself in something of the same reportorial role as Baldwin had on his visits south and, of course, as Evers had in his role as NAACP field secretary. As Ochs's biographer Michael Schumacher notes, "Phil approached his week in Mississippi the way a journalist gathers information for a news story. He carried around a notebook and jotted down his impressions of the people and events around him. He met with the locals and asked them endless questions about their day-to-day lives. The more he saw and heard, the more alarmed he became."[42] The result was the scathing, deeply sarcastic "Here's to the State of Mississippi," which castigates, in pounding chords and eight long verses, the state's cops, judges, schools, and so on, ending with the resounding refrain:

> Oh, here's to the land
> You've torn the heart of.
> Mississippi find yourself
> Another country to be part of.[43]

Ochs had actually studied journalism at Ohio State University, and when the student newspaper refused to publish his radical articles, he started his own underground paper called *The Word*. As Schumacher reports, Ochs said he generated material for his songs from reading news magazines.[44] In "The Need for Topical Music," a 1962 editorial in *Broadside*, Ochs maintained that "[e]very newspaper headline is a potential song."[45] In the introduction to his book of lyrics, *Songs of Phil Ochs*, Ochs writes:

Most of my early songs were straight journalistic narratives of specific events, and the later ones have veered more in the direction of
themes behind the events. All of them, though, are trying to make a
positive point, even the ones that deal with tragic events. However, I
do have to concur with some of the right-wing groups that consider
topical songs subversive. These songs are definitely subversive in the
best sense of the word. They are intended to overthrow as much idi-
ocy as possible, and hopefully to effect some amount of change for
the better.[46]

The first known performance of Ochs's "Too Many Martyrs (Ballad of
Medgar Evers)" took place at the 1963 Newport Folk Festival, where he
joined a star-studded bill that included both Dylan and the first group
of SNCC Freedom Singers, which did then not include Matthew Jones.[47]
Given the dates of the festival, July 26–28, Ochs's song, like Dylan's "Only
a Pawn," must have been written soon after Evers's murder. The festival
drew a crowd of nearly fifty thousand, a huge number in pre-Woodstock
days, and changed the course of American music, paving the way for folk
music to move into the commercial arena. At the festival Ochs, then only
twenty-two, was suffering from such a debilitating migraine that he had
to be hospitalized twice over the course of several days and was advised
against performing. (Schumacher believes that the headache was brought
on by severe performance anxiety, which Ochs would end up suffering
from his entire career.) Despite the fact that he had collapsed several
times from the continuing headache and had undergone a spinal tap in
the hospital, Ochs insisted on singing. He opened his set with "Too Many
Martyrs (Ballad of Medgar Evers)."[48] Biographer Marc Eliot writes that
as Ochs progressed through that song and its follow-up, "Birmingham
Jam," his strength began to return "as if by magic." When he ended with
"The Power and the Glory," people were "stomping and clapping."[49]
Other performances of Ochs's Evers song drew enthusiastic reviews. In
Broadside a letter from a reader, Lucy Foster of Connecticut, reported in
"An Open Letter to Phil Ochs" that in an Ochs performance at a venue
called Thirdside, "We listened to his singing of 'The Power and the Glory,'
'Ballad of William Moore,' 'Medgar Evers,' and 'How Long.' We say to him
'Your songs are great, etc., etc.' However, we wish that we could say more.

If we were more articulate, we would tell Phil Ochs that his topical songs are more than a record of today's happenings and questions. We would tell him that we sense the expression of the beautiful and the not so beautiful in his words."[50] The Newport festival, and the songs Ochs sang there, sealed his place as an important figure on the folk music scene, and although he would always be mired in a contrast with Dylan, purists and progressives would actually prefer Ochs's music for its sincerity and social commitment.

Like the journalist that he prided himself on being, Ochs had done his research on Evers and used that research to interesting effect in his song about the civil rights leader. In addition, like Baldwin's *Blues*, Ochs's song subtly and suggestively links the lives and deaths of Emmett Till and Evers. Although Ochs collaborated on the music for his song with another musician, Bob Gibson, who had played an important role in Ochs's musical development, the words are Ochs's alone and call out to both history and memory—the history of the lynching of black men, which, as I noted earlier, Evers's murder was a part of, and the memory of Evers as "a man" of bravery and historical significance. The level of detail, the moralistic message, and the variations of Ochs's song recall the traditional murder ballad form.

Ochs begins the song with the story of young Medgar's boyhood encounter with lynching in his hometown of Decatur, Mississippi, when he witnessed the aftermath of a lynching of family friend Willie Tingle, whose blood-stained clothes were left near the tree where he was killed.

> In the state of Mississippi, many years ago
> A boy of fourteen years got a taste of Southern law.
> He saw his friend a'hangin', his color was his crime
> The blood upon his jacket put a brand upon his mind.[51]

As the song progresses, it becomes clear that the boy is young Medgar, but if, in 1963, and perhaps today as well, one hears only the first two lines of this first stanza, the name of Emmett Till, murdered at fourteen in Mississippi, would be the first to come to mind. It is especially interesting, then, that Ochs, erroneously but perhaps purposefully, sets young Medgar's age at fourteen when the Tingle lynching occurred. Charles Evers, Medgar's brother, who along with Medgar passed the bloody clothes left at the site of the lynching, puts his own age at ten and his brother's at eight, while Myrlie Evers sets young Medgar's age at "about twelve."[52] Certainly the bloody clothes left a lasting psychological imprint on both boys. Myrlie Evers writes that "Medgar would pass the spot while hunting drawn against his will to see the rotting clothes with those blood stains turning slowly to rust."[53] Charles Evers writes about the effects of the killing on his and his brother's perceptions of race: "The way they treated [Tingle] really got Medgar and me bitter toward white people. We knew we had to do something about it."[54]

The connection between Evers and Till is made concrete in both the chorus and the second stanza of Ochs's song. The first line of the chorus connects the two as interlocking links in a seemingly endless historical chain of "Too many martyrs and too many dead." The first two lines of the second verse further cement the connection: "His name was Medgar Evers and he walked his road alone, / Like Emmett Till and thousands more whose names we'll never know." Although these two lines are from the published version of the song in *Songs of Phil Ochs*, an alternate version of those lines available on YouTube offers a compelling sense of the young Emmett, possibly perceived in the first two lines, as growing into the man Medgar Evers: "Then the boy became a man. The man became a cause / The cause became the hope for the country and its laws."[55] There is a melding of Till and Evers here, as there is in Baldwin's play, along with the sense that the "thousands more" victims are somehow linked to Till's and Evers's shared martyrdom. The song also recalls Evers's dedication to reporting the truth about white-on-black violence in the South. As discussed earlier, it was, in fact, in his relatively new role as NAACP field secretary—he'd taken the post on November 24, 1954—that Evers worked so intensely and successfully to bring to light the 1955 Till murder in Money, Mississippi.

While making Evers's murder a part of the history of lynching, to which Till's death also testified, Ochs's "Too Many Martyrs" calls its listeners to the act of collective memory. This call to collectivity is not surprising coming from Ochs, whose music was mostly about social action and social responsibility. He insists, in the third verse, that "It struck the heart of every man when Evers fell and died." In the fourth and final verse, the reenactment of Evers's burial at Arlington, the lines—which, like those of Matt Jones's Evers ballad, echo the ballad "Jesse James" — suggest collective action: "They laid him in his grave while the bugle sounded clear, / They laid him in his grave when victory was near." But the next two lines burst that bubble of victory and become ironic, even as they resonate with other writings that describe Evers as, above all, "a man": "While we waited for the future with the wisdom of our plans, / The country gained a killer, and the country lost a man." Ochs's music calls its listeners to remember they are part of a nation. It asks, over the Arlington gravesite of Medgar Evers, what kind of nation do they want? What kind of nation is ethically responsible in the face of such a man's unjust death, a death that echoes backward and forward in history?

The barely repressed rage behind the clipped language and hard-driving rhythms of Dylan's "Only a Pawn" and the scathing sarcasm in Ochs's "Too Many Martyrs" give way to sorrow and mourning in Matthew Jones's "The Ballad of Medgar Evers," which he performed with his all-black male quartet, a reincarnation of the original SNCC Freedom Singers, which had been formed by Cordell Hull Reagon of Nashville, Bernice Johnson Reagon's husband. Unlike Dylan, Jones thought of himself as both an organizer and a singer; he understood the relationship between song and the movement. His obituaries quote him as saying: "I am a freedom singer, a freedom fighter. I've always been a freedom fighter. I'll probably go down that way, too. Freedom songs are different than other protest songs because they are really a mantra. The use of repetition allows for the message to be understood. If we sing a powerful statement enough times, like 'This little light of mine. I'm gonna let it shine,' then we can internalize it."[56] Jones, who was born in 1936 and died in 2011, worked for civil rights around the South. By 1964 he had become an SNCC field secretary and director of the second group of the SNCC Freedom Singers, which toured the country that year to raise funds for the organization's efforts in the South. Of the Freedom Singers, Jones later said, "We were organizers first, singers second."[57] Jones never ended an appearance without "The Freedom Chant," an affirmation based on a statement by Fannie Lou Hamer:

> I'm tired of being sick and tired.
> I will not allow anybody at any time

To violate my mind or body
In any shape, form or fashion.
If they do they'll have to deal with ME immediately!
Freedom! Freedom! Freedom![58]

The original Freedom Singers had been pioneers in the larger civil rights music scene. According to music critic Dorian Lynskey, folk singer Pete Seeger went to sing at a church in Albany, Georgia (anticipating giving a talk/class on the history of protest songs), and "Only when he struck up 'We Shall Overcome' did he win the crowd over, and only then by shutting up and letting them sing the song the way they liked it, steeped in the call-and-response rituals of the church." Seeger later suggested to James Forman (SNCC executive secretary at the time) that the organization should assemble a singing group in order to build audiences, spread the word about organizing efforts, and help with fundraising drives.[59]

Cordell Reagon of Albany, Georgia, SNCC field secretary, who had participated in the Freedom Rides and sit-ins in his hometown, organized the original group, which included Rutha Harris, a soprano from Albany, Georgia; Charles Neblett, a bass from Cairo, Illinois; and Bernice Johnson, an alto from Albany, who would become Reagon's wife. From December 1962 until September 1963, Edward Hatfield says, "the group traveled 50,000 miles through forty states in a Buick station wagon, playing at colleges, elementary and high schools, concert halls, living rooms, jails, political rallies, and the March on Washington in August 1963." The music came directly from the black church tradition, with songs being popular church hymns, whose lyrics were revised or modified "to reflect the political aims of the civil rights movement."[60] In a 2010 NPR *Talk of the Nation* interview, Bernice Johnson Reagon, who went on to found the women's group Sweet Honey in the Rock, offered a more expansive view: "When you need to sing, the songs that fit—while you need to sing—come to your mind. . . . The songs were not adapted as consciously as I hear it when people talk about using [them]. . . . It was like the song that you know must name where you are."[61] Besides performing with Dylan in Greenwood, the original Freedom Singers also performed at the 1963 Newport Folk Festival alongside Dylan and Ochs. Although the original Freedom Singers lasted less than a year—they disbanded after recording an album in 1963 — the second group, led by Jones, formed in 1964.

The second incarnation of the SNCC Freedom Singers performed widely at large and small venues, making it difficult to know when they first sang "The Ballad of Medgar Evers" publicly and therefore when it was composed. The date of composition would have to have been after the bombing of the Sixteenth Street Baptist Church in Birmingham on September 15, 1963, which is mentioned in the song, and before the 1965 Atlanta SNCC conference, where it was performed with Jones, almost thirty at the time, singing the verses and the other three singers the chorus. The song's somber, mournful cadence carries the deep, surging rhythms and gravitas of spirituals such as "Steal Away" and "Deep River" and poetry such as Margaret Walker's "For My People" and Langston Hughes's "The Negro Speaks of Rivers." The beginning of the song tells the story of Evers's courage:

> In Jackson, Mississippi in 1963,
> There lived a man who was brave.
> He fought for freedom all of his life.
> But they laid Medgar Evers in his grave.

And the chorus mourns his passing:

> They laid Medgar Evers in his grave.
> They laid Medgar Evers in his grave. (Lord)
> He fought for freedom all of his life,
> But they laid Medgar Evers in his grave.[62]

Like the lyrics of Ochs's "Too Many Martyrs (Ballad of Medgar Evers)," the words seem to derive from the hymns and spirituals about laying Christ in his grave, the song "John Brown's Body" ("lies moldering in the grave"), or even the rollicking murder ballad "Jesse James" by minstrel Billy Gashade, which tells the story of a man named Robert Ford, "that dirty little coward," who shot his friend Jesse for a twenty-five-dollar reward and "laid poor Jesse in his grave."[63] As in "Jesse James," Jones's "Ballad of Medgar Evers," in the convention of the murder ballad, names Evers's killer: "Then a hate-filled white man named Byron De La Beckwith / Laid Medgar Evers in his grave."

As indicated by the first verse, the song puts Evers's life's work in the foreground while mourning his death. Jones knew the details of Evers's killing because he refers to "a high powered rifle" that "tore out [Evers's] heart," and he connects Evers's death to the murder of "Those little children from Birmingham," referring to the four girls who were the victims of the church bombing. The last stanza of the song links Evers to the girls, saying that "Like Christ, they died for you and for me. / They died for you to be free." The tone and cadence of the song are dirgelike throughout, and Jones's shout-out, "Lord," sounds like a wail. Although it has affinities with the murder ballad tradition, the song seems more closely affiliated with African American song traditions; its repeated refrains and allusion to Christ seem designed to be easily beaten out and remembered, with its ponderous cadence and call-and-response refrain. Given Jones and the Freedom Singers' commitment to activism, the song seems designed, first, to mold Evers's and the girls' shared martyrdom as a way of solidifying a sense of the sacrifices made for progress and, second, to give its listeners inspiration to solidify hard-won progress and move forward to embrace new goals, even if it meant making sacrifices themselves. When the Freedom Singers performed the song at the SNCC conference in 1965, much had happened in the ensuing years after Evers's murder, and the events of 1963 had perhaps receded somewhat into the past. Jones wanted the conference attendees to remember the past and realize their responsibilities to the future; "The Ballad of Medgar Evers," with its memorable lines and melody and its affiliation with African American music traditions, was the perfect vehicle to accomplish these goals.

Formally and historically, then, Jones's "Ballad" departs from the songs of the two young white singers from the Midwest; it adheres to some of the conventions of the murder ballad in naming the details of the murder and the murderer and its lines that in part recall the ballad of "Jesse James," but its sonorous, mournful rhythms, deep seriousness, and appeal to human dignity and freedom all seem to derive from African American music traditions going back to slavery. Evers, in the song, "taught words of love, dignity and freedom / He died before he'd be a slave." The song's thick layering of African American history carried its own sedimentary memory and must have made the song seem familiar to its listeners at SNCC rallies; it played an important role in the ongoing and often tragic narrative of black southern history, a narrative that Jones and the Freedom Singers urged must be rewritten and retold in the future.

Another white musician, Richard "Dick" Weissman, who grew up in Philadelphia, wrote, performed, and recorded "Lullaby (for Medgar Evers)," called "Lullaby" on his 1964 Capitol Records album *The Things That Trouble My Mind*. Although Evers's name was not in the title on Weissman's LP, the liner notes clearly identify the connection:

> In 1963, Negroes in America made important advances in the long struggle for their "inalienable," still-promised rights. Medgar Evers, Field Secretary for the N.A.A.C.P., worked tirelessly for his peoples' cause. He was shot outside his home in Jackson, Mississippi on June 12, 1963.
>
> This lullaby, written for his son, also pays tribute to Medgar Evers with the pertinent question it poses: Can a people continuously resist oppression and prejudice and still raise their children without bitterness?

The liner notes also describe Weissman as "one of the top five-string banjo players in the country."[64] With a sophisticated knowledge of African American history and music, Weissman was well suited to write "Lullaby." His major at Goddard College was "Negro History," and his thesis was "Leadbelly, His Life and Music." He had played piano, banjo, and guitar, and, in what would prove a long and varied career, he would move through many facets of the music business and eventually become a professor and music scholar with several books on folk music and the sixties to his credit.[65]

Weissman says he was inspired to write the song because he, unlike Dylan, Ochs, or Collins, had played extensively in the South with his band, the Journeymen,[66] which was popular on college campuses, and had had firsthand experiences with Jim Crow.

> [W]e experienced quite a bit of the racial travail that was going on. For example, we did a concert in Virginia with Odetta at a college, and the hotel at first refused to let her stay there, then agreed when the student from the college offered some fanciful story about her

being African, or an African princess, or something. They let her stay there, but made her use the freight elevator.

At another college concert in Virginia, we went to a party after the show. A black singer–piano player was singing Smoky Robinson's song, "You Really Got a Hold on Me." A blonde co-ed in a low-cut dress was staring down at him. I felt an incredible tension in the room, and felt like some sort of trouble was imminent. I became almost physically sick, afraid for the guy, and had to leave.[67]

Weissman recalls that he wrote the song in December 1963 or January 1964 and recorded the song in January. After seeing what was going on in the South, part of his impetus for writing the Medgar Evers song was his "frustration at being in a musical group that was so safe and un-political, at a time where people were risking their lives in the struggle for freedom and equality." Yet, like Baldwin, Weissman was far from Mississippi when he wrote the song; he was playing with the Journeymen in Los Angeles.[68]

Weissman moved in the same music circles and was friends with Judy Collins at the time he produced his record. In her memoir *Singing Lessons*, Collins writes of her passion for "song hunting": "I learned from my father that snaring the right song is like falling in love, and the feeling of taking in a song and making it my own is an alchemy that has as much to do with faith as with music."[69] Weissman's "Lullaby" was such a song. When Collins decided to sing it at the live recorded performance in New York, she asked him to perform with her; he wasn't able to do so because the Journeymen were working elsewhere that weekend.

Collins writes that she believes "the process of finding songs is as mysterious, unpredictable and magical as the art of songwriting itself."[70] She recorded a more down-tempo version than Weissman's during her first performance of "Lullaby" at New York City's Town Hall on March 21, 1964. It was released on the Elektra Records album *The Judy Collins Concert*. The response to Collins's live performance of what she called "Medgar Evers Lullaby" was enthusiastic. Almost deafening applause followed the song—a haunting, lyrical melody beautifully covered by Collins's bell-like voice. Jack Goddard corroborates the audience's response on the liner notes to the LP: "With every song, the audience grew more profound, their applause louder and more joyously involved. There were songs ranging from the shadowy misery of depressed coal towns to the exuberance of a cowhand's stolen amours, to bitter reflections on American racial strife. . . . She [Collins] had become part of that small but important group of artists who do not divorce themselves from the social currents of our society and because of this Judy Collins had taken her place among the very best of American folksingers."[71] Weissman's original intent in writing the song, he says in retrospect, "was to contrast the very sad lyrics with a sort of inexorable beat that represented the horror of the story, and of the Mississippi of that time." So, while Collins's rendition sounds much more like a traditional lullaby—a slow, lyrical form of irony—Weissman's is hard-driving, pressing up against the soothing function of the lullaby form, much like Dylan's and Ochs's Evers songs, which pushed the boundaries of the ballad. Weissman was, in fact, disappointed in Collins's version. He says, "I was displeased with the slowing down of the tempo, because I felt that it made the song too safely liberal, rather than inducing thought. That wasn't my intention. Judy is an infinitely better singer than I am, but I actually felt that her version didn't capture what I had in mind." Weissman says he regrets he didn't play with Collins for her first performance of the song because he feels he might have persuaded her to push the song in a different direction.[72] A critique of the song as covered by Collins maintains that her album is marred by the "inclusion of the extremely sentimental 'Medgar Evers Lullaby'" and adds, "This song by Richard Weissman pretends to be a lullaby for Medgar Evers' son, about why his father was killed. The racial murder of Medgar Evers was a cruel and shameful event in American history, and does not need cheapening by this kind of treacly writing."[73] It is not clear whether the writer of this assessment, Vivian Claire, is objecting to the lyrics or delivery of the song; clearly she has no sense of the ironic tone Weissman intended.

The song may have stirred Collins's desire to help out in the Mississippi struggle. "I wanted to sing, I wanted to help people," she says in retrospect. "I wanted to do the thing I had been raised up to do: make a difference, or at least try to."[74] Like Ochs in the summer of 1964, she headed south to Evers's state from New York, wanting, she writes, "to be a part of the revolutionary summer," and traveling with other singers "in a beat-up Volkswagen bus through Ruleville, Jackson, Drew and Hattiesburg, Mississippi" to help with voter registration. She must have been there just before Ochs because Chaney, Goodman, and Schwerner had just been abducted in Meridian. She writes of that trip:

> The Southern whites were, it seemed to me, universally furious at the intrusion of this assembly of visitors from the North. We knew murder was in the air, and there were beatings and jailings and threats to our physical health. I trembled at every truck with a gun rack. . . . [The singers] would all join hands and sing together, encouraging our audiences, mostly black, to register and to vote. This was dangerous for them in many parts of the state. We left, to go on to another town, but they had to stay, often to face the hostile hoses of the police, driven from the polling booths, frightened, intimidated. Their bravery succeeded, and during that summer, hundreds of thousands of voters were registered.[75]

Like Ochs's ballad, Weissman's lullaby seems to create this world of hostility and imminent danger. The singer/speaker of the song is presumably Myrlie Evers or a caretaker of the Evers children, who is singing to Evers's son. In the song the child is a baby, an especially bitter irony, probably unintended, since Myrlie Evers miscarried the couple's fourth child soon after her husband's murder. The story format of the murder ballad becomes clear in the first stanza:

> Bye, bye, my baby, I'll rock you to sleep,
> Sing you a sad song, it might make you weep.
> Your daddy is dead, and he'll never come back,
> And the reason they killed him because he was black.[76]

Like many murder ballads, Weissman's lullaby isn't intended to be purely factual. The Evers's younger son, James Van Dyke (Van), was three when his father was killed, not exactly a baby. Nor is the story that the song tells accurate: "Your daddy was walking alone for some air, / And a man in the bushes was waiting right there." (Evers wasn't walking to get some air; he was getting out of his car in his driveway.) And the story continues in the third stanza:

> That man shot your daddy and laughed while he died.
> Your daddy lay dying with tears in his eyes.
> He cried for the things that a man leaves undone,
> And he cried for the dreams that he had for his son.

Also like many murder ballads, the song turns to questions of morality:

> What will you do, son, when you are a man?
> Will you learn to live lonely and hate all you can?
> Will you try to be happy and try not to see
> That all men are slaves till their brothers go free?

The short song presents two equally unethical options—hatred of others and blindness to injustice—and in the progression of the song, the first stanza's focus on Evers's son turns to bleakness, before the first stanza is repeated. Thus the song provides no answers or options. Weissman's lullaby is far from soothing; it is instead profoundly jarring, especially in his own performance of it, which pushes the song to a tempo that is much faster than a traditional lullaby (the song lasts only a minute and a half). The result is a sorrow song that asks hard questions of southerners of the sixties, black and white: What do we tell our children about the world we live in? How does one live ethically in such a world?

At the end of his study of sixties music, *Talkin' 'Bout a Revolution*, Weissman again raises this issue as he asks whether music can indeed bring about social change. Songs (in the sixties at least), he points out, are about three minutes long; he argues, citing "We Shall Overcome" as a notable exception, that it is rare for a song "to capture a major issue in such a short time capsule." Weissman uses the example of Dylan's "Only a Pawn in Their Game"—"a truly profound song," in his judgment—as being far too complex to have garnered mass appeal. He notes that "Pawn" is "a teaching tool, offered to people who do not necessarily want the lesson," and he adds that "'Blowin' in the Wind' is a song that appears to raise issues, but in fact raises only questions, and offers no answers." Yet songs, Weissman believes, while not creating social change, "can certainly be the inspiration that ultimately leads to social change," as the era of the sixties so richly illustrates.[77]

Weissman's thoughts echo those of Nina Simone, who both articulated those sentiments and then belied them with her devastatingly powerful song "Mississippi Goddam," her first protest song. In her 1991 autobiography, *I Put a Spell on You*, Simone discusses her discomfort with protest music. She asks, "How can you take the memory of a man like Medgar Evers and reduce all he was to three and a half minutes and a simple tune? That was the musical side I shied away from; I didn't like 'protest music' because a lot of it was so simple and unimaginative it stripped the dignity away from the people it was trying to celebrate." But Evers's murder and the deaths of the girls at the Sixteenth Street Baptist Church in Birmingham pushed her to become more directly involved with and committed to the civil rights movement, even as they evoked the explosive anger of "Mississippi Goddam."[78] She relates:

> [W]hile Kennedy was on TV talking about the moral crisis in America, Medgar Evers—a field secretary for the NAACP in Jackson, Mississippi—was shot to death on the steps of his home. I heard the news with disgust, but it seemed like just one more bitter news story at a time when there were already too many. At the trial of the white man accused of Medgar Evers' murder, the Governor of Mississippi walked into the courthouse to shake hands with the man in the dock. I noted this at the time, but didn't react to it—I was still turning the other cheek. What I didn't appreciate was that, while Medgar Evers' murder was not the final straw for me, it was the match that lit the fuse.[79]

A few months later, while at home on September 15, she heard news on the radio of the bombing at the Sixteenth Street Baptist Church in Birmingham. Her reflection on the effects of this news sounds much like the young Anne Moody's response to Emmett Till's death; for both Simone and Moody, the murder of young people changed everything:

> It was more than I could take, and I sat struck dumb in my den like St. Paul on the road to Damascus: all the truths that I had denied to myself for so long rose up and slapped my face. The bombing of the little girls in Alabama and the murder of Medgar Evers were like the final pieces of a jigsaw that made no sense until you had fitted the whole

thing together. I suddenly realized what it was to be black in America in 1963, but it wasn't an intellectual connection of the type Lorraine [Hansberry] had been repeating to me over and over—it came as a rush of fury, hatred and determination. In church language, the Truth entered into me and I "came through."[80]

Simone relates that, soon after, her husband at the time, Andrew ("Andy") Stroud, found her in their garage trying to make what she called "a zip gun, a home-made pistol," perhaps in an updated version of Zora Neale Hurston sharpening her oyster knife. His reaction was simply to say, "Nina, you don't know anything about killing. The only thing you've got is music." According to Simone, roughly an hour later, she emerged from her apartment "with the sheet music for 'Mississippi Goddam' in my hand." She writes, "It was my first civil rights song, and it erupted out of me quicker than I could write it down. I knew then that I would dedicate myself to the struggle for black justice, freedom and equality under the law as long as it took."[81]

So, although "Mississippi Goddam," like Malvina Reynolds's "What's Going on Down There?" doesn't mention Evers by name, it is perhaps the angriest of the 1960s songs about him, and it ushered Simone into full battle mode in the movement. Like Jones's "The Ballad of Medgar Evers," but in a vastly different register, Simone's song links Evers's murder and those of the Birmingham girls. While the Jones song is deeply mournful and melodic, Simone's is like a brush fire. Harsh and driving in its rhythms and ending with the explosive shout-out "That's it!" the song was oriented toward live audiences and, though recorded many times, was never recorded in a studio. Audiences in several recorded live performances of the song, for example, a performance at the Martinengo Jazz Club, shout "Too slow," in the verse following Simone's words, "I don't trust you any more / You keep on saying 'Go slow!'" Simone's first performance of "Mississippi Goddam" took place in September 1963 in New York at the Village Gate, which is now considered a historic jazz/Latin club in Greenwich Village, and it was quickly released as a single.[82] As British rock critic and music writer Dorian Lynskey suggests, Simone's performance of "Mississippi Goddam" at Carnegie Hall on March 21, 1964, is the best-known version, and listeners can actually hear the first comical and later uneasy and uncomfortable reaction of the predominantly white audience. In several performances Simone introduces the song thusly: "The name of this song is 'Mississippi Goddam' and I mean *every word of it*." And often she says, "This is a show tune but the show hasn't been written for it yet." As the song progresses and she repeats the line "everybody knows about Mississippi Goddam," she stretches out the "Goddam" further and further until the final lines:

> You don't have to live next to me
> Just give me my equality
> Everybody knows about Mississippi
> Everybody knows about Alabama
> Everybody knows about Mississippi Goddam.

Holding the last word until her breath is gone, she then takes a quick breath and explodes: "That's it!"[83]

The song, which articulates a desperate sense of betrayal and burning rage in a country "full of lies,"[84] is also linked to Simone's awakened sense of personal commitment to the goals of racial justice; Dorian Lynskey believes that Simone may well have sung the song during one of the Selma-to-Montgomery marches organized by SCLS in the spring of 1965, a march that included other entertainers such as Harry Belafonte; Peter, Paul, and Mary; and Sammy Davis Jr.[85] "Mississippi Goddam" was Simone's road-to-Damascus conversion experience; Evers's and the Birmingham girls' deaths had moved her to create an aesthetic outlet for her own murderous rage. The fact that she sang the song again and again, that it become one of her signature songs, speaks to its cathartic qualities, both for herself and others. Whether it changed any minds is doubtful—it wasn't distributed in many parts of the South—but, though it doesn't mention Evers's name, it generated a sizzling energy field, enacted again and again in performance, that kept the issues he fought and died for firmly in the foreground in a way none of these other songs of the sixties did.

Much has changed since Evers's life was taken in the summer of 1963 and Simone fashioned her makeshift gun in her garage and then decided to use music as her weapon, but some contemporary singers and songwriters question just how much. Like other fallen 1960s leaders, Evers is called by name in the music of several contemporary artists, such as the rapper/ hip-hop artist Immortal Technique, who asks, in the third verse of the song "Crossing the Boundary," whether a diamond is "worth the blood of Malcolm and Medgar Evers," or Wu Tang Clan, whose song "I Can't Go to Sleep" has a brief mention of Evers in a rap by Rza, a member of the group and its chief producer.[86] Of more interest is Jackson, Mississippi, rapper David Banner, who sprinkles his songs with references to Evers and other victims he sees as part of the long, bitter history of violence against black men. Ali Neff suggests that Banner's "hypersexed videos" must be understood as complicated expressions of black southern cultural production that create an "alternative script for the expression of Black masculinity, cut from the rich cultural fabric of his native Mississippi." Singing while covered in green paint and with a noose around his neck, Banner, born Levell Crump, "rallies to increase after-school programs [and] exhume the bodies of lynching victims," thereby calling attention to racial injustice in the present as well as the past.[87]

My focus here is two songs built exclusively on Evers's memory. The artists are very different contemporary groups: the urbane duo Dälek from Newark, New Jersey, made up of MC Will Brooks and producer Alap Momin, both African American; and a white newspaper reporter/song-writer/performer from Chattanooga, Tennessee, named Kathy Veazey, who wrote her song for her local group Soul Consolidation after interviewing a man organizing a community cleanup in Signal Mountain, Tennessee, and discovering that he was none other than Byron De La Beckwith. But as different as these songwriters and their songs are in style, substance, and circulation, their message signals the need for a civil rights movement that extends out into the future and the necessity of remembering and testifying to the civil rights struggles of the past. Sacrifices like that of Medgar Evers must be remembered in an amnesiac contemporary world where racism and racial and ethnic violence are still as alive and well as Beckwith was when Veazey stumbled upon him living out his life as if his cold-blooded murder of Evers had never happened.

Based on Dälek's tour schedule during 2009, when "Who Medgar

Evers Was" was released on their album *Gutter Tactics*, the group's performances have spanned the globe. The duo had stops in Japan, France,
Ireland, Germany, Spain, Sweden, the Netherlands, the United Kingdom,
and even Croatia and Slovenia.[88] Although no comments on record from
the group mention Evers specifically, when asked in a 2005 interview how
his ethnicity had influenced his music, MC Dälek indicated he was interested in addressing issues of racial inequity in his music:

> As a minority in America, my ethnicity plays a significant role in my
> every breath and step. Racial and socioeconomic differences are what
> helped create hip-hop culture. It was birthed out of frustration with
> a country and a system that didn't give a fuck about minorities. We
> made ourselves heard and felt, as the downtrodden always do. But
> America was created with institutionalized racism. Things may seem
> better on the surface, but as a whole? No, America still doesn't more
> readily accept racial difference. No, we are not moving forward. We
> haven't moved at all, with or without Bush at the helm.[89]

"Who Medgar Evers Was" reverberates with this level of cynicism ("Guess
we better off if we all play dumb"). The two verses, both of which begin
and end with "Tell the truth, you never knew who Medgar Evers was," and
the chorus contradict each other. The verses are full of despair, bitterness, and a powerful anger ("Only solace lie in the language of drums"),
while the chorus, which is repeated three times between the two verses
but not after the last verse, calls out against forgetting past struggles
and for solidarity for present ones: "Can't forget how they fought or the
struggle / Remove one block, watch us all tumble."[90] Like David Banner's
insistence on remembering the history of violence against black men, of
which Evers is a tragic part, this song lists the martyrs in that lineage: Till,
Evers, King, and so on. Class inequalities abound, with "Silver spoons
only on the tube."

The actual recorded performance of the song sounds as if it was produced in a busy train station; there's an insistent click-clack sound, in-
termittent clangs and clatters, and an occasional explosive noise that
sounds like a machine gun. Overall the sound betrays a nervousness, a
postmodern anxiety about a society in which "More than forty years lower

class stay numb / Martin Luther tried we still in same slum." Much of the cut, which lasts more than eight minutes, is instrumental, and the words to the song are difficult to hear. In this high-energy performance and others, MC Dälek (Brooks) raps while producer Octopus (Momin) paces as he mixes sounds on several computers and occasionally hits the microphone.

Both the Dälek lyrics and performance of "Who Medgar Evers Was" evoke a tension between remembering and forgetting, between "the Boom-Bap [that] sparks revolutions" and "play[ing] dumb." Knowing who Medgar Evers was is "the Boom-Bap" of memory and history, the "one block" that prevents the tumble into cynicism and despair in the face of a contemporary America where "there ain't love." Knowing who Medgar Evers was can save (or take) your life, but not knowing can kill your soul, the song seems to be saying. The postmodern state of memorylessness in the jangled sound of the set seems to recall, in fact, the cyborgian Däleks from the British science fiction TV series *Doctor Who*, who live in a tanklike shell and are bent on universal conquest and domination, whose every emotion, except hatred, has been excised. The duo's DVD *Gutter Tactics* has, in fact, a kind of mutant on the cover, a dark figure with a square metal casing for a head, a rectangular box for a heart, and, in a possible reference to slavery, shackled wrists.

In the mid-1990s, Kathy Veazey and the five men who made up Soul Consolidation were as homegrown and local a group as Dälek is global. One performance shows them playing on the back of a flatbed truck for what appears to be a meager nursing home audience, some in wheelchairs. Pacing back and forth in front of the band is an old African American woman doing a kind of dance/walk. Another taped performance takes place at a barnlike structure in Chattanooga with no discernible audience.

The question of who is alive and who is dead pervades Veazey's haunting folk ballad "I'm Alive," recorded with Soul Consolidation (but never released on CD) in 1995, the year after Beckwith was finally convicted but while his case was still under appeal, with Soul Consolidation at a Nashville nightclub. Unlike Jim Williams's poem, which opened this book by claiming that Evers isn't dead, Veazey's lyrics highlight the fact that his murderer, Byron De La Beckwith, isn't dead but is, in an eerie echo of "Where Is the Voice Coming From?" actually gloating about not being dead. Like Dälek's "Who Medgar Evers Was," Veazey's lyrics and melody carry a strange unworldly quality and suggest that not only was Beckwith alive and well in Tennessee when Veazey had her chance encounter with him in 1985, but racism and racist violence are themselves self-perpetuating, moving into the future with a sinister determination that cannot be stopped.[91]

This impression is fostered and reiterated in the video online, which comes with the instructions "PLEASE READ" preceding the story of how Veazey interviewed Beckwith, knowing only that he was "a man organizing a Signal Mt, Tn community clean up."[92] The visuals of the video include, in this order, a picture of Evers, various members of the band, marchers, Rosa Parks, two men in KKK robes using portable toilets, and a diptych of matching headshots of Beckwith and Evers.

The performance of "I'm Alive" is haunting. As in Welty's story, the narrative is told in the voice of Evers's killer, who repeats, "I'm still alive," "I won't go away," "You can't make me go away." The last statement is spoken rather than sung, rendered ironically in the voice of Paul McKibben, also a vocalist in the group, along with Veazey, and, like three of the five male members of Soul Consolidation, African American. Recalling the traditional murder ballad, in which the murderer himself often spoke, but without the remorse or moral comment of the murder ballad tradition, the song begins with:

> Look at me, I'm happy
> I'm a man that took a chance.
> By laying down in the bushes
> Been laying down ever since.

There are more details of Evers's murder—"Another shot, a family's scream"—and then a leap to the present and the life that Beckwith has led since the murder:

> Way up here on the mountain
> I made a happy home.
> I didn't try to hide it,
> The things that I had done.

Some of the most chilling lyrics to the song strongly imply that an in-finite number of Byron De La Beckwiths will inevitably be reborn and re-cycled through the American family:

> You men stand there and shake your heads.
> You women hide your face
> But somewhere sitting in your lap
> Is one to take my place.

In the vocal rendition, the eeriest part of the song is its closing lines, which repeat ten times over the phrase "I won't go away," and twice "You can't make me go away." Ending with the soft-spoken line "You can't make me go away," rendered in the voice of a black man, the song echoes, as does Dälek's "Who Medgar Evers Was," the deeply ironic edge of Dylan's "Only a Pawn in Their Game."[93] These two songs take up Dylan's speculations about the stubbornness and complexity of racism and their chilling but unavoidable implication: that the story of racial injustice and violence isn't/won't be over. Dylan and Dälek give us an individual victim in Medgar Evers, but no individual villains exist in either the Jim Crow South or postmodern America. Instead, there is an amorphous conglom-eration of forces generated by either smooth-talking, prosperous white men in suits, as in "Pawn," or neoconservative political interests, as in Dälek's "Silver Spoons." In Jacquelyn Dowd Hall's words in her 2004 presidential address to the Organization of American Historians, such forces as these create in the contemporary United States

> [t]he resegregation of the public schools; the hypersegregation of in-ner cities; the soaring unemployment rates among black and Latino youths; the erosion of minority voting rights; the weakening of the labor movement; the wealth and income gap that is returning the United States to pre–New Deal conditions; the unraveling of the social safety net; the ever-increasing ability of placeless capital to move at will; the malignant growth of the "prison-industrial complex," which far outstrips apartheid-era South Africa in incarcerating black men.[94]

In the same address, though, Hall also says that stories emphasizing *individual agency* "dramatiz[e] the hidden history of policies and in-stitutions—the publicly sanctioned choices that continually shape and reshape the social landscape and yet are often invisible to citizens trained in not seeing and in thinking exclusively in ahistorical, personal terms."[95] What Hall seems to be describing is not so much history but historical memory and the stories that memory engenders. Despite its very limited circulation, Veazey's song is important because of its insistence that we remember that one man, Medgar Evers, was murdered in cold blood by another, who for many years was not made to pay for his crime. Veazey insists on both individual and collective accountability: a man like Beckwith shouldn't be allowed to reenter society and organize community cleanups. He should have been punished years before she met him and years before he was actually punished. Dälek's song—echoing much music of the sixties from Ochs to Simone as well as Anne Moody's and Myrlie Evers's memoirs—calls out a roll of victims. Veazey's song suggests that other stories need to be told, the stories of perpetrators, imperviously living out their daily lives, cleaning up garbage when they themselves are the garbage. As different as Dälek's and Veazey's songs are, both dramatize the utter necessity of a long memory and a long revolution. If these two stories were lullabies, none of us should be able to fall asleep.

CHAPTER SIX

The Pocket and the Heart

Scientists tell us that memory calls us into being: memory makes us, builds us, into the people we are. Our actions, our beliefs, the ways we walk, talk, live in the world—these come from memory. This is true on the individual level; it is true collectively and culturally. Without memory there would be nothing I could call *I*, nothing we could call *we*. It is the glue that holds us together psychically and socially; it is the bond to others that comes from inhabiting time.

Memory is also external to the self, residing in place and history. In Toni Morrison's *Beloved*, memory takes on agency, becoming "rememory." And much as Sethe tries to beat back the slavery past, "Sweet Home comes rolling, rolling, rolling out before her eyes."[1] It is in the leaves on the trees, in the terrible trees themselves. Long ago left behind, the plantation lurks around every corner. Sethe has every right and reason to forget the past; there is the living present to contend with, the future to plan for and worry about. But traumatic memory will not be denied; even if neglected, abused, and cast aside, it remains: a present absence, eavesdropping on people's lives and plotting its return.

Summoning all her emotional resources to address the mourners at her husband's funeral, Myrlie Evers said:

> I hope by his death that all will be able to draw some of his strength, courage and determination to finish this fight. My purpose here is to ask a favor of you.
>
> I do not want his death to be in vain. That would be as big a blow as his death itself. I ask you for united action in this effort in memory of my husband.[2]

Myrlie Evers made her plea in a specific time and place, and the action she had in mind was action at the voting booths, lunch counters, schools, libraries, hospitals, bus stations. She wanted to be called "Mrs. Evers" by the white clerks in department stores; she wanted a better, fuller world for her children; she wanted her husband's dream to come true.

In more recent speeches and interviews, Myrlie Evers-Williams has stressed that memory is also a form of action; memory is work. In the case of the Medgar Evers story, as I hope this book has shown, memory can be transmitted from generation to generation by aesthetic work, work that is urgently important because it is self-perpetuating. This aesthetic labor of memory reaches far beyond its authors' intentions for it, and it can reach beyond its authors' limitations and shortcomings. It inclines backward and forward in time; it is historical and it is prescient.

The past is always changing because we see it through a changing lens as we move through time. Art has its own memories of what was and dreams of what might be, its own resonances, and these are self-perpetuating. The memory songs of recent years about Evers could not have been written without the topical music and freedom songs of the sixties. The memoirs and stories and poetry of Evers's own times feed contemporary writers' creative impulses to remember his legacy for the twenty-first century. Carl Dixon, a folk artist in Jackson, Mississippi, whose wooden portrait of Evers is shown in this book, carves his figures of African American heroes from memory, but that memory is fed by other aesthetic objects of memory: parades, sculpture, photographs, stories. In Dixon's hands, memory is chiseled into wood. In these writers' hands, memory becomes story; memory becomes language; memory flows out into the world.

Historical memory needs writers and artists and musicians. Aesthetic labor is made necessary because the traumatic past doesn't just vanish from the individual or collective or national psyche; even if forgotten—*especially* if forgotten—it still haunts us. It carves out its own location, its own "heart's field." Historical memory is a flawed and messy thing, but it doesn't go away because we'd rather it did. Art, music, performance, writing bring us face to face with the human dimensions of traumatic history. The civil rights movement of Evers's time is a story of triumph and a story of trauma; these aesthetic acts of memory—the carving of these faces into the wood or page or musical notes—confront us with the complexity, the multidimensionality, the tangled messiness of history. This is memory's function, to put a face to history. The labor of art is to make us imagine that face as our own. When we forget the past, we also forget part of ourselves. But that part does not go away. As Frank X Walker's poem "Heavy Wait" says of Evers's home state,

> If Mississippi is to love her elephant self
> she needs a memory as sharp as her ivory tusks
> with as many wrinkles as her thick thick past.[3]

It has been a half century since Medgar Evers died on his driveway. Literature, song, and film of the past two decades have continued to imagine and reimagine the "thick thick" story of his life and death; and as Walker's stunning collection of poetry *Turn Me Loose: The Unghosting of Medgar Evers* attests so eloquently today, the writing continues. While this final chapter focuses, as it should, on Walker's poems, it is also a partial compendium of other imaginative memory work from 1990 to the present. Together these writings usher us into a future that, in its own good time, will also become memory.

Such a work is Lucille Clifton's untitled poem, which begins: "the son of medgar / will soon be / older than medgar," published in her appropriately titled collection *The Terrible Stories* in 1996. The Clifton poem echoes Kathy Veazey's song "I'm Alive" in its bitingly ironic picture of Beckwith as an old man:

> he is sick
> his old wife sighs
> he is only a sick old man
>
> medgar isn't
> wasn't
> won't be.[4]

As in Veazey's song, it is the life not lived that is the tragedy and the crime. Evers himself is the terrible absence at the center of Clifton's poem, a man cut down in his prime, who "isn't / wasn't / won't be." While

Jim Williams, whose poem began this book, writes in 1964 of the servant leader Medgar Evers, who will "always live forever" and who always looms larger than life, Clifton, thirty years later, bears witness to the physical erasure of a mortal man.

Clifton's poem "started the fire" that resulted in the most extensive and remarkable work of literature about Evers of the past fifty years: Frank X Walker's poetry collection *Turn Me Loose*.[5] As I said earlier, my serendipitous discovery at the end of 2011 that Walker's book was forthcoming occurred after I had finished this book and was about to send it to the publisher, and it almost seemed, after I read *Turn Me Loose* for the first time with a growing excitement and awe, that it was a flame kindled out of my own uneasy sense, at book's end, of a void around the Medgar Evers story that aesthetic production had yet to fill.[6] In a strange way, *Remembering Medgar Evers: Writing the Long Civil Rights Movement* seemed to have been calling out for Walker's collection; certainly the existence of his book allows this one to rest easy. As different as they are, both volumes, along with Michael Vinson Williams's substantive biography of Evers, which appeared after this book had gone into production, spring from the same commemorative impulse to "unghost" Medgar Evers. Walker relates that, after reading Clifton's poem, he began to ponder

> what level of general knowledge consisted regarding Medgar's life and death. I started casual conversations with people of different ages and confirmed what I suspected might be a broad generational gap regarding his relevance and even his existence. Many of my own students admitted having no idea who he was. And many when asked to recount the victims of assassinations during the civil rights era all started with MLK and Malcolm and ended with the Kennedy brothers and occasionally Fred Hampton.[7] None of them mentioned Medgar Evers. To the degree that he had potentially become invisible to a whole generation of young people just bothered me, so I switched to activist mode and made a decision to attempt a whole collection of poems that worked against that notion of his invisibility.[8]

An English professor, director of African American and Africana Studies at the University of Kentucky, journal editor, Lannan Literary Fellow, and native Kentuckian, Walker works at the intersection of history and dramatic poetry. As with *Turn Me Loose*, the title echoing Evers's last words, Walker is interested in bringing to light the experiences of forgotten or shadowy African American historical figures, thereby re-scripting historical memory. His first two books to do so are *Buffalo Dance: The Journey of York* (2003) and its 2008 sequel, *When Winter Come: The Ascension of York*, both dramatic reimaginings of the Lewis and Clark expedition through the eyes of Clark's personal slave, York, the only black man on the journey. Walker's most recently published book of po-etry, *Isaac Murphy: I Dedicate This Ride* (2010), is about the legendary nineteenth-century jockey, son of a slave.

Turn Me Loose is both a continuation of these earlier volumes and a departure from them that took almost twice the time to research and write than any one of the others.[9] As he progressed in his understand-ing of the Evers story, Walker came to realize that he "couldn't interrogate this specific history without simultaneously interrogating the very roots of racism"—a pursuit that led to a sociological/psychological excavation of Beckwith's background and motives similar to that of Welty's "Where Is the Voice Coming From?" and Baldwin's *Blues for Mister Charlie*. The volume thus fans out from Walker's original impulse to commemorate Evers's historical legacy to a commitment to asking the same kinds of questions the civil rights leader was asking in the fifties and sixties about "conspiracies of silence that continue today."[10]

Turn Me Loose is composed of forty-nine poems in five sections with deeply ironic titles: "Dixie Suite," "Southern Dreams," "Look Away, Look Away . . . ," "Gallant South," and "Bitter Fruit." As Walker explains in his introduction, the primary speakers in the book are Myrlie Evers; Charles Evers; Byron De La Beckwith; Beckwith's wives, Mary Louise ("Willie") and Thelma; "and a sixth voice that works like a Greek chorus." Even the bullet that killed Evers speaks. Interestingly, Medgar Evers's voice is si-lent beyond lifting his final words "turn me loose" in the title and ex-pressing his philosophy of resistance in an epigraph at the beginning of the volume, although, as Walker suggests in his introduction to the book, "his presence, like a ghost, speaks loudly throughout the poems."[11] This presence is felt especially in poems in the voices of Myrlie Evers, who de-scribes her husband as a lover, family man, and committed activist; and

Charles Evers, who in "The Assurance Man" tells of his brother's stubborn vision of Mississippi as having "something beautiful to offer / her sons our freedom."[12] As a whole, the poems tell the story of a terrible loss, a hole shot through the heart of the Mississippi movement for social justice in the early sixties and through the heart of those who loved Evers and what he stood for. Walker's poems probe that wound, its causes and its effects, and in doing so force readers "to interrogate the relationship between ignorance, fear, hatred, racism and violence."[13]

The fact that Evers's presence and possibility hover over these poems, even though he himself does not speak in them, leads to the question of memory and voice: how Evers's physical absence is made palpable, as it is in Clifton's poem, at the same time his remembered presence continues to articulate itself in our own times. (Such a technique recalls the murder of Richard at the beginning of Baldwin's *Blues*, while Richard is brought to life over and over again throughout the play.) The role of memory, then, is paramount to the forward motion of social justice, which, as Walker notes, "Evers and so many others died for, and ultimately the healing and reconciliation [are] still needed."[14] As Michelle Hite so eloquently puts it in her epilogue to Walker's collection, these poems of remembrance make it "necessary to answer the call of Medgar Evers. If we are to finally lay him to rest, to satisfy his request to *turn him loose*, we must remember."[15]

Turn Me Loose confronts the willful or indifferent failure to remember, not just the failure to remember Evers as an important leader in the civil rights struggle but a collective unwillingness to remember the racist heart of southern and American history, a history that is ongoing. Walker says that his research for the Beckwith poems led him, as it does the rap duo Dälek in "Who Medgar Evers Was," to look at racism of the present as well as that of the past in sites such as "racist YouTube videos" and "white supremacist literature." His composition process for the book was incremental and inductive: "As I worked my way through these materials, every time I read something that moved my stomach or my heart, I tried to write something from that place."[16] In Walker's poems, remembering Medgar Evers means re-membering the "thick thick past . . . the entire weight of history"; it also means embracing the kind of "response-ability" that

Kelly Oliver describes—the commitment to a long civil rights movement that continues in the present and out into the future.[17]

Even as *Turn Me Loose* moves toward the vexed task of partial reconciliation through remembrance, there is a riveting tension in these poems created around the issue of what is remembered and by whom. In the poem "One Mississippi, Two Mississippis," Walker writes of present-day dualities of black/white cultural memory:

> You got beautiful gardens
> We got cotton fields
> You got Gulf Shore beaches
> We got river banks
>
> You don't remember lynchings
> We can't forget
> You got blacks
> We got the blues[18]

"One Mississippi, Two Mississippis" appears in the final section, "Bitter Fruit," but the tension between the African American struggle for justice and the racism of white supremacy cuts across the whole volume, beginning on the first page with its dueling epigraphs, one by Evers, on his belief in "a peaceful struggle for justice," and one by Beckwith, on his desire "to do a lot of shooting."[19] It is hard for the mind to hold both of these histories simultaneously, but Frank X Walker's poems, like Margaret Walker's, insist on this doubleness of history and memory; while past and present are held in tension with each other in these poems, they are also one of a piece in the fabric of southern history. The first poem in the volume and in the first section, "Dixie Suite," called "Ambiguity over the Confederate Flag," dips back into the slavery past while alluding to contemporary racially inflected arguments over the meaning of the confederate flag. The poem, formally stunning, divides on the page, as Baldwin does on the stage, the "two Mississippis" into white and black, with a script that reads both vertically and horizontally:

> In the old south *life was full of work*
> we would sit on the veranda *from sunup to sundown*

Split squarely down the middle, the poem marches down the page to the closing line that unites it:

those were good ol' days   *for plantation owners*

not having to use the whip   *sharecropping and extending debt*

was more civilized   *was almost more profitable*

than slavery[20]

This is historical memory that is as split as the two columns of this poem, made whole only by history, only in the word "*slavery*." The question the poem poses—what can close the chasm of memory between black and white—hovers throughout the volume; it is the question that is "turned loose" to wander the pages to come.

The next poem, "What Kills Me," spoken by the Myrlie Evers persona and echoing many of her writings and public statements, implicitly asks the question that drives Walker's book: Why has Evers been largely forgotten? The Myrlie Evers of this poem declares that

> When people talk about the movement
> as if it started in '64, it erases every
> body who vanished on the way home
> from work or school and are still listed
>
> as missing. . . .
> It mutes every unsung voice in Mississippi
> that dared to speak up . . .

Finally she says,

> It means he lived and died for nothing.
> And that's worse than killing him again.[21]

Evers's connection to unnamed martyrs of the movement, his absorption into their "unsung" heroism, shows Walker's understanding of the man Evers was, a leader who was part of a larger whole, a man who enabled the work of others and told their stories.

Throughout *Turn Me Loose* Walker's poetry works against forgetting and partial, incomplete remembrance. Just as we are not allowed to forget

Evers, neither can we forget Beckwith and the sheer evil of his obsession with racial purity. In a series of chilling "Byron de la Beckwith Dreaming" poems, we follow Beckwith down into the sewer of his unconscious as he dreams of engendering a bloodied "mongrel baby" and throwing it into the Mississippi River, of pulling "a long black snake" out of his pants for his wife Willie to fondle.[22] In "Southern Sports" Beckwith speaks of the "sheer joy of causing them pain" — the entertainment value and sexual va-lence — of racial violence:

All you need is some body wearing
the color you've been taught to hate

some body threatening to take
what's rightfully yours

and a little girl with her thighs exposed
held high in the air and screaming.[23]

These poems also reveal the human propensity for seeing and not see-ing, knowing and not knowing, which allows the villains of history such as Beckwith to go about their business for lifetimes, unreported and unpun-ished. Walker assails that kind of blindness throughout the volume but especially in the poems written in the voice of Willie De La Beckwith. In "Fire Proof," for example, Willie says she burned the clothes her husband told her to burn and

just pretended I didn't know

what gunpowder smelled like
or why he kept his rifles so clean.

. . . .

He often confused hatred with desire.

But if you ain't never set a man on fire,
felt him explode, then die in your arms
honey, you got no idea what I'm talking about.[24]

This is a particularly chilling poem, not only for its attention to "look-ing away" and the collapse of sex and racial violence in the final stanza, but also because of the way that "honey" seems to refer to Myrlie Evers, who did indeed feel her husband "die in her arms," from the bullet from Willie's husband's rifle. The address "honey" points to the next poem in the "Southern Dreams" section, "Listening to Music," narrated in Myrlie Evers's voice. The poem tells about everyday life in the Evers household, the nights when the Myrlie of the poem would turn on the radio and listen to "Sam Cooke / and Ray Charles or Bobby Blue Bland" as she waited up for her husband to come home and they "melted together in the dark, beneath the covers."[25]

In "Fire Proof" Willie seems to be addressing this Myrlie persona, as she does in a later poem in the collection, "Bighearted," in which Willie explains to Myrlie Evers that Beckwith did her a "courtesy" by

> opening up a hole
>
> in that boy's black back and not his face,
> allowing you and your children the dignity
>
> of an open casket . . .[26]

This cutting tension between the book's Myrlie Evers and Willie De La Beckwith reflects their dueling values and the legacies those values have imprinted on the face of Mississippi history. Myrlie's husband comes home late from lifting people up, Willie's from burning people up. Again and again, Walker juxtaposes the two wives, showing the oppositions between their husbands' valor and violence through the wives' stories of their marriages. For example, following on the heels of the poem "Stand By Your Man," in which Willie challenges those who question her loyalty to her husband by saying they "ain't never heard / Tammy Wynette sing,"[27] is Myrlie's own love song, "Husbandry," in which she says, poignantly and resonantly, "He spent every penny of his strength organizing / for a hate-free day and we didn't waste a single night."[28] The Myrlie Evers of these poems describes nights of love and days of dignified, righteous work; Willie, nights of burned clothes, the smell of gunpowder and blood, and sex driven by violence.

Walker's book is filled with acts of memory. Myrlie Evers remembers her husband coming home to the sweet sounds of Motown, Charles Evers remembers that his little brother was "bullheaded,"[29] the bullet that killed the civil rights leader remembers its path from rifle to melon, the chorus remembers Emmett Till's murder, the section titles of the book remember (and re-member) songs as different as "Dixie" and "Strange Fruit." Mississippi "must never ever ever forget,"[30] Walker writes in the final poem, but how does one own the truth of history and provide "a final accounting"? What "final accounting" does Walker want twenty-first-century readers to take from these poems, and what responsibilities does such an accounting entail?

In the poem called "A Final Accounting" in the last section of the book, Walker returns to the question of who can own history, writing: "you can fill all the libraries with your version / of facts, call it history, and still not own the truth."[31] Such a statement recalls Leigh Raiford and Renee Romano's observations about the nature of consensus memory and the shaping of civil rights history and suggests, as they do, that what is re-membered about the past has everything to do with power in the present. In her epilogue to *Turn Me Loose*, Hite writes that Evers's ghost "high-lights the liveliness of history";[32] Walker's volume, in its thickness of de-tail and drama, demands that we pay attention to that "*liveliness*," which won't stay put, keeps insinuating itself into the present. Grim reminders of that fact came as I was completing this volume during the summer of 2011 and news arrived from Jackson of the racial murder of James Craig Anderson, forty-eight, a black gay family man, being robbed, beaten, and then run over by a group of white teenagers, who set upon Anderson be-cause he was African American, and then later, in March 2012, when the story of Trayvon Martin broke.[33]

But the hope and fortitude that Medgar Evers practiced right up to his death a half century ago is also still lively. A change in southern history, as the title of Walker's final poem of the volume attests, has been a "Heavy Wait" — a "heavy wait" for Mississippi, the South, to "Move, in any direc-tion, as long as it is forward," even as "her elephant self" bears "the entire weight of history / and southern guilt on her massive head."[34]

As heavy as that weight is and as long as we have waited for that for-ward motion, *Turn Me Loose* in the end strikes a chord of hope, a hope that hinges on the linked power of memory and the imagination. The next-to-last poem of the collection, "Gift of Time," recounts, in Myrlie Evers's voice, the imagined story of the boy who grew into Byron De La Beckwith, a "little Byron" before he fell in love with guns

before he lost his mother
and his childhood

before he needed a reason to hate
to feel threatened

With a breathtaking generosity of imagination, the Myrlie Evers of the poem speculates in the closing lines that "before all that, little Byron was good. / He was clean. He was innocent." Such a statement, and such a poem, takes us by surprise in a book in which the despicable Beckwith, along with his wives, has had his say over and over, and none of it has been anything remotely close to good. The Myrlie of this poem, though, re-members the little boy Beckwith once was, considers what forces "collaps[ed] in on him / like August heat and no fan" to make him into the man who would go on to kill her husband. She re-members this white boy out of the strength given her by her own plentiful, joyous "stores of memories / that a bullet couldn't quit." Out of her own capacity for memory and imagination, out of her own capacity for love, she understands "how faith could be restored."[35] Just as "Heavy Wait" cautions against forgetting, "Gift of Time" suggests that "trouble don't last always." Yet it is through the muck and mire of memory that forward motion must thread its uneasy way, and Walker never lets us forget the "bitter fruit" of the racial violence that Evers fought against so valiantly.

While *Turn Me Loose* unquestionably stands as the most important work of literature written on the Medgar Evers story, two recent novels, Kathryn Stockett's *The Help* (2009) and *The Queen of Palmyra* (2010), which I was moved to write after completing much of the research for this book, present Evers as a significant part of their narratives as they focus on the causes and effects of white racism. Set in Jackson, *The Help* considers the chilling effect of Evers's murder on Aibileen and Minny, the two primary African American characters of the book. Both are domestic servants telling their stories of being "the help" in response to a request from a young white woman named Skeeter, who plans to publish the black women's stories in a book. In a chapter written from Aibileen's point of view, Aibileen and Minny are listening to a radio announcer telling of

Evers's death and Minny says: "Things ain't never gone change in this town, Aibileen. We living in hell, we *trapped*. Our *kids* is trapped." This sense of entrapment and fear pervades their conversation; in Aibileen's narrative they become even more fearful that their contribution to Skeeter's project will lead to brutal punishment:

> Minny stare at the door the kids went through. Sweat's drilling down the sides a her face.
>
> "What they gone do to us, Aibileen? If they catch us . . ."
>
> I take a deep breath. She talking about the stories. "We both know. It be bad."
>
> "But what would they do? Hitch us to a pickup and drag us behind? Shoot me in my yard front a my kids? Or just starve us to death?"

This sense of fear and foreboding echoes the terror and anxiety expressed by Anne Moody and Myrlie Evers in their memoirs. As Aibileen feels the tears start, she thinks, "It's all them white peoples that breaks me, standing around the colored neighborhood. White peoples with guns, pointed at colored peoples. Cause who gone protect our peoples? Ain't no colored policemans."[36]

But these two women, fearful though they be, continue to tell their stories. A day after the Evers funeral, Aibileen, who is devoted to her three-year-old white charge, Mae Mobley, is rocking the child, saying a prayer for Myrlie Evers, and wishing she'd gotten off work to go to the funeral: "I rock and pray, feeling so sad. I don't know, something just come over me. The words just come out." What comes over Aibileen is a story that she commences to tell Mae Mobley about a white girl and an African American girl. The two children compare skin, hair, noses, and toes, and come to the conclusion: "So we's the same. Just a different color." Aibileen's story, told to a little white girl, ends with the two children becoming friends.[37] Evers's murder, then, incites Aibileen's fear but also initiates a response in the form of an alternate story: a story of unweighted difference and friendship between a black child and a white child, which, while unrealistic in Jim Crow Mississippi, pursues the kind of vision Evers brought to his life's work.

The Queen of Palmyra began with research on this book, and the Evers story is the novel's bedrock.[38] Set in "Millwood," Mississippi, a small town outside Jackson, in the summer of 1963, *The Queen of Palmyra* is the story of a ten-year-old white girl named Florence Forrest, whose father, Win Forrest—a working-class version of Byron De La Beckwith—is Nighthawk, or enforcer, of the local Klan chapter. In the opening sentence, an adult Florence tells her readers, "I need you to understand how ordinary it all was," yet in middle age she herself remains haunted by her father's racial violence and her own "necessary, willed blindness" to it. Unlike her rebellious mother, Martha, who early on tries to warn the black community of Klan actions, young Florence sees and doesn't see, knows and doesn't know; her journey is coming to perceive her own father as the monster he is.

The novel is organically intertwined with Evers and his time and place. It features actual racist articles from Jackson's *Clarion-Ledger*. A prominent character, an African American woman student activist from Tougaloo named Eva Greene, is based on Anne Moody. Eva becomes Florence's summer tutor and mentor, and it is she who explains to the girl Evers's importance to the black community and the complicated reasons behind his murder; the exchange that follows between the young idealistic black woman and the naive white girl is a turning point of the novel. A venomous letter warning against the evils of integration written by Florence's father is based on a similar letter by Beckwith.

Upon finding her father's letter and, like Moody, a Klan flyer with a picture of Evers and others crossed out, young Florence, already affiliated with the black characters in the novel, comes to a crucial understanding (less sophisticated than Myrlie Evers's but cut from the same cloth) of the gendered component of her father's elevation of her as a white girl "with an angel halo and wings" as a key component of his virulent racism. She comes to hate her own white skin, feeling "such a train wreck of madness plow right through me that it made me want to rip my own self to pieces because I couldn't live inside the girl he saw me as. . . . I wanted to cut myself open and step out of my skin and leave it like a pile of dirty clothes on the floor. Then I could say to him, here, take it, and give me back the rest, give me the inside part and let me be."[39] But disavowing her own story as a white girl in Jim Crow Mississippi is its own kind of blindness. At the close of the story, the adult Florence, assaulted by the past, can't see her way through her own story, which is also Eva Greene's.

Confronted by the dirty windshield of southern history, the best Florence can do is peer through it, keep her hands on the wheel, and try to stay on the road, trusting in the possibility of another narrative of history that she herself must deliver.

History, as Florence Forrest knows, can take sharp turns. Such a turn is today's fertile and bustling web, where a wealth of materials about Evers has burgeoned even as this book has progressed over the years. The web makes the Medgar Evers Institute possible, bringing people and groups together who not only perpetuate his memory but turn memory into social action. The Internet offers commentary, pictures, music, and historical and educational materials. Messy, disorganized, and sometimes frustrating to dig through, it nonetheless has thrust the Evers story into the twenty-first century in a way that nothing else has.

Likewise, the films about Evers have had an impact that may reach far beyond their shortcomings. Two feature-length films, *For Us, the Living* (1990), taken from Myrlie Evers's autobiography and narrated in her persona's voice, and the 1996 Rob Reiner film *Ghosts of Mississippi*, the story of Beckwith's final trial and conviction, coupled with the 1989 film *Mississippi Burning* about the Philadelphia murders of the three civil rights workers, brought questions of belated witnessing and overdue justice into play on the big screen. *For Us, the Living*, directed by Michael Schultz and starring Howard Rollins Jr. and Irene Cara, focuses on Evers's life's work, although it begins and ends with his death.[40] The more polished and widely screened *Ghosts of Mississippi* centers on Beckwith's third trial and the work of Assistant District Attorney Bobby DeLaughter in obtaining a conviction in the case. Like *Mississippi Burning*, Reiner's film, despite his good intentions in adapting Maryanne Vollers's book of the same name, has been justly accused of being a white man's story of white men's heroism and right-doing that marginalizes or erases African American activists in the civil rights movement and focuses on white characters as saviors.[41] On the other hand, the film, although it slighted Myrlie Evers-Williams's dogged pursuit of justice over the decades, introduced Medgar Evers for the first time to hundreds of thousands of viewers. Moreover, the making of the film in Jackson and the complete refurbishment of the vacant Evers house in order to use it in the movie produced a cathartic effect in that city that resulted in more attention to Evers's memory locally and created out of a boarded-up shell the Evers House Museum, which Tougaloo University now manages and opens to the public.[42]

The Evers story casts new shadows in the light of the election of an African American president and a changed southern landscape. In a January 2009 issue of *Glamour*, Evers's twin grandnieces, Courtney and Corrie Cockrell, tell an interviewer about the thrill of Barack Obama's election. They grew up in a family full of stories about the bravery, heroism, and martyrdom of their great-uncle. Corrie Cockrell describes the delight she felt when she received her acceptance letter to the University of Mississippi law school almost fifty years after her revered great-uncle Medgar had been denied admission. She recalls finding a plaque in his honor outside the law library: "I called my granddaddy right away on my cell phone and said, 'I'm standing in front of a tribute to Uncle Medgar! At Ole Miss!'" Her sister, Courtney, who also was attending Ole Miss at the time of the interview, adds: "I check out that plaque on campus all the time. I'll walk by it on my way into the library and just give it a little wink: 'Hi, Uncle Medgar! Look what we did!'"[43]

We will never know all the stories about Medgar Evers. Here are two.

On June 12, 1963, at 10:40 a.m., the black-owned Collins Funeral Home turned over the personal effects from the pockets of Medgar Evers to his doctor, A. B. Britton, to give to Myrlie Evers. The items included a billfold with $6.02 in it, a pen emblem in a plastic box, a Deposit Guaranty deposit book and account card, one fountain pen, one ballpoint pen, an address book, a comb, and two white handkerchiefs—ordinary things, things that many of us might be carrying around in our pockets.[44]

Soon after Evers's pockets were emptied of their commonplace contents, a man named Lester J. Martin sent Myrlie Evers two poems written in response to her husband's death. One of them, "Salute to Medgar Evers," begins with this verse:

You could find the most meaningful word to describe him
You could write it with Ink of Gold,
You could scribe a thousand words of his Greatness
Yet all of him could never be told.[45]

At the beginning of this book I asked where remembrance of Medgar Evers and his plural singularity might lead, and what role aesthetic production might have had and continues to have in perpetuating his legacy. Against the backdrop of a treacherous time and place, Evers's potency as a leader lay in his ability to be ordinary and extraordinary at the same time, to be a hero but also to be a man disguised as a fieldworker his struggling people could whisper their stories of trouble to and know that those stories, bravely told and carefully recorded, might lead to something larger than themselves, might even make them heroes, too.

"All of him could never be told," but one thing we can know, we can remember, is Medgar Evers's astute understanding of stories as tools of social change. He did not write with gold ink; he simply wrote with one of the ordinary pens in his pocket, whether that pocket were in a dress shirt his wife had carefully ironed or in a pair of fieldworker's overalls. But he served as scribe to the greatness of others. Their stories, and his, translate an ethics of collective social struggle based in memory, an ethics that lies at the heart of many of the writings and songs examined in this book and an ethics that continues to script itself onto twenty-first-century human rights struggles.

They—the stories and the writings—translate the complexity, the texture of Evers's heroism; and, more expansively, of the human struggle to be better than we know how to be. They, like the man himself, show us what's in the pocket and what's in the heart, and what ordinary people, like ourselves, are capable of.

ACKNOWLEDGMENTS

Many people and institutions have contributed expertise, energy, and support to this decade-long project. I am especially indebted to Myrlie Evers-Williams, who generously gave of her long memory and immense store of wisdom in conversations crucial to the project.

This undertaking was bracketed by the work of two brilliant graduate assistants; I'm enormously grateful for their heartfelt commitment to this project. For the early work, I thank (now Professor) Mary Alice Kirkpatrick for her considerable research skills and long hours at the microfilm machine, her irreverent humor in the face of adversity, and her deep knowledge of African American literature and history. Elizabeth Gale Greenlee's unflagging efforts in researching songs and lyrics of the sixties brought forth crucial material for the music chapter. Many photographs in the volume are the result of her eagle eye, and her calm and resolute efforts resolved a tangle of permissions issues at the end of the project. Jameela Dallis and Danielle Hartman Johnson helped tremendously in the mid-years of the work. I am particularly indebted to Jameela for her research into the life of Anne Moody.

I am also very grateful to various institutions and organizations for allowing me to present this material in lecture form over the years and receive valuable responses from far-flung colleagues. I especially thank Mercer University for inviting me to give the Lamar Memorial Lectures, especially to David and Kris Davis, whose hospitality knows no bounds. I thank Emory University and Barbara Ladd for asking me to give the Biennial Lecture in Southern Literature and Culture, and the UNC Center for the Study of the American South and Sally Greene and Harry Watson for inviting me to share my ideas in a Hutchins Lecture with some of the foremost experts on 1960s Mississippi. I particularly thank Bill Ferris, Patricia Derian Carter, and Hodding Carter III for their insights after that lecture. I also owe a huge debt of gratitude to Bill Ferris for his unerring way of having everyone's contact information at his fingertips. I thank the Society for the Study of Southern Literature and the Berry College Southern Women Writers Symposium for asking me to present some of this material in keynote lectures.

Many others have been helpful at crucial junctures. To Maryemma Graham, I owe a debt of gratitude for helping locate material in Margaret Walker's journals; Suzanne Marrs generously assisted with Welty archival materials and showed me through Welty's house. I thank Rebecka Rutledge Fisher for important information about African American civil rights music and Billie Rutledge Killens for her musical ear. Danielle Eliot alerted me to Lucille Clifton's poem on Evers. Bernard Herman sent Bob Dylan material, and Sally Greene sent important information on Anne Moody and James Baldwin. Over the course of several conversations, Ali Neff helped me understand the importance of present-day southern hip-hop, especially at the local level. Erin Thornton shared her thesis on Evers's funeral arrangements. I thank Linda Wagner-Martin for a steady flow of newspaper clippings under my office door and James Coleman and Fred Hobson for their continuing support of this project.

No undertaking of this kind can move forward without the help of multiple library and archival staffs. I thank those at the University of North Carolina Music Library and Southern Folklife Collection; the Mississippi Department of Archives and History, especially Forrest Galey and Alanna Patrick; the Margaret Walker Center at Jackson State University, especially Angela D. Stewart; and the Amistad Research Center, especially Andrew Salinas. Brenda Poke of the Washington County Library in Greenville, Mississippi, went far beyond the call of duty and pored over microfilm of the *Delta Democrat-Times* to find an important interview with Myrlie Evers. Archivist Minnie Watson showed me through the Medgar Evers Museum several times over, and her poignant stories of the Everses' life as a family brought history to life. Over time, Tommy Dixon at UNC Davis Library has put me in touch with many valuable materials pertinent to this book.

A special thanks to Frank X Walker, who allowed me to read his brilliant poetry sequence about Medgar Evers while it was in typescript, and to Randall Horton for putting me in touch with Frank and his important work. One of the most gratifying aspects of writing this book was to read Frank's *Turn Me Loose: The Unghosting of Medgar Evers* while still in manuscript and Michael Vinson Williams's much-needed and wonderfully informative biography of Evers, *Medgar Evers: Mississippi Martyr*, which came out in 2011, after this book had been written. I am grateful to Michael Vinson Williams for answering several late-breaking queries about source materials and correcting several inaccuracies. I also thank singers and songwriters Dick Weissman and Kathy Veazey for e-mail conversations about the origins of their songs about Evers.

The University of North Carolina at Chapel Hill has strongly supported this project; I appreciate the research leave and the Institute for the Arts and Humanities semester-long fellowship, without which this book would still be in process. I'm especially grateful for the insights of my colleagues at the IAH, who read parts of the book and offered valuable advice.

I couldn't have hoped for more helpful or supportive editors than Nancy Grayson, whose unflagging enthusiasm for this project put the wind in my sails more than once; Beth Snead, who patiently answered each and every question and kept the whole endeavor on track; and Jon Davies, who provided sage counsel when the book was in production and in the end turned the tide of permissions gathering. I thank Lori Rider for her careful editorial eye. John McLeod and his staff have worked hard to introduce the book to potential readers.

As always, I'm deeply grateful to Ruth Salvaggio for her bedrock support in ways large and small over the long haul of this project and others.

The author also thanks the following rightsholders for permission to quote extensively from their work:

Lucille Clifton, "the son of medgar." From *Collected Poems of Lucille Clifton*. Copyright © 1996 by Lucille Clifton. Reprinted with the permission of the Permissions Company, Inc., on behalf of BOA Editions Ltd., www.boaedition.org.

Dälek, "Who Medgar Evers Was." Words and music by Dälek. Copyright 2009. Reprinted courtesy of the artists.

Bob Dylan, "Only a Pawn in Their Home." Copyright © 1963, 1964 by Warner Bros. Inc.; renewed 1991, 1996 by Special Rider Music. All Rights Reserved. International copyright secured. Reprinted by permission.

Medgar Wiley Evers and Myrlie Evers-Williams, quotes from the Medgar Wiley and Myrlie Evers Papers. Courtesy of the Medgar Wiley and Myrlie Beasley Evers Papers, Mississippi Department of Archives and History, and Myrlie Evers-Williams (Z/2231.000/S).

Matthew Jones, "The Ballad of Medgar Evers." Copyright 1963, 1993 Matthew Jones (ASCAP). Copyright 1993 Wisdom Train, ASCAP.

Phil Ochs, "Here's to the State of Mississippi." Words and music by Phil Ochs. Copyright 1966. Renewed by WB Music Corp. (ASCAP). All rights reserved. Used by permission.

Phil Ochs, "Too Many Martyrs (Ballad of Medgar Evers)." Words and music by Phil Ochs and Bob Gibson, copyright © 2000 Barricade Music, Inc., and Robert Josiah Music, Inc. All rights for Barricade Music, Inc., controlled and administered by Almo Music Corp. All rights for Robert Josiah Music, Inc., administered by Wixen Music Publishing, Inc. All rights reserved. Used by permission. Reprinted by permission of Hal Leonard Corporation.

Malvina Reynolds, "What's Going On Down There?" Words and Music by Malvina Reynolds, copyright 1964. Schroder Music Company, renewed 1992. Used by permission.

Nina Simone, "Mississippi Goddam." Words and music by Nina Simone. Copyright 1964 (renewed) WB Music Corp. All rights reserved. Used by permission.

Kathy Veazey, "I'm Alive." Courtesy of the artist.

Frank X Walker, excerpts from *Turn Me Loose: The Unghosting of Medgar Evers* (Athens: University of Georgia Press, forthcoming). Courtesy of Frank X Walker.

Margaret Walker, three excerpts from journals dated June 13 and 15, 1963. Margaret Walker Center, Jackson State University.

Dick Weissman, "Lullaby (for Medgar Evers)." Words and music by Dick Wiessman, TRO — © Copyright 1964 (Renewed) Ludlow Music, Inc., New York, N.Y. International copyright secured. Made in USA. All rights reserved including performance for profit. Used by permission.

Eudora Welty, quotes and manuscript for "1st original," marginalia, and subsequent drafts of "Where Is the Voice Coming From?" Courtesy of the Eudora Welty Collection, Mississippi Department of Archives and History. Reprinted by permission of Russell & Volkening as agents for the author. Copyright 1963 by Eudora Welty.

Jim Williams, "A Keen for Medgar." From *Freedomways* 5, no. 2 (1965). Courtesy of Esther Cooper Jackson.

NOTES

Jim Williams's "A Keen for Medgar Evers," used as an epigraph for this book, is from *Freedomways: A Quarterly Review of the Negro Freedom Movement* 5, no. 2 (Spring 1965): 263.

CHAPTER 1. "He leaned across tomorrow": Medgar Evers and the Future

1. The term "servant leader" is from Manning Marable, introduction to *The Autobiography of Medgar Evers: A Hero's Life and Legacy Revealed through His Writings, Letters, and Speeches*, ed. Myrlie Evers-Williams and Manning Marable (New York: Basic Civitas Books, 2005), xxi.

2. Gwendolyn Brooks, "Medgar Evers, for Charles Evers," in *Every Shut Eye Ain't Asleep: An Anthology of African Americans since 1945*, ed. Michael S. Harper and Anthony Walton (Boston: Little Brown, 1994), 49, lines 14–16.

3. Historian Michael Vinson Williams's much-needed, substantive biography of Evers, *Medgar Evers: Mississippi Martyr* (Fayetteville: University of Arkansas Press, 2011), was published after this book had gone into production.

4. Jacqueline Dowd Hall, "The Long Civil Rights Movement and the Political Uses of the Past," *Journal of American History* (March 2005): 1263. Hall questions the dominant narrative of the U.S. civil rights movement as a neatly contained period and instead argues for a more expansive conceptualization of civil rights that is "harder to simplify, appropriate, and contain" (1235).

5. Myrlie Evers-Williams, interview by the author, June 12, 2010. The letters to Myrlie Evers after her husband's death that are contained in the Myrlie Evers Archives are incomplete. There were about as many hate letters as there were condolence letters, and those are not included.

6. Ralph Ellison, *Invisible Man* (New York: Vintage, 1995), 581.

7. Eudora Welty, "Place in Fiction," in *The Eye of the Story* (1978; repr., New York: Vintage International, 1990), 118.

8. Medgar Evers (as told to Francis H. Mitchell), "Why I Live in Mississippi," *Ebony*, November 1958, 65–70. Reprinted in Evers-Williams and Marable, *Autobiography of Medgar Evers*, 111.

9. Myrlie Evers with William Peters, *For Us, the Living* (1967; repr., Jackson: University Press of Mississippi, 1996), 259. Myrlie Evers's name was changed to Evers-Williams when she married Walter Williams in 1975. I use both names, Evers and Evers-Williams, depending on the time in which she is speaking or writing.

10. Evers-Williams and Marable, eds., *Autobiography of Medgar Evers*, 286.

11. Margaret Walker, "Jackson, Mississippi," in *This Is My Century: New and Collected Poems* (Athens: University of Georgia Press, 1989), 62.

12. In Jackson today the spatial demarcations between black and white areas remain clear-cut. As in many U.S. cities, most whites have moved to the suburbs of the city and return only to work, if that. The remaining white neighborhoods contain few African Americans.

13. Adam Nossiter, *Of Long Memory: Mississippi and the Murder of Medgar Evers* (Cambridge, Mass.: DaCapo, 2002), 96.

14. A series of correspondences in the Amistad Research Center in New Orleans reveals that in the winter and spring of 1954, NAACP officials, including attorneys Thurgood Marshall and Robert Carter and Field Secretary Daniel Byrd, closely directed Evers, who had graduated from Alcorn College, in an attempt to break the back of Jim Crow at the University of Mississippi. When his attempts failed, they decided he would be more useful to the cause as a paid employee of the NAACP than as a law student.

15. Myrlie Evers with Peters, *For Us, the Living*, 226.

16. Susan Weill, *In a Madhouse's Din: Civil Rights Coverage by Mississippi's Daily Press, 1948–1968* (Westport, Conn.: Praeger, 2002), 93; David R. Davies and Judy Smith, "Jimmy Ward and the Jackson *Daily News*," in *The Press and Race: Mississippi Journalists Confront the Movement*, ed. David R. Davies (Jackson: University Press of Mississippi, 2001), 85.

17. Davies and Smith, "Jimmy Ward," 82–87.

18. John R. Tisdale, "Medgar Evers (1925–1963) and the Mississippi Press," PhD dissertation, University of North Texas, Dec. 1996, 60.

19. Arthur J. Kaul, "Hazel Brannon Smith and the *Lexington Advertiser*," in Davies, *The Press and Race*, 255.

20. Nossiter, *Of Long Memory*, 95–96.

21. James W. Silver, *Mississippi: The Closed Society* (New York: Harcourt, Brace & World, 1963), 151.

22. Hall, "Long Civil Rights Movement," 1247.

23. Medgar Evers, "Negro Forced Out—Economic Pressure," March 16, 1955, Series 14, Box 3, Folder 6, Medgar Evers Archives, Mississippi Department of

Archives and History, Jackson, Miss. Ironically, this is the same box that contains Evers's investigation of the Emmett Till murder.

24. Quoted in Nossiter, *Of Long Memory*, 68.

25. Quoted in Myrlie Evers with Peters, *For Us, the Living*, 281.

26. Ibid., 183–84.

27. Tisdale, "Medgar Evers," 62.

28. Myrlie Evers with Peters, *For Us, the Living*, 211.

29. Tom Dent, "Portrait of Three Heroes," in "Mississippi: Opening the Closed Society," special issue, *Freedomways: A Quarterly Review of the Negro Freedom Movement* 5, no. 2 (Spring 1965): 256–58.

30. Myrlie Evers, "Interview: Myrlie B. Evers," by Fred Beauford, *The Crisis*, June/July 1988, 30. The issue of *The Crisis* in which this interview appeared commemorated the twenty-fifth anniversary of Evers's death and included his May 20, 1963, address on stations WLBT and WJTV in Jackson and, in addition, an article called "Jackson: 25 Years Later."

31. Medgar Evers, "Killing of Clinton Melton, Negro, by Elmer Kimbel, White," December 1955, Series 2, Box 3, Folder 14, Medgar Evers Archives, Mississippi Department of Archives and History, Jackson, Miss. Adam Nossiter took this phrase for his book title, *Of Long Memory: Mississippi and the Murder of Medgar Evers*. Nossiter mentions the report but cites only the final sentence of the quotation above. Nossiter, *Of Long Memory*, 53.

32. Medgar Evers, report on Edward Duckworth murder, 1956, Series 2, Box 3, Folder 14, Medgar Evers Archives, Mississippi Department of Archives and History, Jackson, Miss.

33. Myrlie Evers with Peters, *For Us, the Living*, 238.

34. Tisdale, "Medgar Evers," 39.

35. Evers-Williams, "Unsung Civil Rights Hero," interview by Farai Chideya, NPR, October 18, 2007.

36. I am indebted to Erin Thornton, who first called my attention to the extensive NAACP management of Evers's funeral and burial services, detailed in Myrlie Evers with Peters, *For Us, the Living*, and in Maryanne Vollers, *Ghosts of Mississippi: The Murder of Medgar Evers, the Trials of Byron De La Beckwith, and the Haunting of the New South* (Boston: Little, Brown, 1995).

37. Vollers, *Ghosts of Mississippi*, 163. The lawyers who defended Beckwith were Hardy Lott, Stanny Sanders, and Hugh Cunningham, the latter in the same law firm as then–former governor Ross Barnett, who made it a practice to stroll in and out of the courtroom and at one point shook Beckwith's hand and greeted him warmly in the presence of the jury.

38. Nossiter, *Of Long Memory*, i–ii. Although at least three black men in Mississippi alone had been killed for attempting to register voters, they were relatively unknown outside their home counties.

39. Myrlie Evers with Peters, *For Us, the Living*, 5–6.

40. Nossiter, *Of Long Memory*, 200–201. DeLaughter's account of the third Beckwith trial is *Never Too Late: A Prosecutor's Story of Justice in the Medgar Evers Case* (New York: Scribner, 2001). In 2009, when he was fifty-five, DeLaughter, who had been a judge before being removed from the bench, found himself facing an eighteen-month prison sentence for obstruction of justice in a bribery case. He was released from prison in 2011.

41. Minnie Watson, interview by the author, February 23, 2006. According to Minnie Watson, Tougaloo University curator and guide of the Medgar Evers Museum (the Evers home), the Everses selected the lot in the first African American subdivision in Jackson because it was not at the end of the street with an easy escape route for a possible attacker to a busy street nearby, but was more safely situated between two houses. Medgar Evers expressed worries, however, about the weed-infested lot across the street.

42. Vollers, *Ghosts of Mississippi*, 126–27.

43. Myrlie Evers miscarried within a month after her husband's death. See Myrlie Evers-Williams with Melinda Blau, *Watch Me Fly: What I Learned on the Way to Becoming the Woman I Was Meant to Be* (Boston: Little, Brown, 1999), 66, 78.

44. Vollers, *Ghosts of Mississippi*, 126–29.

45. Watson, interview by the author, February 23, 2006. Minnie Watson maintains that, because all ambulances were "out on call," neighbors brought Evers to University Hospital. There "two administrators told them he couldn't be treated there because they didn't treat colored and they didn't have any colored blood. Then a white doctor came out of the door and said he would treat him, to bring him in, so they did. . . . They did let Medgar Evers's doctor in, but he could not help in any way because he couldn't practice at University Hospital."

46. Leigh Raiford and Renee C. Romano, "Introduction: The Struggle over Memory," in *The Civil Rights Movement in American Memory* (Athens: University of Georgia Press, 2006), xiv; Renee C. Romano, "Narratives of Redemption: The Birmingham Church Bombing Trials and the Construction of Civil Rights Memory," in Raiford and Romano, *Civil Rights Movement*, 111, 116.

47. Nossiter, *Of Long Memory*, 263.

48. Michael Vinson Williams, *Medgar Evers: Mississippi Martyr* (Fayetteville: University of Arkansas Press, 2011), 53, 57.

49. Ibid., 232.

50. Ibid., 308–9.

51. Vollers, *Ghosts of Mississippi*, 331.

52. Dälek, vocal performance of "Who Medgar Evers Was," on *Gutter Tactics*, Ipecac Recordings, 2009, compact disc.

53. Marable, introduction to *Autobiography of Medgar Evers*, ed. Evers-Williams and Marable, xxi–xxii.

54. Evers-Williams, "Unsung Civil Rights Hero."

55. Myrlie Evers-Williams, interview by Amy Goodman, *Democracy Now!*, June 12, 2008.

56. Evers-Williams, preface to *Autobiography of Medgar Evers*, ed. Evers-Williams and Marable, xiv.

57. Evers-Williams, interview by the author, June 12, 2010.

58. Eudora Welty, "A Conversation between Cleanth Brooks and Eudora Welty," in *More Conversations with Eudora Welty*, ed. Peggy Whitman Prenshaw (Jackson: University Press of Mississippi, 1996), 156.

59. Nossiter, *Of Long Memory*, 61.

60. Evers-Williams and Marable, *Autobiography of Medgar Evers*, 15–16.

61. Myrlie Evers with Peters, *For Us, the Living*, 17; Charles Evers, *Evers* (New York: World Publishing Co., 1971), 59.

62. Russ Castronovo, "Beauty along the Color Line: Lynching, Aesthetics, and the *Crisis*," *PMLA* 121, no. 5 (2006): 1450.

63. Toni Morrison, *Playing in the Dark: Whiteness and the Literary Imagination* (Cambridge, Mass.: Harvard University Press, 1992), 53.

64. Marable, introduction to *Autobiography of Medgar Evers*, ed. Evers-Williams and Marable, xxiii.

65. Hall, "Long Civil Rights Movement," 1234–35, 1263. In her allusion to making civil rights harder, Hall is referring to Kevin Mattson's title "Civil Rights Made Harder," *Reviews in American History* 30, no. 4 (December 2002): 663–70.

66. Christopher Metress, "Making Civil Rights Harder: Literature, Memory, and the Black Freedom Struggle," in special issue on History, Memory, and Mourning, *Southern Literary Journal* 40, no. 2 (Spring 2008): 140–41.

67. Raiford and Romano, "Introduction," in *Civil Rights Movement*, xiv.

68. Jefferson Humphries, *Southern Literature and Literary Theory* (Athens: University of Georgia Press, 1990), xii.

69. Raiford and Romano, "Introduction," in *Civil Rights Movement*, xv.

70. Hall, "Long Civil Rights Movement," 1235.

71. Raiford and Romano, "Introduction," in *Civil Rights Movement*, xxi, xvii.

72. Brooks Barnes, "From Footnote to Fame in Civil Rights History," *New*

York Times, November 26, 2009, http://www.nytimes.com/2009/11/26
/books/26colvin.html.

73. Diana Taylor, *The Archive and the Repertoire: Performing Cultural Memory in the Americas* (Durham, N.C.: Duke University Press, 2003), 2. Taylor uses the phrase "acts of transfer" to describe the effects of performance-based practices and events, which she contrasts to texts; conversely, in my analysis of the Jackson newspapers, I think of texts as being performative forms of cultural work, in that they reiterate and sometimes initiate performances of race.

74. Iwona Irwin-Zarecka, *Frames of Remembrance: The Dynamics of Collective Memory* (New Brunswick, N.J.: Transaction Publishers, 1994), 9.

75. See Larry J. Griffin and Peggy G. Hargis's study of the racial divide between African Americans and whites, both southern and nonsouthern, regarding which cultural events are remembered and which events are considered important to remember: "Surveying Memory: The Past in Black and White," in special issue on History, Memory, and Mourning, *Southern Literary Journal* 40, no. 2 (Spring 2008): 42–69.

76. As this book has progressed over the past decade, the necessity of updating this list has saddened and angered me.

77. Frank X Walker, "Heavy Wait," in *Turn Me Loose: The Unghosting of Medgar Evers* (Athens: University of Georgia Press, forthcoming), 60. All references are to the typescript.

78. Hall, "Long Civil Rights Movement," 1233.

79. As Benedict Anderson notes, "All profound changes in consciousness, by their very nature, bring with them their characteristic amnesias. Out of such oblivions, in specific historical circumstances, spring narratives." See Anderson, *Imagined Communities: Reflections on the Origin and Spread of Nationalism* (New York: Verso, 1991), 204.

80. Nossiter, *Of Long Memory*, 250.

81. In contrast, the suburb of Brandon is 80 percent white.

82. There are currently plans to renew Farish Street and draw new businesses to the neighborhood.

83. Taylor, *Archive and the Repertoire*, 82.

84. Kelly Oliver, *Witnessing: Beyond Recognition* (Minneapolis: University of Minnesota Press, 2001), 136.

85. Myrlie Evers with Peters, *For Us, the Living*, 246–48.

86. See, for example, Cathy Caruth, *Unclaimed Experience: Trauma, Narrative, and History* (Baltimore: Johns Hopkins University Press, 1996), and Shoshana Felman, "Education and Crisis, or the Vicissitudes of Teaching," in *Trauma:*

Explorations in Memory, ed. Cathy Caruth (Baltimore: Johns Hopkins University Press, 1995), 13–60.

87. See Ruth Leys, *Trauma: A Genealogy* (Chicago: University of Chicago Press, 2000).

88. In his widely cited essay "Between Memory and History: *Les Lieux de Mémoire*," French historian Pierre Nora suggests that such sites of memory are necessary because in the forgetful contemporary world there are no longer "real environments of memory" (in "Memory and Counter-Memory," special issue, *Representation* 26, no. 1 [Spring 1989]: 8).

89. In *Family Frames: Photography, Narrative, and Postmemory* (Cambridge, Mass.: Harvard University Press, 1997), Marianne Hirsch discusses intergenerational memory in the context of the Holocaust.

90. Brett Ashley Kaplan, *Unwanted Beauty: Aesthetic Pleasure in Holocaust Representation* (Urbana: University of Illinois Press, 2007), 167.

91. Toni Morrison, "Rootedness: The Ancestor as Foundation," in *Black Women Writers (1950–1980)* ed. Mari Evans (New York: Anchor/Doubleday, 1984), 345.

92. Kai Erickson, "Notes on Trauma and Community," in Caruth, *Trauma: Explorations in Memory*, 185, 187.

93. In the days that followed Evers's murder, between nine hundred and one thousand adults and teenagers were arrested and held in livestock pens at the fairgrounds; many were brutalized by police. Black leaders, many of them ministers, along with children carrying miniature American flags, were arrested.

94. Dominick LaCapra discusses the difference between "working through" and "acting out" past trauma in *History and Memory after Auschwitz* (Ithaca, N.Y.: Cornell University Press, 1998), 45.

95. I am here referring to Dori Laub's discussion of the three levels of witnessing: "the level of being a witness to oneself within the experience; the level of being a witness to the testimonies of others; and the level of being a witness to the process of witnessing itself" ("An Event without a Witness," in Caruth, *Trauma: Explorations in Memory*, 75).

96. Interestingly, Massengill's book is dedicated to Morris.

97. Frank X Walker, "Legal Lynching," in *Turn Me Loose*, 34.

98. I am very grateful to Randall Horton for telling me about Walker's book in process and introducing me to the poet, who graciously made his manuscript available to me so that it could be discussed in this volume.

99. Michelle Hite, epilogue to Frank X Walker, *Turn Me Loose*, 60. I thank Michelle Hite for making her manuscript available before publication.

100. Kelly Oliver, *Witnessing*, 7.

101. Myrlie Evers with Peters, *For Us, the Living*, 5.

102. W. James Booth, "The Color of Memory: Reading Race with Ralph Ellison," *Political Theory* 36, no. 5 (October 2008): 703.

103. Many of the condolence letters, memorials, and poems in the Myrlie Evers Archives at the Mississippi Department of Archives and History use that term.

CHAPTER 2. Where Are the Voices "Coming From"?:
James Baldwin, Margaret Walker, Eudora Welty, and
the Question of Location

1. Fern Marja Eckman, *The Furious Passage of James Baldwin* (New York: J. B. Lippincott, 1966), 173.

2. David Leeming, *James Baldwin: A Biography* (New York: Alfred A. Knopf, 1994), 217.

3. Eckman, *Furious Passage of James Baldwin*, 175; Leeming, *James Baldwin*, 218.

4. Leeming, *James Baldwin*, 352.

5. Eudora Welty and Walker Percy, "'Southern Imagination': An Interview with Eudora Welty and Walker Percy by William F. Buckley, Jr.," in *Conversations with Eudora Welty*, ed. Peggy Whitman Prenshaw (Jackson: University Press of Mississippi, 1984), 101.

6. Personal journals by Margaret Walker, Journal #68, June 13, 1963; June 15, 1963, Margaret Walker Center, Jackson State University (hereafter MWC).

7. Eudora Welty, "Place in Fiction," in *The Eye of the Story: Selected Essays and Reviews* (1978; repr., New York: Vintage, 1990), 118.

8. Toni Morrison, prefatory remarks, author reading of *Beloved*, Virginia Polytechnic Institute and State University, Blacksburg, Virginia, May 6, 1988.

9. Myrlie Evers with William Peters, *For Us, the Living* (1967; repr., Jackson: University Press of Mississippi, 1996), 204, 205.

10. Minnie Watson, interview by the author, February 23, 2006.

11. Myrlie Evers with Peters, *For Us, the Living*, 287, 299, 302; Myrlie Evers, interview by Nicholas Hordern, *Delta Democrat-Times*, July 13, 1971, 4; Watson, interview by the author, February 23, 2006.

12. Myrlie Evers, "Interview: Myrlie B. Evers," by Fred Beauford, *The Crisis*, June/July 1988, 30.

13. Myrlie Evers, interview by Nicholas Hordern, 3.

14. Maryanne Vollers, *Ghosts of Mississippi: The Murder of Medgar Evers, the Trials of Byron De La Beckwith, and the Haunting of the New South* (New York: Little, Brown, 1995), 122.

15. Myrlie Evers, interview by Nicholas Hordern, 4. Ellipses in original.

16. Leeming, *James Baldwin*, 216.

17. Ibid., 221.

18. Reviewers criticized the production as being too zealous in its polemic. For a full discussion of the history of the productions of *Blues* and the reviewers' criticisms, see W. J. Weatherby, "Baldwin on Broadway," in *James Baldwin: Artist on Fire: A Portrait* (New York: Donald I. Fine, 1989), 236–55.

19. James Baldwin, "Notes for *Blues*," in *Blues for Mister Charlie* (1964; repr., New York: Vintage, 1995), xv.

20. James Baldwin, "Conversation: Ida Lewis and James Baldwin," in *Conversations with James Baldwin*, ed. Fred L. Standley and Louis H. Pratt (Jackson: University Press of Mississippi, 1989), 84, 85.

21. James Baldwin, "Letters from a Journey," *Harper's Magazine* 226, no. 1356 (May 1963): 49.

22. Baldwin, "Notes for *Blues*," in *Blues for Mister Charlie*, xiv.

23. Trudier Harris, *The Scary Mason-Dixon Line: African American Writers and the South* (Baton Rouge: Louisiana State University Press, 2009), 40.

24. Baldwin, "Notes for *Blues*," in *Blues for Mister Charlie*, xv.

25. For a description of the London performance, see Weatherby, "Baldwin on Broadway," 253. See Leeming, *James Baldwin*, 231–42, for another detailed discussion of the inception and production of the play.

26. "James Baldwin 1924–1987," in *Drama Criticism*, edited by Lawrence J. Trudeau (Detroit: Gale Research, 1991), 1:1–20; Calvin C. Hernton, "Critical Commentary," *Drama Criticism*, 1:22.

27. Eckman, *Furious Passage of James Baldwin*, 171.

28. Baldwin, "Notes for *Blues*," in *Blues for Mister Charlie*, xv. In a 1980 interview, Baldwin notes of Evers: "I was working on *Blues for Mister Charlie* and he was helpful with that." See Baldwin, "James Baldwin, an Interview," by Wolfgang Binder, in Standley and Pratt, *Conversations with James Baldwin*, 206.

29. Quoted in Eve Auchincloss and Nancy Lynch Handy, "Disturbers of the Peace" in *Black, White, and Gray: Twenty-one Points of View on the Race Question*, ed. Bradford Daniel (New York: Sheed and Ward, 1964), 195.

30. James Baldwin, "Nobody Knows My Name: A Letter from the South," in *James Baldwin: Collected Essays*, ed. Toni Morrison (New York: Library of America, 1998), 198.

31. James Baldwin, "The Artist's Struggle for Integrity," in *The Cross of*

Redemption: Uncollected Writings, ed. Randall Kenan (New York: Pantheon, 2010), 42.

32. Harris, *Scary Mason-Dixon Line*, 39.

33. Baldwin, "Letters from a Journey," 49.

34. James Campbell, *Talking at the Gates: A Life of James Baldwin* (Berkeley: University of California Press, 1991), 191.

35. Baldwin, *Blues for Mister Charlie*, 49–50.

36. Emmanuel S. Nelson feels that the play's "sad picture of a divided humanity" has implications for Baldwin's vision of self and the search for self-identity. See Nelson, "James Baldwin's Vision of Otherness and Community," *MELUS* 10, no. 2 (Summer 1983): 27.

37. Baldwin, *Blues for Mister Charlie*, 83.

38. Louis Phillips, "The Novelist as Playwright: Baldwin, McCullers, and Bellow," in *Modern American Drama: Essays in Criticism*, ed. William F. Taylor (Deland, Fla.: Everett Edwards, 1968), 147.

39. Quoted in *Ebony*, "*Blues for Mister Charlie*," 19, no. 8 (June 1964), 190.

40. Hernton, "Critical Commentary," 22.

41. Carlton W. Molette, "James Baldwin as a Playwright," in *James Baldwin: A Critical Evaluation*, ed. Therman B. O'Daniel (Washington, D.C.: Howard University Press, 1977), 183–88; repr., *Drama Criticism*, 1:6. Nonetheless, the split in audience perceptions seems, in part, to be mirrored in the reviews of the play. In its review article of "*Blues for Mister Charlie*," *Ebony* proclaimed that, by and large, negative responses to the play had come from white observers, whereas "Negroes, as well as many other whites who saw the play, have been almost unanimous in the [*sic*] praise. While sensitive to artistic criticism, Baldwin is unperturbed by the latter controversy—he had expected a certain 'white backlash'" (190). Overall the play received negative reviews, most of which charged that it was too polemical and reproduced the very stereotypes that it castigated.

42. Baldwin, *Blues for Mister Charlie*, Act One, 15.

43. Ibid., Act Two, 77.

44. Medgar Evers (as told to Francis H. Mitchell), "Why I Live in Mississippi," *Ebony*, November 1958, 69; repr. in *The Autobiography of Medgar Evers: A Hero's Life and Legacy Revealed through His Writings, Letters, and Speeches*, ed. Myrlie Evers-Williams and Manning Marable (New York: Basic Civitas Books, 2005), 111–21.

45. Baldwin, "Artist's Struggle for Integrity," 47.

46. Harris, *Scary Mason-Dixon Line*, 34; Nelson, "James Baldwin's Vision," 29.

47. Baldwin, *Blues for Mister Charlie*, Act One, 17.

48. Baldwin, "*The Black Scholar* Interviews James Baldwin," *Black Scholar* 5 (December 1973–January 1974): 33–42; repr. in Standley and Pratt, *Conversations with James Baldwin*, 145.

49. Suzanne Marrs, e-mail to author, September 28, 2005.

50. Margaret Walker, "A Mississippi Writer Talks," interview by John Griffin Jones, in *Conversations with Margaret Walker*, ed. Maryemma Graham (Jackson: University Press of Mississippi, 2002), 89; Anne Moody, *Coming of Age in Mississippi* (New York: Dell, 1968), 273.

51. Margaret Walker, "Mississippi Writer Talks," 88.

52. Watson, interview by the author, February 23, 2006.

53. Margaret Walker, personal journals, Journal #68, June 13, 1963, MWC.

54. Welty and Percy, "Southern Imagination," 83.

55. Doris Betts, "Killers Real and Imagined," *Southern Cultures* (Winter 1999): 6.

56. Welty and Percy, "Southern Imagination," 101.

57. Suzanne Marrs, *Eudora Welty: A Biography* (New York: Harcourt, 2005), 298–306. It is interesting to note that many of the calls Welty received were from progressive individuals chastising her for not doing more to combat white domination in her state.

58. Ibid., 305.

59. Eudora Welty, "Where Is the Voice Coming From?," in *The Collected Stories of Eudora Welty* (New York: Harcourt Brace, 1980), 604.

60. In "The Constitution of the White Knights of the Ku Klux Klan of the Sovereign Realm of Mississippi," the "Nighthawk" is a lesser officer of the klavern (number 11 in the pecking order of officers). He wears a black rather than a white robe and is responsible for security and order. See William H. McIhany, *Klandestine* (New Rochelle, N.Y.: Arlington House, 1975), 159.

61. For example, see Welty and Percy, "Southern Imagination," 101; see also Welty, "An Interview with Eudora Welty/29 July 1977," by Jean Todd Freeman, in *Conversations with Eudora Welty*, 183.

62. Welty, "Where Is the Voice Coming From?," 606.

63. Margaret Walker, "Southern Song: An Interview with Margaret Walker/1986," interview by Lucy M. Freibert, in Graham, *Conversations with Margaret Walker*, 112.

64. Margaret Walker, "Delta," in *This Is My Century: New and Collected Poems* (Athens: University of Georgia Press, 1989), 19.

65. Margaret Walker, "October Journey," in *This Is My Century*, 93.

66. Margaret Walker, "For Andy Goodman — Michael Schwerner — and James Chaney," in *This Is My Century*, 73.

67. Margaret Walker, "Jackson, Mississippi," in *This Is My Century*, 63.

68. Welty, "Where Is the Voice Coming From?," 606–7.

69. "Micah" is one of two Walker poems about Evers. The second is the sonnet "Medgar Evers, 1925–1963: Arlington Cemetery," in *This Is My Century*, 176, a poem about Evers's burial site, where "he will have neighbors good and true / Who have given their lives for freedom, too" (lines 13–14).

70. Walker, "Micah," in *This Is My Century*, 83.

71. Klaus Koch, *The Prophets* (Philadelphia: Fortress, 1982), 102.

72. Eric William Heaton, *A Short Introduction to the Old Testament Prophets* (Rockport, Mass.: Oneworld, 1996), 89.

73. Cathy Caruth, *Unclaimed Experience: Trauma, Narrative, and History* (Baltimore: Johns Hopkins University Press, 1996), 7–9.

74. Margaret Walker, "Mississippi Writer Talks," 89.

75. Maryemma Graham and Deborah Whaley, "Introduction: The Most Famous Person Nobody Knows," in *Fields Watered with Blood: Critical Essays on Margaret Walker*, ed. Maryemma Graham (Athens: University of Georgia Press, 2001), 1.

76. Walker, personal journal, Journal #68, Saturday morning, June 15, 1963, MWC.

77. Maryemma Graham, e-mail to author, January 31, 2006.

78. Eudora Welty, *One Writer's Beginnings* (Cambridge, Mass.: Harvard University Press, 1983), 39.

79. Welty, "A Conversation with Eudora Welty," interview by Tom Royals and John Little, in *Conversations with Eudora Welty*, 266.

80. Welty, "A Visit with Eudora Welty," interview by Barbara Lazear Ascher, *Yale Review* 74 (November 1984), repr. in *More Conversations with Eudora Welty*, edited by Peggy Whitman Prenshaw (Jackson: University Press of Mississippi, 1995), 85.

81. Welty, *The Collected Stories of Eudora Welty* (1980), Box 14, Folders 1, 3, 5, Welty (Eudora Alice) Collection, Mississippi Department of Archives and History, Jackson, Miss.

82. For an alternative explanation, see Ann Romines's "A Voice from a Jackson Interior: Eudora Welty and the Politics of Filial Piety," which argues that certain of Welty's multiple titles illustrate her own mixed feelings about being the primary caregiver for her elderly mother. The essay appears in an excellent collection, *Eudora Welty and Politics: Did the Writer Crusade?*, ed. Harriet Pollack

and Suzanne Marrs (Baton Rouge: Louisiana State University Press, 2001), 109–22.

83. Eudora Welty, "The Art of Fiction XLVII: Eudora Welty/1972," interview by Linda Kuehl, *Paris Review* 55 (Fall 1972), repr. in *Conversations with Eudora Welty*, 83.

84. Ibid., 84; Eudora Welty, "Eudora Welty at Home," interview by Clarence Brown, repr. in *More Conversations with Eudora Welty*, 230; Eudora Welty, "An Afternoon with Miss Welty," interview by Joseph Dumas, *Mississippi Magazine*, May/June 1994, repr. in *More Conversations with Eudora Welty*, 283.

85. Eudora Welty, "From the Unknown," in *Creative Writing and Rewriting: Contemporary American Novelists at Work*, ed. John Kuehl (New York: Appleton-Century-Crofts, 1967), 4.

86. Welty, "Art of Fiction XLVII," 83.

87. For example, "the Yum Yum Drive-In and Trailer Camp" was only changed to "the Kum Back Drive-In and Trailer Camp" from the first galley (dated June 26) to the published story (July 6), a significant revision historically because Betty Coley, a waitress at the Yum Yum Steak House near the Everses' house, was reported to have testified she might have seen someone resembling Beckwith at the restaurant and also walking in the area from which the shots were fired (*Clarion-Ledger*, February 1, 1964).

88. Welty, *Collected Stories of Eudora Welty* (1980), Box 14, Folder 1, Welty Collection. One of Barnett's partners, Hugh Cunningham, was a defense attorney for Beckwith (*Clarion-Ledger*, February 7, 1964).

89. Betts counts forty-five pages of typescript ("Killers Real and Imagined," 8).

90. Welty, "Art of Fiction XLVII," 83.

91. Ibid., 83 ("The Voice"); Welty and Percy, "Southern Imagination" ("real story"); Welty, "Afternoon with Miss Welty," 283.

92. Myrlie Evers, "Interview," by Fred Beauford, 30.

93. Lester J. Martin Jr., "A Man," Myrlie Evers Archives Subgroup 2, Series 20, Box 3, Folder 48, Mississippi Department of Archives and History, Jackson, Miss.

CHAPTER 3. "Agitators" and Aesthetics:
Jackson's Newspapers and the Battle for Collective Memory

1. Malvina Reynolds, vocal performance of "What's Going On Down There?" by Malvina Reynolds, 1964, renewed 1992, on *Malvina Reynolds Sings the Truth*, Columbia CS-9414, 33 ⅓ rpm. Used by permission.

2. Myrlie Evers with William Peters, *For Us, the Living* (1967; repr., Jackson: University Press of Mississippi, 1996), 265.

3. John R. Tisdale, "Medgar Evers (1925–1963) and the Mississippi Press," PhD dissertation, University of North Texas, Dec. 1996, 71.

4. "NAACP Leader Slain in Jackson; Protests Mount," *New York Times*, June 13, 1963, 12; Tisdale, "Medgar Evers," 34, 37.

5. Susan Weill, *In a Madhouse's Din: Civil Rights Coverage by Mississippi's Daily Press, 1948–1968* (Westport, Conn.: Praeger, 2002), 93.

6. For the discussion of women in prison, see Charles M. Hills's column, "Affairs of the State," *Clarion-Ledger*, June 20, 1963, 12A.

7. Minor's comments are quoted in David R. Davies and Judy Smith, "Jimmy Ward and the *Jackson Daily News*," in *The Press and Race: Mississippi Journalists Confront the Movement*, ed. David R. Davies (Jackson: University Press of Mississippi, 2001), 107–8.

8. Hills, "Affairs of the State," *Clarion-Ledger*, June 12, 1963, 5A.

9. Tisdale, "Medgar Evers," 104, 41.

10. Mitchell's comments came in a September 22, 2007, speech in which he accepted the John Peter and Anna Catherine Zenger Journalism Award from the University of Arizona Department of Journalism. Jerry Mitchell, acceptance speech at the Annual Meeting of the Arizona Newspapers Association, Scottsdale, Ariz., September 22, 2007. www.journalism.arizona.edu/news /zengerspeech.php.

11. Quoted in Weill, *In a Madhouse's Den*, 92.

12. Caryl A. Cooper, "Percy Greene and the *Jackson Advocate*," in Davies, *The Press and Race*, 56.

13. Quoted in Julius E. Thompson, *Percy Greene and the* Jackson Advocate: *The Life and Times of a Radical Conservative Newspaperman, 1897–1977* (Jefferson, N.C.: McFarland, 1994), 69.

14. Cooper, "Percy Greene," 73.

15. Tisdale, "Medgar Evers," 137–38.

16. Cooper, "Percy Greene," 73–75.

17. Percy Greene, "Editorial," *Jackson Advocate*, June 22, 1963, 4.

18. John R. Salter, Jr., *Jackson, Mississippi: An American Chronicle of Struggle and Schism* (Hicksville, N.Y.: Exposition Press, 1979), 29.

19. Julius E. Thompson, *The Black Press in Mississippi, 1865–1985* (Gainesville: University Press of Florida, 1993), 74. Thompson notes that by 1966 circulation had increased to 5,340.

20. Ginger Rudeseal Carter, "Hodding Carter, Jr., and the *Delta Democrat-Times*" in Davies, *The Press and Race*, 284.

21. Salter, *Jackson, Mississippi*, 30.

22. My focus on spring and summer of 1963 precludes discussion of another white-owned newspaper in Jackson, the more moderate *State-Times*, a publication started in the mid-fifties by local businessmen. It had lost so much advertising by 1961 that it was gobbled up by the Hedermans.

23. Diana Taylor, *The Archive and the Repertoire: Performing Cultural Memory in the Americas* (Durham, N.C.: Duke University Press, 2003), 1 ("acts of transfer"); Leigh Raiford and Renee C. Romano, "Introduction: The Struggle over Memory," in *The Civil Rights Movement in American Memory* (Athens: University of Georgia Press, 2006), xiv.

24. Tisdale, "Medgar Evers," 39, quoting the *Mississippi Free Press*, May 28, 1963.

25. Taylor, *Archive and the Repertoire*, 24.

26. Nicholas Hordern, "USA: 'This Is the Island! Here You Will Die!'" *New African*, July 2003, 64.

27. For example, the Wisconsin Historical Society archives in Madison and the University of Arkansas at Fayetteville.

28. I am referring to Pierre Nora's term in his classic article "Between Memory and History: *Les Lieux de Mémoire*," in "Memory and Counter-Memory," special issue, *Representations* 26, no. 1 (Spring 1989): 7–24.

29. Nicholas Abraham and Maria Torok, *The Shell and the Kernel: Renewals of Psychoanalysis*, trans. Nicholas T. Rand (Chicago: University of Chicago Press, 1994).

30. Avery F. Gordon, *Ghostly Matters: Haunting and the Sociological Imagination* (Minneapolis: University of Minnesota Press, 1997), 7.

31. Kim Severson, "Weighing Race and Hate in a Mississippi Killing," *New York Times*, August 22, 2011, 1. www.nytimes.com/2011/08/23/us/jackson.html?pagewanted=all, 8/24/11.

32. Myrlie Evers-Williams's assessment of the newspapers' changed politics is particularly interesting. See Myrlie Evers-Williams, interview by Jim Lehrer, *Online NewsHour*, PBS, April 23, 2002, http://www.pbs.org/newshour/media/clarion/myrlie_evers.html.

33. Davies and Smith, "Jimmy Ward," 106.

34. Tisdale, "Medgar Evers," 138–39.

35. "History of *The Clarion-Ledger*," last modified March 8, 2011, http://www.clarionledger.com/article/99999999/ABOUT02/40708005.

36. The website for the *Jackson Advocate*; www.jacksonadvocate.com.

37. "Jackson Free Press," Wikipedia, last modified August 15, 2011, http://en.wikipedia.org/wiki/Jackson_Free_Press.

38. "Mississippi Alt-Weekly Revealed Indicted Klansman Was Still Alive," news release on Association of Alternative Newsmedia official website, http://www.aan.org/news/mississippi.

39. Although there are many studies of southern print media during the civil rights movement, their focus is on the histories and content of the newspapers, not on their aesthetic components.

40. Hills, "Affairs of the State," *Clarion-Ledger*, June 12, 1963, 5.

41. Hills, "Affairs of the State," *Clarion-Ledger*, June 14, 1963, 4.

42. "NAACP Leader Slain in Jackson; Protests Mount," *New York Times*, June 13, 1963, 12.

43. "Jackson Negroes Clubbed as Police Quell Marchers," *New York Times*, June 14, 1963, 1, 15.

44. The two stories were titled "Move In on Race Agitators" and "Agitators Are Warned of U.S. Court Decision." Underneath those stories was the headline "Alabama Negroes Enjoined in Gadsden Demonstrations," and under it "Still Seeking Evers Killer." *Clarion-Ledger*, June 15, 1963, 1.

45. Jimmy Ward, "Covering the Crossroad," *Jackson Daily News*, June 15, 1963, 1.

46. Editorial, *Jackson Daily News*, June 15, 1963, 6.

47. *Jackson Daily News*, June 24, 1963, 1.

48. *Clarion-Ledger*, June 13, 1963, 12.

49. *Clarion-Ledger*, June 20, 1963, 1.

50. "Evers Gets Hero's Burial in Arlington," *Washington Post*, June 20, 1963, 18.

51. An interesting sidebar: Although the paper is filled with stories about black people far and wide, whites dominate its advertisements. Five of the seven ads in the first section of the June 15 issue, for example, feature individuals with light skin tone and phenotypically white features, especially in ads for beauty products.

52. *Jackson Advocate*, June 15, 1963, 1, 8.

53. Percy Greene, "Mississippi and Mississippians As History Repeats Itself," *Jackson Advocate*, June 15, 1963, 8.

54. See, for example, the *New York Times*'s June 20 three-column picture of soldiers holding the American flag over Evers's coffin during burial ceremonies at Arlington and the *Washington Post*'s June 18 front-page, three-column picture of Evers's body being borne in a hearse through the streets of the nation's capital.

55. Interestingly, as Julius E. Thompson points out, Greene, "a constant

tormentor of black male leaders such as Medgar Evers, Robert Moses, Martin Luther King, Jr., and others," seldom attacked black women in the *Jackson Advocate*. See Thompson, *Percy Greene*, 102.

56. According to Tisdale, the ultraconservative Hedermans "ran" the Chamber. See Tisdale, "Medgar Evers," 41.

57. As Cooper points out, Greene's reluctance to support a fully desegregated school system was long-standing, dating back to 1954 when, in August 28 and September 4 editorials, he supported separate but equal systems. See Cooper, "Percy Greene," 67.

58. Ibid., 60–64.

59. Ibid., 81.

60. Thompson, *Percy Greene*, 84.

61. Ibid., 102–3.

62. Cooper, "Percy Greene," 69.

63. See Thompson, *The Black Press in Mississippi*, and Julian Williams, "Truth Shall Make You Free," *Journalism History* 32, no. 2 (Summer 2006): 106–13, for complete histories of the *Free Press*. Williams's article focuses primarily on the newspaper between 1961 and 1963.

64. Tisdale, "Medgar Evers," 43.

65. Editorial, *Mississippi Free Press*, July 14, 1962, 2.

66. Ibid.

67. Aaron Henry, "Dear Medgar," *Mississippi Free Press*, July 13, 1964, 4.

68. Julian Williams, whose study, "Truth Shall Make You Free," spans 1961 to 1963, claims that the *Mississippi Free Press* failed to cover the full Jackson movement, possibly because of the national NAACP's opposition to the demonstrations. I see no evidence of any such failure in the paper's issues relating to Evers, although, as Williams notes, Evers felt torn between local groups' efforts to integrate Jackson sites and the NAACP's emphasis on voter registration in lieu of sit-ins or demonstrations. An example of front-and-center coverage of the Jackson movement may be found in the June 8, 1963, issue, which led with the one-inch headline: "POLICE JAIL OVER 600; Mass Protests Will Continue; Charge Police with Brutality." The story describes "hundreds of armed, helmeted police officers wielding clubs and rifles arrest[ing] over 500 children last Friday and Saturday as they marched in the Negro section of Jackson in a demand for equal rights" (1).

69. "Where Lies the Blame?" *Mississippi Free Press*, June 15, 1963, 2.

70. *Mississippi Free Press*, June 13, 1964, 1.

71. Maryanne Vollers, *Ghosts of Mississippi: The Murder of Medgar Evers, the*

Trials of Byron De La Beckwith, and the Haunting of the New South (Boston: Little, Brown, 1995), 208, 212.

72. Verna Bailey, "Medgar Wylie," *Mississippi Free Press*, June 13, 1964, 4–5.

73. *Mississippi Free Press*, June 22, 1963, 1.

74. Two columns, it should be noted, seem much larger in the *Mississippi Free Press*, which was only five columns across, than in the other papers, which were eight columns wide.

75. Aaron Henry, interview with *Mississippi Free Press*, June 29, 1963, 1.

76. *Mississippi Free Press*, July 13, 1963, 1.

77. *Mississippi Free Press*, January 25, 1964, 7.

78. *Mississippi Free Press*, April 25, 1964, 1, 4.

79. "'No More Bus Insults; We're Going to Walk'; Woman Reports Nasty Driver; Mass Meeting Votes to Stay Off," *Mississippi Free Press*, April 25, 1964, 1.

80. Ibid.

CHAPTER 4. "It wears, it tears at the root of your heart":
Medgar Evers and the Civil Rights Memoir

1. Eudora Welty, "Place in Fiction," in *The Eye of the Story: Selected Essays and Reviews* (1978; repr., New York: Vintage International, 1990), 118.

2. Kelly Oliver, *Witnessing: Beyond Recognition* (Minneapolis: University of Minnesota Press, 2001), 85.

3. Ibid., 98–99. These are observations made in a more specific way in the context of slave narratives by scholars such as William L. Andrews and Frances Smith Foster.

4. Anne Moody, interview with Debra Spencer, February 19, 1985, Archive # OHP403, 24, 5, typescript, Mississippi Department of Archives and History Oral History Collection, Jackson, Miss.

5. Brett Ashley Kaplan, *Unwanted Beauty: Aesthetic Pleasure in Holocaust Representation* (Urbana: University of Illinois Press, 2007), 167.

6. Shoshana Felman, "Camus' *The Plague*, or a Monument to Witnessing," in *Testimony: Crises of Witnessing in Literature, Psychoanalysis, and History*, ed. Shoshana Felman and Dori Laub, M.D. (New York: Routledge, 1992), 114. Yet, as Kaplan makes clear in the context of aesthetic representations of the Holocaust (for example, Nazi monuments), the relation of aesthetic production to ethics can cut both ways: at best, aesthetic mourning produces works "that mourn losses from traumatic histories in beautiful ways that expand our understanding of the events themselves," urging us to think critically about difficult histories

(Kaplan, *Unwanted Beauty*, 167). At the same time aesthetics, in the context of Evers's life and death, even the visual representations (layout, placement of stories, and pictures) in newspapers owned by members of the Mississippi Citizens' Council, can be fascist—subverting, assaulting, and attempting to manipulate alternative political imaginaries and the social movements driven by them.

7. W. Fitzhugh Brundage, *The Southern Past: A Clash of Race and Memory* (Cambridge, Mass.: Harvard University Press, 2005), 137.

8. Thomas Larsen, *The Memoir and the Memoirist: Reading and Writing Personal Narrative* (Athens: Ohio University Press, 2007), 129–30.

9. Myrlie Evers with William Peters, *For Us, the Living* (1967; repr., Jackson: University Press of Mississippi, 1996), 295.

10. Angela Pulley Hudson, "Mississippi Lost and Found: Anne Moody's Autobiograph(ies) and Racial Melancholia," *A/B: Auto/Biography Studies* 20, no. 2 (2005): 294.

11. In her essay on Moody, Hudson rightly points us back to Freud's 1917 essay "Mourning and Melancholia" to mark the difference between the two forms of emotion by emphasizing "the persistent and pathological nature of melancholia as compared with mourning" (ibid., 282).

12. Myrlie Evers with Peters, *For Us, the Living*, 284.

13. Ibid., 285.

14. Moody, interview by Debra Spencer, 47. The typed transcript of this interview is seventy-seven pages. It is, to my knowledge, the only extant interview with Moody after she left Mississippi in 1963. An interview with activist and writer Tom Dent, given a day after Spencer's, is listed as being in the archives of the Amistad Library at Tulane and the Tougaloo University library, but neither library has been able to locate a copy.

15. Moody, interview by Debra Spencer, 48.

16. In Moody's interview with Debra Spencer, she describes her response to a *New Yorker* editor who tried to persuade her to omit the cursing in the memoir: "I said, 'Are you kidding?' What would my mother sound like without her 'shits'. . . I would destroy the whole book if I did that" (65).

17. Anne Moody, *Coming of Age in Mississippi* (New York: Dell, 1968), 249–50.

18. Ibid., 263.

19. Ibid., 254.

20. Myrlie Evers with Peters, *For Us, the Living*, 172.

21. Both quotations in Myrlie Evers-Williams and Manning Marable, eds.,

The Autobiography of Medgar Evers: A Hero's Life and Legacy Revealed through His Writings, Letters, and Speeches (New York: Basic Civitas Books, 2005), 16.

22. Moody, *Coming of Age in Mississippi*, 123.

23. Ibid., 121, 125–26.

24. Moody, interview by Debra Spencer, 2. In *Coming of Age in Mississippi* (125), Moody gives her age as fourteen going on fifteen.

25. Moody, *Coming of Age in Mississippi*, 278.

26. Ibid., 280–81.

27. Ibid., 328.

28. Ibid., 340–41.

29. Moody, interview by Debra Spencer, 24.

30. Moody, *Coming of Age in Mississippi*, 384.

31. Moody, interview by Debra Spencer, 50.

32. Minnie Watson, interview by author, February 23, 2006. In the interview Watson, curator of the Medgar Evers House and Museum, said that Moody had been given a residency and house at Tougaloo for her 1985 visit but left Mississippi suddenly before her time in the residency was complete.

33. John Donovan's cheery introduction belies this subject matter. John Donovan, introduction to *Mr. Death and Other Stories* by Anne Moody (New York: Harper & Row, 1975), vi–vii.

34. Myrlie Evers with Peters, *For Us, the Living*, 204–5.

35. Ibid., 264.

36. Myrlie Evers-Williams, interview by author, June 7, 2010. Much of this history would be revisited in Evers-Williams's coauthored second memoir, *Watch Me Fly* (1999), which focuses on her more recent life with her children, her position as chair of the NAACP, and Beckwith's final trial.

37. Myrlie Evers with Peters, *For Us, the Living*, 100.

38. In the interview, I asked Evers-Williams about her collaboration with William Peters. She said she had been working on the memoir for quite some time and had amassed voluminous notes, which a friend had typed. She then revised the typed manuscript and got in touch with Peters, a reporter for the *New York Post* and CBS, who, like several prominent newspaper and wire service reporters from other areas, had worked with Evers on news stories. Peters had also interviewed Evers for CBS in the summer of 1962. Evers-Williams said, "I needed someone who was a good editor — Bill and Medgar had become good acquaintances when he covered civil rights activities. I had pages and pages of writing. We met, spent a week together revising the manuscript. The book came from the heart and we worked together. We got along well. He got the publisher, Doubleday."

39. Myrlie Evers with Peters, *For Us, the Living*, 347.

40. Receipts, Subgroup 2, Series 21, Folder 9, Medgar Evers Archives, Mississippi Department of Archives and History, Jackson, Miss. Receipts for life insurance policies in the Evers Archives indicate that payments were stopped to Universal Life Insurance Company (last payment of $17.54 paid on May 2, 1963); Collins Burial Association (last payment of $7.50 paid on May 22, 1963); and Security Life Insurance (after ninety-four weekly entries of sixty-five cents each, on April 16, 1963). At the time of his death, the NAACP was paying Evers a gross salary of $271.15 every two weeks.

41. Myrlie Evers with Peters, *For Us, the Living*, 295.

42. Ibid., 131.

43. Ibid., 121.

44. Ibid., 125–26, 129.

45. Ibid., 130.

46. Ibid., 279–80.

47. Ibid., 267.

48. Ibid., 273.

49. Ibid., 271.

50. Ibid., 303.

51. Ibid., 306.

52. Ibid., 347.

53. Myrlie Evers-Williams with Melinda Blau, *Watch Me Fly: What I Learned on the Way to Becoming the Woman I Was Meant to Be* (Boston: Little, Brown, 1999), 78–79.

54. Myrlie Evers with Peters, *For Us, the Living*, 331–32.

55. Evers-Williams, interview by the author, June 7, 2010. Evers-Williams received masses of mail after her husband's assassination. About half were condolence letters, and the other half were hate letters. The condolence letters are in the Myrlie Evers-Williams Archive at the Mississippi Department of Archives and History in Jackson.

56. Myrlie Evers with Peters, *For Us, the Living*, 310–11.

57. Moody, *Coming of Age in Mississippi*, 384.

58. Myrlie Evers with Peters, *For Us, the Living*, 377.

59. Ibid., 374–75.

60. Ibid., 376.

61. Kai Erickson, "Notes on Trauma and Community," in *Trauma: Explorations in Memory*, ed. Cathy Caruth (Baltimore: Johns Hopkins University Press, 1995), 185–87.

62. In the days that followed Evers's murder, around a thousand adults and

teenagers were arrested and held at the fairgrounds; many were brutalized by police. Black leaders, many of them ministers, were arrested, along with children carrying miniature American flags.

63. I am here referring to Dori Laub's discussion of the three levels of witnessing in relation to the Holocaust experience: "the level of being a witness to oneself within the experience, the level of being a witness to the testimonies of others, and the level of being a witness to the process of witnessing itself." See Laub, "An Event Without a Witness," in Caruth, ed., *Trauma: Explorations in Memory*, 61.

64. Kelly Oliver, *Witnessing*, 206.

65. Willie Morris, introduction to Myrlie Evers with Peters, *For Us, the Living*, x, xiii.

66. Ibid., xviii.

67. Interestingly, Massengill's book is dedicated to Morris.

68. Willie Morris, *The Ghosts of Medgar Evers: A Tale of Race, Murder, Mississippi, and Hollywood* (New York: Random House, 1998), 27.

69. Ibid., 271.

70. Ibid., 11.

71. Ibid., 9–10.

72. Ibid., 11.

73. Ibid., 271–72.

74. Ibid., 189.

75. Ibid., 58.

76. Ibid., 58–59.

77. Eudora Welty, "Where Is the Voice Coming From?," in *The Collected Stories of Eudora Welty* (New York: Harcourt Brace, 1980), 604.

78. Morris, *Ghosts of Medgar Evers*, 266.

79. Pierre Nora, "Between Memory and History: *Les Lieux de Mémoire*," trans. Marc Roudebush, in "Memory and Counter-Memory," special issue, *Representations* 26, no. 1 (Spring 1989), 7–24. Nora argues that we need to erect sites of memory because we have lost rituals of remembrance.

CHAPTER 5. Music and Medgar Evers: The Heartbeat of Memory

The epigraph is from page 82 of Taylor's book.

1. Eudora Welty, "Place in Fiction," in *The Eye of the Story* (1978; repr., New York: Vintage International, 1990), 118.

2. Dick Weissman, *Talkin' 'Bout a Revolution: Music and Social Change in America* (New York: Backbeat Books, 2010), 208.

3. Kerran L. Sanger, *"When the Spirit Says Sing!": The Role of Freedom Songs in the Civil Rights Movement* (New York: Garland, 1995), 17–19.

4. Ibid. (both quotations), 17. In the liner notes to the CD collection *Voices of the Civil Rights Movement*, Reagon interestingly discusses black music in terms relating to movement or physicality. She refers, for example, to "the *agility* of the singer, the ability . . . to *scoop* and *glide*" (my emphasis). See *Voices of the Civil Rights Movement: Black American Freedom Songs, 1960–1966*, Smithsonian Folkways, 1997, compact disc, liner notes.

5. The term *broadside* is taken from sixteenth-century single-sheet printings of ballads, also called penny sheets.

6. Lester was a professor of African American studies at the University of Massachusetts, a prolific author of adult and children's books, and a singer/musician active in the movement. He coauthored with Pete Seeger *The Folksinger's Guide to the 12-String Guitar as Played by Leadbelly* (1965). There are no page numbers in this article.

7. Although Myrlie Evers does not mention the name of the closing song at her husband's funeral, many other sources identify it as "We Shall Overcome."

8. Bob Dylan, "Only a Pawn in Their Game," *Lyrics, 1962–1985* (New York: Knopf, 1985), 98. The song lyrics are on pages 97–98; future quotations reference this version and those pages. Ali Neff, teaching notes, generously shared with the author.

9. Matthew Jones, vocal performance of "The Ballad of Medgar Evers," on *Voices of the Civil Rights Movement*.

10. This doesn't mean that these were the only songs about Evers. The January 1, 1964, issue of *Broadside*, for example, contains a ballad by Randall Wilbur called "Medgar Evers," which is meant to be set to the tune of "Jesse James." It has the same refrain as the Jones song. There is no record of its being performed. Ochs and Gibson's song was called by both titles; the form of the title used here comes from Phil Ochs, *Songs of Phil Ochs* (New York: Appleseed Music, 1964), 29. Ochs wrote the words and collaborated with Gibson on the music. Ochs performed the song.

11. Ochs's was published in volume 29 and Dylan's in 33.

12. I am grateful to Rebecka Rutledge Fisher for helping me understand Jones's song and its roots and to Billie Rutledge Killens for helping in the attempt to trace the origins of the melody. On the black ballad, Harold Courlander suggests that black folk singers absorbed and adapted English, Irish, Scottish, and, in Louisiana, French ballad styles into the "main flow" of African American musical tradition, "where a style characterized by allusion and interpolation usually remained supreme. Indirection of statement and selective

imagery tended to substitute for unbroken continuity of story line" (*Negro Folk Music, U.S.A.* [New York: Columbia University Press, 1963], 176).

13. See Olive Woolley Burt, *American Murder Ballads and Their Stories* (New York: Oxford University Press, 1958), for a discussion of the lullaby as part of the murder ballad tradition.

14. Roger Abrahams and George Foss, *Anglo American Folksong Style* (Englewood Cliffs, N.J.: Prentice Hall, 1968), 38; see note 12 on the circuitousness of the black ballad style.

15. Burt, *American Murder Ballads*, xxi.

16. Ibid., ix–x.

17. Ibid., 127, 202. Burt's treatment of race and ethnicity primarily focuses on murder ballads surrounding the "massacres" of whites by Native Americans. In *Songsters and Saints: Vocal Traditions on Race Records* (Cambridge: Cambridge University Press, 1984), cited later in this chapter, Paul Oliver also discusses the "Stagolee" ballad (238).

18. Mike Marqusee, *Chimes of Freedom: The Politics of Bob Dylan's Art* (New York: New Press, 2003), 74.

19. Quoted in Robert Shelton, *No Direction Home: The Life and Music of Bob Dylan* (New York: William Morrow, 1986), 170.

20. Marqusee, *Chimes of Freedom*, 76.

21. Pete Seeger, *The Incomplete Folksinger* (New York: Simon & Schuster, 1972), 247.

22. Marqusee, *Chimes of Freedom*, 76–77; Shelton, *No Direction Home*, 179.

23. Marqusee, *Chimes of Freedom*, 76; Shelton, *No Direction Home*, 179.

24. Quoted in Shelton, *No Direction Home*, 179.

25. Howard Sounes, *Down the Highway: The Life of Bob Dylan* (New York: Grove Press, 2001), 134–35.

26. Bob Spitz, *Dylan: A Biography* (New York: McGraw-Hill, 1987), 309.

27. Marqusee, *Chimes of Freedom*, 76–77. As Marqusee says in a footnote to the statement above, Beckwith wasn't exactly a "pawn in their game" since he eluded justice in the Evers murder for thirty years.

28. "Northern Folk Singers Help Out at Negro Festival in Mississippi," *New York Times*, July 7, 1963, 25. See "'Only a Pawn in Their Game' 1962–1964," The Pop History Dig, www.pophistorydig.com/?p=654, December 7, 2011.

29. Marqusee, *Chimes of Freedom*, 78.

30. Shelton, *No Direction Home*, 179; Marqusee, *Chimes of Freedom*, 78.

31. Greil Marcus, *Bob Dylan: Writings, 1968–2010* (New York: Public Affairs, 2010), 408.

32. Marqusee, *Chimes of Freedom*, 6–7.

33. Ibid., 9.

34. Quoted in Aidan Day, *Jokerman: Reading the Lyrics of Bob Dylan* (Oxford: Basil Blackwell, 1988), 4.

35. See, for example, "The Death of Emmett Till" and "The Lonesome Death of Hattie Carroll."

36. Betsy Bowden, *Performed Literature: Words and Music by Bob Dylan* (Bloomington: Indiana University Press, 1982), 10.

37. Ibid., 9–12. Interestingly, as Bowden points out, the last verse to Ochs's song contains the sentence "the times are changing mighty fast," which Dylan would take (my term, not hers) for his 1963 hit "The Times They Are A-Changin'" (10).

38. Marc Eliot, *Death of a Rebel: A Biography of Phil Ochs* (1979; repr., New York: Franklin Walls, 1989), 64, 94.

39. See Ochs's obituary in the picture section of Michael Schumacher's biography, *There but for Fortune: The Life of Phil Ochs* (New York: Hyperion, 1996), 210–11.

40. Phil Ochs, "Interviews with Phil Ochs," audio recording in *Broadside Ballads*, vol. 11, Folkways Records, FW05321, 1976. In the same interview, Ochs says of Dylan: "He's been such a large part of my psyche."

41. Schumacher, *There but for Fortune*, 86.

42. Ibid., 87.

43. Ochs, "Here's to the State of Mississippi," on *I Ain't Marching Anymore*, Elektra, 1965, 33 1/3 rpm. Ochs would eventually revise the song to the equally scathing "Here's to the State of Richard Nixon." The song has mutated many times to fit various political figures and situations. Schumacher describes the controversies around the song (*There but for Fortune*, 88). Eliot notes that the song was nominated by the Canadian Federation of English Teachers for "Song of the Year" (*Death of a Rebel*, 102).

44. Schumacher, *There but for Fortune*, 54.

45. Quoted in Eliot, *Death of a Rebel*, 59.

46. Ochs, *Songs of Phil Ochs*, 4.

47. Dorian Lynskey, *33 Revolutions per Minute: A History of Protest Songs from Billie Holliday to Green Day* (New York: Ecco, 2011), 60. As discussed later, Jones and his all-male quartet were the second group of SNCC Freedom Singers, which was formed in 1964 after the first group disbanded.

48. Schumacher, *There but for Fortune*, 62.

49. Eliot, *Death of a Rebel*, 67. In volume 31 of *Broadside* (dated September

1963), Josh Dunson wrote an article titled, "Workshops Key to Newport '63." In the article he explained that the workshops were more intimate gatherings of the musicians with roughly five hundred to six hundred audience members. He described the workshops as "informal jam sessions" and even mentioned that the festival included a workshop devoted to ballads (n.p.). While Dunson didn't provide a lengthy review of Ochs's participation at the festival, he nevertheless mentioned Ochs's performance of "Ballad of Medgar Evers": "The city bred music of Phil Ochs drew the only standing ovation of the workshop, a real tribute to this talented young writer. He had been ill for several weeks with severe headaches and dizziness, and his first song 'Medgar Evers,' though well received, lacked his usual power of delivery" (n.p.).

50. *Broadside* 29, July 1963, n.p.

51. Ochs, "Too Many Martyrs (Ballad of Medgar Evers)," in *Songs of Phil Ochs*, 29. All further references to the song are to this volume and page number, although circulating versions vary slightly.

52. Charles Evers, *Evers* (New York: World, 1971), 59; Myrlie Evers with William Peters, *For Us, the Living* (1967; repr., Jackson: University Press of Mississippi, 1996), 17.

53. Myrlie Evers with Peters, *For Us, the Living*, 18.

54. Charles Evers, *Evers*, 59.

55. Ochs, "Too Many Martyrs (Ballad of Medgar Evers)." See also the YouTube video of the audio recording, http://www.youtube.com/watch?v=h1T25D2CLrE.

56. John Pietaro, "Matthew Jones, Freedom Singer, Civil Rights Activist: 1936–2011," The Cultural Worker (blog), April 2, 2011, http://theculturalworker .blogspot.com/2011/04/obituary-matt-jones.html; "Freedom Singers Member Matt Jones Crosses Over," *Frost Illustrated*, April 13, 2011, http://www .frostillustrated.com/full.php?sid=8632&current_edition=2011-4-13.

57. Quoted in Pietaro, "Matthews Jones," n.p.

58. Pietaro, "Matthew Jones," n.p.

59. Lynskey, *33 Revolutions per Minute*, 44.

60. Edward A. Hatfield, "Freedom Singers," *New Georgia Encyclopedia*, Georgia Humanities Council, last modified November 28, 2007, accessed June 23, 2011, http://www.georgiaencyclopedia.org/nge/Article.jsp?id=h-3670&hl=y.

61. "A Freedom Singer Shares the Music of the Movement," *Talk of the Nation*, NPR, February 11, 2010, accessed June 24, 2011, http://www.npr.org /templates/story/story.php?storyId=123599617.

62. Transcription of Matthew Jones and the Freedom Singers, "The Ballad of Medgar Evers," in *Voices of the Civil Rights Movement*. All quotations are from

this version of the song and from this source. "The Ballad of Medgar Evers" by Matthew Jones, 1963, 1993 (ASCAP), copyright 1993 Wisdom Train (ASCAP).

63. Liner notes of Bruce Springsteen, *We Shall Overcome: The Seeger Sessions*, Columbia, 2006, compact disc. Ochs's "Too Many Martyrs," performed in late July 1963 at the Newport Folk Festival, also uses the line, so the words could also be a riff on Ochs's song.

64. Front and back covers of Dick Weissman, *The Things That Trouble My Mind*, Capitol Records, 1964, 33 ⅓ rpm.

65. Weissman, e-mail message to author, July 10, 2011.

66. Weissman and John Phillips started the Journeymen in early 1961.

67. Weissman, e-mail message to author, July 10, 2011.

68. Ibid.

69. Judy Collins, *Singing Lessons* (New York: Pocket Books, 1998), 126.

70. Ibid.

71. Jack Goddard, liner notes to Judy Collins, *The Judy Collins Concert*, recorded at Town Hall, New York City, March 21, 1964, Elektra Records, 33 ⅓ rpm.

72. Weissman, e-mail message to author, July 10, 2011.

73. Vivian Claire, *Judy Collins* (New York/London: Finish Books, 1977), 47.

74. Collins, *Singing Lessons*, 122.

75. Ibid., 130. Here, Collins's assessment of the effectiveness of the voter drives of the summer of 1964 is much more positive than the statistics from Greenwood after Dylan's visit there.

76. Weissman, "Lullaby," on *The Things That Trouble My Mind*. All references to the song are from this album.

77. Weissman, *Talkin' 'Bout a Revolution*, 321.

78. Nina Simone and Stephen Cleary, *I Put a Spell on You: The Autobiography of Nina Simone* (Cambridge, Mass.: Da Capo Press, 2003), 88–90.

79. Ibid., 88–89.

80. Ibid., 89.

81. Ibid., 89–90.

82. David Brun-Lambert, *Nina Simone: The Biography* (London: Aurum, 2010), 112.

83. Nina Simone, vocal performance of "Mississippi Goddam," by Nina Simone, recorded live at Carnegie Hall in 1964, on *Nina Simone in Concert*, Philips/Verve, 2006, compact disc. This is Simone's first album to feature the song as recorded live at Carnegie Hall in 1964, though it was released previously as a single. Since "Mississippi Goddam" became one of her signature songs, it is included on many of her albums.

84. Simone, vocal performance of "Mississippi Goddam."

85. Lynskey, *33 Revolutions per Minute*, 78, 83.

86. Immortal Technique, "Crossing the Boundary," 3rd verse, on *Revolutionary*, Vol. 2, Viper Records, compact disc, released November 18, 2003; Wu Tang Clan, "I Can't Go to Sleep," on *The W*, Sony, compact disc, released November 21, 2000.

87. I am grateful to Ali Neff for bringing Banner to my attention and providing me with information about him. These quotations are from her teaching notes.

88. Dälek's website (n.d., new website under construction), accessed June 25, 2011, Deadverse.com.

89. Scott Thill, "We Are Not Moving Forward: An Interview with Dälek." *Morphizm.com*. November 29, 2005, accessed June 25, 2011, http://www.morphizm.com/recommends/interviews/Dalek05.html.

90. For lyrics, see the website www.songlyrics.com (n.d.), http://www.songlyrics.com/Dalek/who-medgar-evers-was-lyrics. All references are to this source.

91. Kathy Veazey, e-mail to author, February 28, 2012.

92. Soul Consolidation, "I'm Alive, 1995 (Medgar Evers)," YouTube video with audio recording, uploaded April 9, 2008, accessed August 3, 2011, http://www.youtube.com/watch?v=Rped_F9lU-A.

93. The Veazey lyrics vary from the 1995 vocal rendition on YouTube (see n. 92) and the lyrics Veazey sent to the author, which end instead with the one line "I won't go away." Veazey, e-mail to author, February 28, 2012.

94. Jacqueline Dowd Hall, "The Long Civil Rights Movement and the Political Uses of the Past," *Journal of American History* 91, no. 4 (March 2005): 1261.

95. Ibid., 1262–63.

CHAPTER 6. The Pocket and the Heart

1. Toni Morrison, *Beloved* (New York: New American Library, 1987), 6.

2. "Mrs. Evers Asks United Action in Dramatic Plea at Rally," *Jet*, June 27, 1963, 17.

3. Frank X Walker, "Heavy Wait," in *Turn Me Loose: The Unghosting of Medgar Evers: Poems* (Athens: University of Georgia Press, forthcoming), 60 (all page numbers are from the typescript). I am much indebted to Frank X Walker for sharing his manuscript with me before publication.

4. Lucille Clifton, untitled poem, *The Terrible Stories* (Brockport, N.Y.: BOA Editions, 1996), 39.

5. Frank X Walker, e-mail message to author, November 2, 2011, in which he states: "It was a poem by Lucille Clifton that started the fire. . . . I carried that poem around with me for days."

6. As I said in the introduction to this volume, I am very much indebted to Randall Horton for letting me know about Walker's forthcoming book and introducing us over e-mail.

7. Chicago activist and Black Panther Fred Hampton (1948–69) was killed while sleeping, after having been drugged by a police plant, when police raided his apartment. The circumstances of his murder have been described in the documentaries *The Murder of Fred Hampton* and *Eyes on the Prize*.

8. Frank X Walker, e-mail message to author, November 2, 2011.

9. Ibid. Walker says that while these earlier book projects took around two years to complete, the Evers book took almost four.

10. Frank X Walker, introduction to *Turn Me Loose*, 6.

11. Ibid.

12. Frank X Walker, "The Assurance Man," in *Turn Me Loose*, 58.

13. Frank X Walker, e-mail message to author, November 18, 2011.

14. Frank X Walker, introduction to *Turn Me Loose*, 6.

15. Michelle Hite, epilogue to Frank X Walker, *Turn Me Loose*, 7. I am very grateful to Michelle Hite and Frank X Walker for providing me with a copy of her epilogue in advance of publication.

16. Frank X Walker, e-mail message to author, November 2, 2011.

17. Kelly Oliver, *Witnessing: Beyond Recognition* (Minneapolis: University of Minnesota Press, 2001), 206.

18. Frank X Walker, "One Mississippi, Two Mississippis / after Thomas Sayers Ellis," in *Turn Me Loose*, 52.

19. Frank X Walker, *Turn Me Loose*, 2.

20. Frank X Walker, "Ambiguity Over the Confederate Flag," in *Turn Me Loose*, 8.

21. Frank X Walker, "What Kills Me," in *Turn Me Loose*, 9.

22. Frank X Walker, "Byron de la Beckwith Dreaming III," in *Turn Me Loose*, 40.

23. Frank X Walker, "Southern Sports," in *Turn Me Loose*, 13.

24. Frank X Walker, "Fire Proof," in *Turn Me Loose*, 17.

25. Frank X Walker, "Listening to Music," in *Turn Me Loose*, 18.

26. Frank X Walker, "Bighearted," in *Turn Me Loose*, 46.

27. Frank X Walker, "Stand By Your Man," in *Turn Me Loose*, 23.

28. Frank X Walker, "Husbandry," in *Turn Me Loose*, 24.

29. Frank X Walker, "The Assurance Man," in *Turn Me Loose*, 58.

30. Frank X Walker, "Heavy Weight," in *Turn Me Loose*, 60.

31. Frank X Walker, "A Final Accounting" in *Turn Me Loose*, 52.

32. Hite, epilogue to Frank X Walker, *Turn Me Loose*, 4.

33. Kim Severson, "Weighing Race and Hate in a Mississippi Killing," *New York Times*, August 22, 2011, 1. www.nytimes.com/2011/08/23/us/jackson.html 8/24/11.

34. Frank X Walker, "Heavy Wait" in *Turn Me Loose*, 60.

35. Frank X Walker, "Gift of Time," in *Turn Me Loose*, 59.

36. Kathryn Stockett, *The Help* (New York: Amy Einhorn, 2009), 196.

37. Ibid., 200.

38. While it is inadvisable to analyze one's own novel, I discuss it here because of its close and fulsome connection to the Evers story.

39. Minrose Gwin, *The Queen of Palmyra* (New York: HarperCollins/Harper Perennial, 2010), 323.

40. *For Us, the Living* is unfortunately available only in VHS.

41. For a fuller discussion of the history and criticism of such films, see Jennifer Fuller, "Debating the Present through the Past: Representations of the Civil Rights Movement in the 1990s," in *The Civil Rights Movement in American History*, ed. Leigh Raiford and Renee C. Romano (Athens: University of Georgia Press, 2006), 167–96.

42. More recently, an episode of the AMC television drama *Mad Men* probes the relationship between Evers's death and the limited lives of white females in the sixties, using Evers's death as a cultural anchor. See Matthew Weiner and Kater Gordan, "The Fog," *Mad Men*, season 3, episode 5, directed by Phil Abraham, aired September 13, 2009 (Santa Monica, Calif.: Lionsgate, 2010), DVD.

43. Sheila Weller, "We've Waited Our Whole Lives for This," *Glamour*, January 2009, 91.

44. Letters and Memorials, Box 3, Folder 48, Myrlie Beasley Evers Archives, Mississippi Department of Archives and History (Z/2231.000/S).

45. Ibid., Box 3, Folder 48.

BIBLIOGRAPHY

PRIMARY SOURCES
Literature, Interviews, and Other Writing

Bailey, Verna. "Medgar Wylie." *Mississippi Free Press*. June 13, 1964, 4–5.
Baldwin, James. "The Artist's Struggle for Integrity." *Freedomways*, 1963.
Reprinted in *The Cross of Redemption: Uncollected Writings*, edited by Randall Kenan, 41–47. New York: Pantheon, 2010.
———. "*The Black Scholar* Interviews James Baldwin." By *The Black Scholar*, December 1973–January 1974. Reprinted in *Conversations with James Baldwin*, 142–58.
———. *Blues for Mister Charlie (a play)*. 1964. New York: Vintage International, 1995.
———. "Conversation: Ida Lewis and James Baldwin." Interview by Ida Lewis. New York: Essence Communications, Inc., 1970. Reprinted in *Conversations with James Baldwin*, 83–92.
———. *Conversations with James Baldwin*. Edited by Fred L. Standley and Louis H. Pratt. Jackson: University Press of Mississippi, 1989.
———. "James Baldwin, an Interview." By Wolfgang Binder. San Germán, Puerto Rico: Inter American University of Puerto Rico, 1980. Reprinted in *Conversations with James Baldwin*, 190–209.
———. "Letters from a Journey." *Harper's Magazine*, May 1963, 48–52.
———. "Nobody Knows My Name: A Letter from the South." *Partisan Review*, Winter 1959. Reprinted in *James Baldwin: Collected Essays*, edited by Toni Morrison, 197–208. New York: Library of America, 1998.
Barnes, Brooks. "From Footnote to Fame in Civil Rights History." *New York Times*, November 26, 2009. http://www.nytimes.com/2009/11/26/books/26colvin.html.
Brooks, Gwendolyn. "Medgar Evers, for Charles Evers." In *Every Shut Eye Ain't Asleep: An Anthology of African Americans since 1945*, edited by Michael S. Harper and Anthony Walton, 49. Boston: Little, Brown, 1994.

Campbell, Clarice. *Civil Rights Chronicles: Letters from the South*. Jackson: University Press of Mississippi, 1997.

Clarion-Ledger. "History of *The Clarion-Ledger*." Last modified March 8, 2011. http://www.clarionledger.com/article/99999999/ABOUT02/40708005.

Clifton, Lucille. *The Terrible Stories*. Brockport, N.Y.: BOA Editions, 1996.

Collins, Judy. *Singing Lessons: A Memoir of Love, Loss, Hope, and Healing*. New York: Pocket Books, 1998.

Donovan, John. Introduction to *Mr. Death and Other Stories* by Anne Moody, vi–vii. New York: Harper & Row, 1975.

Dunson, Josh. "Workshops Key to Newport '63." *Broadside* 31 (September 1963): n.p.

Ebony. "Blues for Mr. Charlie." 19, no. 8 (June 1964): 188–93.

Ellison, Ralph. *Invisible Man*. New York: Vintage, 1995.

Evers, Charles. *Evers*. New York: World, 1971.

Evers, Medgar. NAACP reports and correspondence. Medgar Wiley Evers and Myrlie Beasley Evers Papers (Z/2231.000/S). Mississippi Department of Archives and History, Jackson, Miss.

———. "Why I Live in Mississippi." *Ebony*, November 1968. Reprinted in *The Autobiography of Medgar Evers: A Hero's Life and Legacy Revealed through His Writings, Letters, and Speeches*, edited by Myrlie Evers-Williams and Manning Marable, 111–21. New York: Basic Civitas Books, 2005.

Evers, Myrlie. "Interview: Myrlie B. Evers." By Fred Beauford. *The Crisis*, June/July 1988, 28–36.

———. Interview. By Amy Goodman. *Democracy Now!* June 12, 2008.

———. Interview. By Nicholas Hordern. *Delta Democrat-Times*, June 13, 1971, pp. 4–5.

———. Medgar Evers personal effects. Letters and Memorials, Box 3, Folder 48, Myrlie Beasley Evers Papers. Special Collections Section, Mississippi Department of Archives and History, Jackson, Miss.

Evers, Myrlie, with William Peters. *For Us, the Living*. 1967. Reprint, Jackson: University Press of Mississippi, 1996.

Evers-Williams, Myrlie. Interview. By Jim Lehrer, *Online NewsHour*, PBS, April 23, 2002. http://www.pbs.org/newshour/media/clarion/myrlie_evers.html.

———. Interview. By Minrose Gwin. June 12, 2010.

———. "Unsung Civil Rights Hero: Myrlie Evers-Williams." Interview by Farai Chideya. NPR. October 18, 2007. http://www.npr.org/templates/story/story.php?storyId=15405815.

Evers-Williams, Myrlie, with Melinda Blau. *Watch Me Fly: What I Learned on the Way to Becoming the Woman I Was Meant to Be*. Boston: Little, Brown, 1999.

Evers-Williams, Myrlie, and Manning Marable, eds. *The Autobiography of Medgar Evers: A Hero's Life and Legacy Revealed through His Writings, Letters, and Speeches*. New York: Basic Civitas Books, 2005.

Frost Illustrated. "Freedom Singers Member Matt Jones Crosses Over." April 13, 2011. http://www.frostillustrated.com/full.php?sid=8632&current_edition=2011-04-13.

Graham, Maryemma, and Deborah Whaley. "Introduction: The Most Famous Person Nobody Knows." In *Fields Watered with Blood: Critical Essays on Margaret Walker*, edited by Maryemma Graham, 1–8. Athens: University of Georgia Press, 2001.

Greene, Percy. Editorial. *Jackson Advocate*, June 22, 1963, p. 4.

———. "Mississippi and Mississippians as History Repeats Itself." *Jackson Advocate*, June 15, 1963, p. 8.

Gwin, Minrose. *The Queen of Palmyra*. New York: HarperCollins/Harper Perennial, 2010.

Henry, Aaron. "Dear Medgar." *Mississippi Free Press*, June 13, 1964, p. 2.

———. Interview. *Mississippi Free Press*, June 29, 1963, p. 1.

Hills, Charles M. "Affairs of the State." *Clarion-Ledger*, June 12, 1963, p. 5.

———. "Affairs of the State." *Clarion-Ledger*, June 14, 1963, p. 4.

———. "Affairs of the State." *Clarion-Ledger*, June 20, 1963, p. 12A.

Hite, Michelle. Epilogue to *Turn Me Loose: The Unghosting of Medgar Evers* by Frank X Walker. Unpublished manuscript.

Hordern, Nicholas. "USA: 'This Is the Island! Here You Will Die!'" Interview with Myrlie Evers-Williams. *New African*, July 2003, p. 60–65.

Hudson, Winson, and Constance Curry. *Mississippi Harmony: Memoirs of a Freedom Fighter*. New York: Palgrave Macmillan, 2002.

Jackson Advocate. "Medgar Evers Slain by Bullet from Sniper's Rifle." June 15, 1963, pp. 1, 8.

Jackson Daily News. Editorial. June 15, 1963, p. 6.

Jet. "Mrs. Evers Asks United Action in Dramatic Plea at Rally." June 27, 1963, 16–17.

Kuehl, John, ed. *Creative Writing and Rewriting: Contemporary American Novelists at Work*. New York: Appleton-Century-Crofts, 1967.

Lester, Julius. "Freedom Songs in the North." *Broadside* 42 (March 20, 1964): n.p.

Martin, Lester J., Jr. "Salute to Medgar Evers," poem sent to Myrlie Evers. Letters and Memorials, Box 3, Folder 48, Myrlie Beasley Evers Papers. Mississippi Department of Archives and History, Jackson, Miss.

Mississippi Free Press. "*After Long Delay* Beckwith Trial Begins; Conviction Doubtful." January 25, 1964, p. 7.

———. "Beckwith Home Free; Posts $10,000 Bond." April 25, 1964, pp. 1, 4.

———. Editorial statement. July 14, 1962, p. 2.

———. "Henry on Beckwith: 'Court Won't Indict.'" June 13, 1963, p. 1.

———. "'No More Bus Insults; We're Going to Walk'; Woman Reports Nasty Driver; Mass Meeting Votes to Stay Off." April 25, 1964, p. 1.

———. "Police Jail Over 600; Mass Protests Will Continue; Charge Police with Brutality." June 8, 1963, p. 1.

———. "Police Power Meets Protesters during Days of Demonstrations." June 22, 1963, pp. 1, 3.

———. "Where Lies the Blame?" June 15, 1963, p. 2.

———. "Young Mother, Young children—No Husband, No Father / What Price Freedom / The Medgar Evers Family / one year after the murder." June 13, 1964, p. 1.

Mitchell, Jerry. Acceptance speech for John Peter and Catherine Zenger Journalism Award. Annual Meeting of Arizona Newspapers Association, Scottsdale, Ariz. September 22, 2007. www.journalism.arizona.edu/news/zengerspeech.php.

Moody, Anne. *Coming of Age in Mississippi.* New York: Dell, 1968.

———. Interview by Debra Spencer, February 19, 1985. Archive #OHP403, 24, 5, typescript. Mississippi Department of Archives and History Oral History Collection, Jackson, Miss.

———. *Mr. Death and Other Stories.* New York: Harper & Row, 1975.

Morris, Willie. *The Ghosts of Medgar Evers: A Tale of Race, Murder, Mississippi, and Hollywood.* New York: Random House, 1998.

———. Introduction to Myrlie Evers with Peters, *For Us, the Living,* ix–xviii.

Morrison, Toni. *Beloved:* New York: New American Library, 1987.

———. Prefatory remarks to author reading of *Beloved* at Virginia Polytechnic Institute and State University, Blacksburg, Virginia. May 6, 1988.

New York Times. "Jackson Negroes Clubbed As Police Quell Marchers." June 14, 1963, pp. 1, 15.

———. "NAACP Leader Slain in Jackson; Protests Mount." June 13, 1963, p. 12.

———. "Northern Folk Singers Help Out at Negro Festival in Mississippi." July 7, 1963, p. 25.

Severson, Kim. "Weighing Race and Hate in a Mississippi Killing." *New York Times*. August 22, 2011, accessed August 24, 2011. http://www.nytimes.com /2011/08/23/us/23jackson.html?pagewanted=all.

Simone, Nina, and Stephen Cleary. *I Put a Spell on You: The Autobiography of Nina Simone*. Cambridge, Mass.: Da Capo Press, 2003.

Stockett, Kathryn. *The Help*. New York: Amy Einhorn, 2009.

Walker, Frank X. *Turn Me Loose: The Unghosting of Medgar Evers*. Unpublished manuscript.

Walker, Margaret. *Conversations with Margaret Walker*. Edited by Maryemma Graham. Jackson: University Press of Mississippi, 2002.

———. Journals. Margaret Walker Center, Jackson State University. Jackson, Miss.

———. "A Mississippi Writers Talks/1982," Interview. By John Griffin Jones. *Mississippi Writers Talking*. Jackson: University Press of Mississippi, 1983. Reprinted in *Conversations with Margaret Walker*, 72–91.

———. *On Being Female, Black, and Freed: Essays by Margaret Walker, 1932–1991*. Edited by Maryemma Graham. Knoxville: University of Tennessee Press, 1997.

———. *Prophets for a New Day*. Detroit: Broadside Press, 1970.

———. "Southern Song: An Interview with Margaret Walker." By Lucy M. Freibert. *Frontiers* 9, no. 3. University of Nebraska Press, 1987. Reprinted in *Conversations with Margaret Walker*, 98–112.

———. *This Is My Century: New and Collected Poems*. Athens: University of Georgia Press, 1989.

Walton, Anthony. *Mississippi: An American Journey*. New York: Vintage Books, 1996.

Ward, Jimmy. "Covering the Crossroad." *Jackson Daily News*. June 15, 1963, p. 1.

Washington Post. "Evers Gets Hero's Burial in Arlington." June 20, 1963, p. 18.

Watson, Minnie. Interview. By Minrose Gwin. February 23, 2006.

Weller, Sheila. "We've Waited Our Whole Lives for This." *Glamour*. January 2009, 91.

Welty, Eudora. "An Afternoon with Miss Welty/1994." Interview. By Joseph Dumas. *Mississippi Magazine*, May/June 1994. Reprinted in *More Conversations with Eudora Welty*, 281–88.

———. "The Art of Fiction XLVII: Eudora Welty/1972." Interview. By Linda Kuehl. *Paris Review* 55, Fall 1972. Reprinted in *Conversations with Eudora Welty*, 74–91.

———. "A Conversation between Cleanth Brooks and Eudora Welty." *Humanities*

9, September/October 1988. Reprinted in *More Conversations with Eudora Welty*, 154–57.

———. "A Conversation with Eudora Welty/Summer 1978." Interview. By Tom Royals and John Little. *Bloodroot* no. 6, Spring 1979. Reprinted in *Conversations with Eudora Welty*, 252–67.

———. *Conversations with Eudora Welty*. Edited by Peggy Whitman Prenshaw. Jackson: University Press of Mississippi, 1984.

———. "Eudora Welty at Home/1992." Interview. By Clarence Brown. *Bostonia*, Fall 1992. Reprinted in *More Conversations with Eudora Welty*, 222–30.

———. "1st Original," *The Collected Stories*, Box 14, Folders 1, 3, and 5. Eudora Welty Archive. Mississippi Department of Archives and History, Jackson, Miss. Reprinted by permission of Russell & Volkening as agents for the author. Copyright 1963 by Eudora Welty.

———. "From the Unknown/Where Is the Voice Coming From?" In *Creative Writing and Rewriting: Contemporary American Novelists at Work*, edited by John Kuehl, 4–18. New York: Appleton-Century-Crofts, 1967.

———. "An Interview with Eudora Welty/29 July 1977." By Jean Todd Freeman. *Conversations with Writers II*. Detroit: Gale Research, 1978. Reprinted in *Conversations with Eudora Welty*, 172–200.

———. *More Conversations with Eudora Welty*. Edited by Peggy Whitman Prenshaw. Jackson: University Press of Mississippi, 1996.

———. *One Writer's Beginnings*. Cambridge, Mass.: Harvard University Press, 1983.

———. "Place in Fiction." In *The Eye of the Story* by Eudora Welty, 116–33. 1978. Reprint, New York: Vintage International, 1990.

———. "A Visit with Eudora Welty/1984." Interview by Barbara Lazear Ascher. *Yale Review* 74, November 1984. Reprinted in *More Conversations with Eudora Welty*, 79–86.

———. "Where Is the Voice Coming From?" In *The Collected Stories of Eudora Welty*, 603–7. New York: Harcourt Brace, 1980.

Welty, Eudora, and Walker Percy. "'The Southern Imagination': An Interview with Eudora Welty and Walker Percy by William F. Buckley, Jr./1972." PBS telecast, December 24, 1972. Reprinted in *Conversations with Eudora Welty*, 92–114.

Wilbur, Randall. "Medgar Evers." *Broadside* 37 (January 1, 1964): n.p.

Williams, Jim. "A Keen for Medgar Evers." In *Freedomways: A Quarterly Review of the Negro Freedom Movement* (Special Issue: Mississippi: Opening the Closed Society) 5, no. 2 (Spring 1965): 263.

Music and Audiovisual Recordings

Collins, Judy. Vocal performance of "Medgar Evers Lullaby" by Dick Weissman. On *The Judy Collins Concert*. Elektra Records, 1964, 33 ⅓ rpm. Originally recorded live at Town Hall, New York City, March 21, 1964.

Dälek. Vocal performance of "Who Medgar Evers Was" by Dälek. On *Gutter Tactics*. Ipecac Recordings, 2009, compact disc.

Dylan, Bob. *Lyrics, 1962–1985*. New York: Knopf, 1985.

———. Vocal performance of "Only a Pawn in Their Game" by Bob Dylan. On *The Times They Are A-Changin'*. Columbia CL 2105, 1964, 33 ⅓ rpm.

Goddard, Jack. Liner notes to *The Judy Collins Concert* performed by Judy Collins. Elektra Records, 1964, 33 ⅓ rpm.

Immortal Technique. Vocal performance of "Crossing the Boundary." On *Revolutionary, Vol. 2*. Viper Records, released November 18, 2003, compact disc.

Jones, Matthew. Vocal performance of "The Ballad of Medgar Evers" by Matthew Jones. On *Voices of the Civil Rights Movement: Black American Freedom Songs, 1960–1966*. Washington, D.C.: Smithsonian Folkways, 1997, compact disc. Originally released by Smithsonian Institution Press in 1980. Copyright 1963, 1993 Matthew Jones (ASCAP). Copyright 1993 Wisdom Train (ASCAP).

Ochs, Phil. "Ballad of Medgar Evers." *Broadside* 29 (July 1963): n.p.

———. "Interviews with Phil Ochs." Audio recording in *Broadside Ballads*, vol. 11, Folkways Records, FW05321, 1976.

———. *Songs of Phil Ochs*. New York: Appleseed Music, 1964.

———. Vocal performance of "Ballad of Medgar Evers" ("Too Many Martyrs") by Phil Ochs and Bob Gibson. On *Newport Broadside: Topical Songs at the Newport Folk Festival 1963*. Vanguard VRS-9144, 33 ⅓ rpm. Recorded live at the Newport Folk Festival, July 26–28, 1963.

———. Vocal performance of "Here's to the State of Mississippi" by Phil Ochs. On *I Ain't Marching Anymore*. Elektra, 1965, 33 ⅓ rpm. Lyrics available on Phil Ochs home page, http://web.cecs.pdx.edu/~trent/ochs, accessed March 27, 2012.

Ochs, Phil, and Bob Gibson. "Too Many Martyrs" ("Ballad of Medgar Evers"). In *Songs of Phil Ochs* by Phil Ochs, 30. New York: Appleseed Music, 1964.

Reagon, Bernice Johnson. "A Freedom Singer Shares the Music of the Movement." Interview with *Talk of the Nation*. NPR, February 11, 2010, accessed June 24, 2011. http://www.npr.org/templates/story/story.php ?storyId=123599617.

Reiner, Rob, Director. *Ghosts of Mississippi*. Castle Rock Entertainment. Culver City, Calif.: Columbia TriStar Home Video, 1997. DVD.

Reynolds, Malvina. Vocal performance of "What's Going On Down There?" Words and music by Malvina Reynolds. On *Malvina Reynolds Sings the Truth*, Columbia CS-9414, 33⅓ rpm. 1964 Schroder Music Co., renewed 1992. Used by permission.

Schultz, Michael, Director. *For Us, the Living: The Story of Medgar Evers*. Fries Entertainment. Troy, Mich.: Anchor Bay Entertainment, 1990. VHS.

Simone, Nina. Vocal performance of "Mississippi Goddam" by Nina Simone. On *Nina Simone in Concert*, Philips/Verve, 2006, compact disc. Originally recorded live at Carnegie Hall in 1964.

Springsteen, Bruce. *We Shall Overcome: The Seeger Sessions*, Columbia, 2006, compact disc. Originally recorded in sessions held in 1997, 2005, and 2006.

Veazey, Kathy. Lyrics to "I'm Alive." E-mail to author, February 28, 2012.

———. "Soul Consolation, 'I'm Alive,' 1995 (Medgar Evers)." Lyrics and music. YouTube video with audio recording, uploaded April 9, 2008, accessed August 3, 2011. http://www.youtube.com/watch?v=Rped_F9lU-A.

Voices of the Civil Rights Movement: Black American Freedom Songs, 1960–1966. Smithsonian Folkways, 1997, compact disc.

Weiner, Matthew, and Kater Gordan, "The Fog," *Mad Men*, season 3, episode 5, directed by Phil Abraham, aired September 13, 2009. Santa Monica, Calif.: Lionsgate, 2010, DVD.

Weissman, Dick. Vocal performance of "Lullaby (for Medgar Evers)." Words and music by Dick Weissman. On *The Things that Trouble My Mind*. Capitol Records, 1964, 33⅓ rpm. TRO 1964 (renewed) Ludlow Music International Copyright Secured. All rights reserved including public performance for profit. Used by permission.

Wu Tang Clan. Vocal performance of "I Can't Go to Sleep." On *The W*. Sony, compact disc. Released November 21, 2000.

SECONDARY SOURCES

Abraham, Nicholas, and Maria Torok. *The Shell and the Kernel: Renewals of Psychoanalysis*. Translated by Nicholas T. Rand. Chicago: University of Chicago Press, 1994.

Abrahams, Roger, and George Foss. *Anglo American Folksong Style*. Englewood Cliffs, N.J.: Prentice Hall, 1968.

Anderson, Benedict. *Imagined Communities: Reflections on the Origin and Spread of Nationalism*. New York: Verso, 1991.

Association of Alternative Newsmedia. "Mississippi Alt-Weekly Revealed Indicted Klansman Was Still Alive." January 24, 2007, accessed April 11, 2012. http://www.altweeklies.com/aan/mississippi-alt-weekly-revealed -indicted-klansman-was-still-alive/Article?oid=177909.

Auchincloss, Eve, and Nancy Lynch Handy. "Disturbers of the Peace." In *Black, White and Gray: Twenty-one Points of View on the Race Question*, edited by Bradford Daniel, 190–209. New York: Sheed and Ward, 1964.

Betts, Doris. "Killers Real and Imagined." *Southern Cultures* (Winter 1999): 5–13.

Booth, James W. "The Color of Memory: Reading Race with Ralph Ellison." *Political Theory* 36, no. 5 (October 2008): 683–707.

Bowden, Betsy. *Performed Literature: Words and Music by Bob Dylan*. Bloomington: Indiana University Press, 1982.

Brown, Jennie. *Medgar Evers*. Melrose Square Black American Series. Los Angeles: Melrose Square, 1994.

Brun-Lambert, David. *Nina Simone: The Biography*. London: Aurum, 2010.

Brundage, W. Fitzhugh. *The Southern Past: A Clash of Race and Memory*. Cambridge, Mass.: Harvard University Press, 2005.

Burt, Olive Woolley. *American Murder Ballads and Their Stories*. New York: Oxford University Press, 1958.

Campbell, James. *Talking at the Gates: A Life of James Baldwin*. Berkeley: University of California Press, 1991.

Carter, Ginger Rudeseal. "Hodding Carter, Jr., and the *Delta Democrat-Times*." In Davies, *The Press and Race*, 265–93.

Caruth, Cathy. *Unclaimed Experience: Trauma, Narrative, and History*. Baltimore: Johns Hopkins University Press, 1996.

———, ed. *Trauma: Explorations in Memory*. Baltimore: Johns Hopkins University Press, 1995.

Castronovo, Russ. "Beauty along the Color Line: Lynching, Aesthetics, and the Crisis." *PMLA* 121, no. 5 (October 2006): 1443–59.

Chafe, William H., Raymond Gavins, and Robert Korstads, eds., Paul Ortiz, Robert Parrish, Jennifer Ritterhouse, Keisha Roberts, and Nicole Waligora-Davis, associate eds. *Remembering Jim Crow: African Americans Tell about Life in the Segregated South*. New York: The Free Press, 2001.

Claire, Vivian. *Judy Collins*. New York/London: Finish Books, 1977.

Conley, Tom. "Translator's Introduction" to *The Writing of History*, by Michel de Certeau, vii–xxiv. Translated by Tom Conley. New York: Columbia University Press, 1988.

Cooper, Caryl A. "Percy Greene and the *Jackson Advocate*." In Davies, *The Press and Race*, 55–83.

Courlander, Harold. *Negro Folk Music, U.S.A.* New York: Columbia University Press, 1963.

Davies, David R., ed. *The Press and Race: Mississippi Journalists Confront the Movement*. Jackson: University Press of Mississippi, 2001.

Davies, David R., and Judy Smith. "Jimmy Ward and the Jackson *Daily News*." In Davies, *The Press and Race*, 85–109.

Day, Aiden. *Jokerman: Reading the Lyrics of Bob Dylan*. Oxford: Basil Blackwell, 1988.

DeLaughter, Bobby. *Never Too Late: A Prosecutor's Story of Justice in the Medgar Evers Case*. New York: Scribner, 2001.

Dent, Tom. "Portrait of Three Heroes." In "Mississippi: Opening the Closed Society." Special issue, *Freedomways: A Quarterly Review of the Negro Freedom Movement* 5, no. 2 (Spring 1965): 250–62.

Dittmer, John. *Local People: The Struggle for Civil Rights in Mississippi*. Urbana: University of Illinois Press, 1994.

Eckman, Fern Marja. *The Furious Passage of James Baldwin*. New York: M. Evans in association with J. B. Lippincott, 1966.

Eliot, Marc. *Death of a Rebel: A Biography of Phil Ochs*. 1979. New York: Franklin Walls, 1989.

Erickson, Kai. "Notes on Trauma and Community." In Caruth, *Trauma: Explorations in Memory*, 183–99.

Felman, Shoshana. "Camus' *The Plague*, or a Monument to Witnessing." In Felman and Laub, *Testimony*, 93–119.

———. "Education and Crisis, or the Vicissitudes of Teaching." In Caruth, *Trauma: Explorations of Memory*, 13–60.

Felman, Shoshana, and Dori Laub, M.D. *Testimony: Crises of Witnessing in Literature, Psychoanalysis, and History*. New York: Routledge, 1992.

Freeman, Roland L., ed. Photographs by Roland L. Freeman. *Margaret Walker's "For My People": A Tribute*. Jackson: University Press of Mississippi, 1992.

Friedlander, Saul. *Memory, History, and the Extermination of the Jews of Europe*. Bloomington: Indiana University Press, 1993.

Fuller, Jennifer. "Debating the Present through the Past: Representations of the

Civil Rights Movement of the 1990s." In Raiford and Romano, *Civil Rights Movement*, 167–96.

Gitay, Yehoshua, ed. *Prophecy and Prophets: The Diversity of Contemporary Issues in Scholarship*. Atlanta: Scholars Press, 1997.

Gordon, Avery F. *Ghostly Matters: Haunting and the Sociological Imagination*. Minneapolis: University of Minnesota Press, 1997.

Griffin, Larry J., and Peggy G. Hargis. "Surveying Memory: The Past in Black and White." Special issue on History, Memory and Mourning, *Southern Literary Journal* 40, no. 2 (Spring 2008): 42–69.

Halbwachs, Maurice. *The Collective Memory*. Trans. Francis Ditter and Vida Yazdi Ditter. Introduction by Mary Douglas. New York: Harper Colophon, 1980. First published in French in 1950 by Presses Universitaires de France.

Hall, Jacqueline Dowd. "The Long Civil Rights Movement and the Political Uses of the Past." *Journal of American History* (March 2005): 1233–63.

Harris, Trudier. *The Scary Mason-Dixon Line: African American Writers and the South*. Baton Rouge: Louisiana State University Press, 2009.

Hatfield, Edward A. "Freedom Singers," *New Georgia Encyclopedia*, Georgia Humanities Council, last modified November 28, 2007, accessed June 23, 2011. http://www.georgiaencyclopedia.org/nge/Article.jsp?id=h-3670&hl=y.

Heaton, E. W. *The Old Testament Prophets*. Atlanta: John Knox Press, 1977.

———. *A Short Introduction to the Old Testament Prophets*. Rockport, Mass.: Oneworld, 1996.

Helsinger, Elizabeth. "Using and Abusing Fiction." In *Questions of Evidence: Proof, Practice, and Persuasion across the Disciplines*, edited by James Chandler, Arnold I. Davidson, and Harry Harootunian, 352–57. Chicago: University of Chicago Press, 1994.

Hendrickson, Paul. *Sons of Mississippi: A Story of Race and Its Legacy*. New York: Vintage, 2003.

Hernton, Calvin C. "Critical Commentary." *Amistad I*, 1970. Excerpt reprinted in *Drama Criticism*, vol. 1, edited by Lawrence J. Trudeau, 22–24. Detroit: Gale Research, 1991.

Hillers, Delbert R. *Treaty-Curses and the Old Testament Prophets*. Thesis, Pontifical Biblical Institute, Rome, 1964.

Hirsch, Marianne. *Family Frames: Photography, Narrative and Postmemory*. Cambridge, Mass.: Harvard University Press, 1997.

Hudson, Angela Pulley. "Mississippi Lost and Found: Anne Moody's Autobiograph(ies) and Racial Melancholia." *A/B: Auto/Biography Studies* 20, no. 2 (2005): 282–96.

Humphries, Jefferson. *Southern Literature and Literary Theory*. Athens: University of Georgia Press, 1990.

Irwin-Zarecka, Iwona. *Frames of Remembrance: The Dynamics of Collective Memory*. New Brunswick, N.J.: Transaction Publishers, 1994.

"James Baldwin 1924–1987." In *Drama Criticism* vol. 1, edited by Lawrence J. Trudeau, 1–20. Detroit: Gale Research, 1991.

Kaplan, Brett Ashley. *Unwanted Beauty: Aesthetic Pleasure in Holocaust Representation*. Urbana: University of Illinois Press, 2007.

Kaul, Arthur J. "Hazel Brannon Smith and the *Lexington Advertiser*." In Davies, *The Press and Race*, 233–64.

Klein, Kerwin Lee. "On the Emergency of *Memory* in Historical Discourse." *Representations* no. 69 (Winter 2000): 127–50.

Koch, Klaus. *The Prophets*. Philadelphia: Fortress, 1982.

LaCapra, Dominick. *History and Memory after Auschwitz*. Ithaca, N.Y.: Cornell University Press, 1998.

———. *Writing History, Writing Trauma*. Baltimore: Johns Hopkins University Press, 2001.

Larsen, Thomas. *The Memoir and the Memoirist: Reading and Writing Personal Narrative*. Athens: Ohio University Press, 2007.

Laub, Dori. "An Event without a Witness." In Caruth, *Trauma: Explorations in Memory*, 61–75.

Leeming, David. *James Baldwin: A Biography*. New York: Knopf, 1994.

Leys, Ruth. *Trauma: A Genealogy*. Chicago: University of Chicago Press, 2000.

Lynskey, Dorian. *33 Revolutions per Minute: A History of Protest Songs from Billie Holiday to Green Day*. New York: Ecco, 2011.

McIhany, William H. *Klandestine*. New Rochelle, N.Y.: Arlington House, 1975.

Marcus, Greil. *Bob Dylan: Writings, 1968–2010*. New York: Public Affairs, 2010.

Marqusee, Mike. *Chimes of Freedom: The Politics of Bob Dylan's Art*. New York: New Press, 2003.

Marrs, Suzanne. *Eudora Welty: A Biography*. New York: Harcourt, 2005.

———. *The Welty Collection: A Guide to the Eudora Welty Manuscripts and Documents at the Mississippi Department of Archives and History*. Jackson: University Press of Mississippi, 1988.

Massengill, Reed. *Portrait of a Racist: The Man Who Killed Medgar Evers*. New York: St. Martin's Press, 1994.

Mattson, Kevin. "Civil Rights Made Harder." *Reviews in American History* 30, no. 4 (December 2002): 663–70.

Metress, Christopher. "Making Civil Rights Harder: Literature, Memory, and the Black Freedom Struggle." Special issue on History, Memory and Mourning, *Southern Literary Journal* 40, no. 2 (Spring 2008): 138–50.

Molette, Carlton W. Untitled essay. Previously published as "James Baldwin as a Playwright," in *James Baldwin: A Critical Evaluation*, edited by Therman B. O'Daniel, 183–88. Washington, D.C.: Howard University Press, 1977. Reprinted in *Drama Criticism* vol. 1, edited by Lawrence J. Trudeau, 4–6. Detroit: Gale Research, 1991.

Morris, Willie. *The Ghosts of Medgar Evers: A Tale of Race, Murder, Mississippi, and Hollywood*. New York: Random House, 1998.

Morrison, Toni. *Playing in the Dark: Whiteness and the Literary Imagination*. Cambridge, Mass.: Harvard University Press, 1992.

———. "Rootedness: The Ancestor as Foundation." In *Black Women Writers (1950–1980)*, edited by Mari Evans, 339–45. New York: Anchor/Doubleday, 1984.

Murrain, Ethel. *The Mississippi Man and His Message: A Rhetorical Analysis of the Cultural Themes in the Oratory of Medgar Wiley Evers, 1957–1963*. PhD diss., University of Southern Mississippi. Ann Arbor: UMI, 1990.

Neff, Ali. "David Banner." Teaching notes.

Neilsen, Melany. *Even Mississippi*. Tuscaloosa: University of Alabama Press, 1989.

Nelson, Emmanuel S. "James Baldwin's Vision of Otherness and Community." *MELUS* 10, no. 2 (Summer 1983): 27–31.

Nora, Pierre. "Between Memory and History: *Les Lieux de Mémoire*," trans. Marc Roudebush, in "Memory and Counter-Memory," special issue, *Representation* 26, no. 1 (Spring 1989): 7–24.

Nossiter, Adam. *Of Long Memory: Mississippi and the Murder of Medgar Evers*. Cambridge, Mass.: Da Capo Press, 2002.

Oliver, Kelly. *Witnessing: Beyond Recognition*. Minneapolis: University of Minnesota Press, 2001.

Oliver, Paul. *Songsters and Saints: Vocal Traditions on Race Records*. Cambridge: Cambridge University Press, 1984.

Phillips, Louis. "The Novelist as Playwright: Baldwin, McCullers, and Bellow." In *Modern American Drama: Essays in Criticism*, edited by William F. Taylor, 145–62. Deland, Fla.: Everett Edwards, 1968.

Pietaro, John. "Matthew Jones, Freedom Singer, Civil Rights Activist: 1936–2011," The Cultural Worker (blog), April 2, 2011. http://theculturalworker .blogspot.com/2011/04/obituary-matt-jones.html.

Pollack, Harriet, and Suzanne Marrs, eds. *Eudora Welty and Politics: Did the Writer Crusade?* Baton Rouge: Louisiana State University Press, 2001.

Raiford, Leigh, and Renee C. Romano, eds. *The Civil Rights Movement in American Memory*. Athens: University of Georgia Press, 2006.

———. "Introduction: The Struggle over Memory." In Raiford and Romano, *Civil Rights Movement*, xi–xxiv.

Reagon, Bernice Johnson. Liner notes, *Voices of the Civil Rights Movement: Black American Freedom Songs, 1960–1966*. Smithsonian Folkways, 1997, compact disc.

Romano, Renee C. "Narratives of Redemption: The Birmingham Church Bombing Trials and the Construction of Civil Rights Memory." In Raiford and Romano, *Civil Rights Movement*, 96–134.

Romines, Ann. "A Voice from a Jackson Interior: Eudora Welty and the Politics of Filial Piety." In Pollack and Marrs, *Eudora Welty and Politics*, 109–22.

Salter, John R., Jr. *Jackson, Mississippi: An American Chronicle of Struggle and Schism*. Hicksville, N.Y.: Exposition Press, 1979.

Sanger, Kerran L. *"When the Spirit Says Sing!": The Role of Freedom Songs in the Civil Rights Movement*. New York: Garland, 1995.

Schumacher, Michael. *There but for Fortune: The Life of Phil Ochs*. New York: Hyperion, 1996.

Seeger, Pete. *The Incomplete Folksinger*. New York: Simon & Schuster, 1972.

Shelton, Robert. *No Direction Home: The Life and Music of Bob Dylan*. New York: William Morrow, 1986.

Silver, James W. *Mississippi: The Closed Society*. New York: Harcourt Brace & World, 1963.

Sounes, Howard. *Down the Highway: The Life of Bob Dylan*. New York: Grove Press, 2001.

Spitz, Bob. *Dylan: A Biography*. New York: McGraw-Hill, 1987.

Taylor, Diana. *The Archive and the Repertoire: Performing Cultural Memory in the Americas*. Durham, N.C.: Duke University Press, 2003.

Thill, Scott. "We Are Not Moving Forward: An Interview with Dälek." Morphizm.com. November 29, 2005, accessed June 25, 2011. http://www .morphizm.com/recommends/interviews/Dalek05.html.

Thompson, Julius Eric. *The Black Press in Mississippi, 1865–1985*. Gainesville: University Press of Florida, 1993.

———. *Percy Greene and the* Jackson Advocate: *The Life and Times of a Radical Conservative Black Newspaperman, 1897–1977*. Jefferson, N.C.: McFarland, 1994.

Tisdale, John R. "Medgar Evers (1925–1963) and the Mississippi Press." PhD diss., University of North Texas, 1996.

Vollers, Maryanne. *Ghosts of Mississippi: The Murder of Medgar Evers, the Trials of Byron De La Beckwith, and the Haunting of the New South*. Boston: Little, Brown, 1995.

Weatherby, W. J. "Baldwin on Broadway." In *James Baldwin: Artist on Fire: A Portrait*, 236–55. New York: Donald I. Fine, 1989.

Weill, Susan. *In a Madhouse's Din: Civil Rights Coverage by Mississippi's Daily Press, 1948–1968*. Westport, Conn.: Praeger, 2002.

Weissman, Dick. *Talkin' 'Bout a Revolution: Music and Social Change in America*. New York: Backbeat Books, 2010.

Whitehead, Don. *Attack on Terror: The FBI against the Ku Klux Klan in Mississippi*. New York: Funk & Wagnalls, 1970.

Williams, Julian. "The Truth Shall Make You Free." *Journalism History* 32, no. 2 (Summer 2006): 106–13.

Williams, Michael Vinson. *Medgar Evers: Mississippi Martyr*. Fayetteville: University of Arkansas Press, 2011.

Zelitzer, Barbie. *Covering the Body: The Kennedy Assassination, the Media, and the Shaping of Collective Memory*. Chicago: University of Chicago Press, 1992.

INDEX